D1216709

Southern
Women

Southern
Women

Histories and Identities

edited by

Virginia Bernhard

Betty Brandon

Elizabeth Fox-Genovese

and Theda Perdue

University of Missouri Press
Columbia and London

5 4 3 2 1   96 95 94 93 92

Library of Congress Cataloging-in-Publication Data

Southern women : histories and identities / edited by Virginia
    Bernhard . . . [et al.].
        p.   cm.
    Includes index.
    ISBN 0-8262-0868-1 (alk. paper)
    1. Women—Southern States—History—Congresses. I. Bernhard,
    Virginia, 1937–
    HQ1438.A13S623   1992
    305.4'0975—dc20   92-28762
                                                                CIP

Designer: *Kristie Lee*
Typesetter: *Connell-Zeko Type & Graphics*
Printer and Binder: *Thomson-Shore, Inc.*
Typefaces: *Palatino and Tiffany Light*

Different versions of Jacquelyn Dowd Hall's and Darlene Clark Hine's essays
originally appeared in *Signs: Journal of Women in Culture and Society* 14, no. 4
(Summer 1989): 902–11 and 912–20, published by the University of Chicago
Press.

✤CONTENTS

Roseanne V. Camacho

Darlene Clark Hine

Southern
Women

✄ EDITORS' INTRODUCTION

In the South, as elsewhere, women's identities have always been fashioned by the communities to which they have belonged, even as women's experiences and values have shaped the life of the community. But as Jacquelyn Hall notes in the opening essay of this volume, southern women's history has been slow to emerge as a recognized interest within southern history and American women's history. A primary aim of the first Southern Conference on Women's History, sponsored by the Southern Association for Women Historians at Converse College, Spartanburg, South Carolina, in June 1988, was to encourage and recognize new work in southern women's history. The gratifying response to the call for papers permitted us, in planning this volume, to select from a wide variety of papers on topics ranging from women rebels in seventeenth-century Virginia to woman suffrage in Texas. Although this volume does not pretend to offer a comprehensive narrative history of southern women, it does demonstrate that the outlines of such a general history are beginning to take shape. And within those outlines are emerging new questions about the identities of southern women as products of their discrete and collective histories, and about the significance of these histories in shaping the history of the South.

In different ways, each of the essays in this volume explores aspects of what it meant to be a southern woman, that is, the distinct dimensions of southern women's identities. The plural reflects a growing awareness of the diversity of southern women and the diversity of the discrete histories of women who have in their various ways participated in a common regional history. Thus the "partial truths" of these essays suggest that, diversity notwithstanding, southern women have shared the constraints and the commitments of their region as a whole, and that the South's history cannot be understood independent of its women's specific contributions. The subjects of the essays, which range from the colonial period to the mid-twentieth century, include women of different classes and races, women of rural and urban backgrounds, women as individuals and as members of groups, women as they struggle to represent them-

1

selves, and women as they have been represented by the ideology of their region. Separately and together, these works challenge any monolithic view of American women's experience even as they challenge the view of southern history as an exclusively male affair.

Few events in southern history have been more unthinkingly accepted as male affairs than Bacon's Rebellion, which bears the name of its male leader. But, as Susan Westbury in her essay on women's participation in the Rebellion notes, women as well as men were partisans: "politics crossed gender as well as class lines." A woman wrote one of the earliest narratives of the Rebellion; wives of Virginia planters carried messages, wrote letters, confronted hostile forces who invaded their homes, and, in one instance, were forced to serve as hostages against an attack by their husbands. One rebel's wife even offered her life for her husband's, saying that she, not he, had been guilty of treason.

As a civil war, Bacon's Rebellion drew women "willy-nilly" into the vortex. But Westbury also insists that if many were swept up by the rush of events, others participated because of their personal political commitments. Notably, wives of rebels of all classes took a much more active part than did the wives of men loyal to Governor Berkeley. Thus Westbury, in charting the importance of heretofore neglected gender roles in the Rebellion, explores a new dimension of the experience of seventeenth-century southern women. In so doing, she invites comparisons with the roles and politics of women in other regions and, like Abigail Adams, challenges future historians to "remember the ladies."

Westbury, in effect, underscores the too frequently neglected truth that women constitute active members of any community. But her convincing evidence that some early southern women manifested active political commitments and that at least some of them translated those commitments into action also points to the specific possibilities of a still fluid seventeenth-century Chesapeake society. In contrast, by the eighteenth century the idea of "separate spheres" had begun to shape gender roles and to limit women's opportunities. Eighteenth-century society, preferring to view women as passive, fostered an image of them as invariably apolitical regardless of their actual behavior. Following the American Revolution, as Kathy Roe Coker demonstrates, loyalist men were punished, but their female relatives were not. If property was confiscated, however, women often petitioned the state for redress. Thus, although Coker's examination of the claims of loyalist women in South Carolina after the war confirms the prevalence of ideas about women's apolitical nature, it also confirms that in some cases women's behavior did not conform to the ideal. A few women, in pressing their claims, dared to step outside prescribed gender roles to voice their own political opinions, and others, by the very act of challenging the state to regain control of a male relative's property, belied common assumptions about women's passivity and helplessness.

As the eighteenth century gave way to the nineteenth, both the idea of separate spheres and the flouting of gender prescriptions persisted. With the consolidation of slavery as a social system, gender conventions that relegated women to the dominance of men within households became even more rigid. The ideal of the southern lady, which was to cast such a long shadow over the identities of southern women, increasingly imprisoned elite white women within the constraints of their class, race, and gender. To these women, according to prevailing ideology, accrued the responsibility of upholding the values of southern civilization as envisioned by slaveholding men.[1] And, in an overwhelmingly rural, hierarchical slave society, elite women frequently observed the prescriptions in part out of their own political conviction and in part out of respect for the dangers that threatened a woman who did not. But in the South, even more than in the North, prevailing gender conventions imperfectly captured the realities of different women's lives.

The conventions of gender expressed an ideal of women's fragility and men's strength that has appropriately been described as the myth of the southern lady. In reality, not even the majority of slaveholding women's lives conformed to that myth, much less the lives of nonslaveholding white and black slave women. To be sure, southern men of all classes and races subscribed to a general belief in women's subordination to men, which southern churches, customs, and laws reinforced. But for the majority of southern women of all classes and races, subordination to men did not translate into leisured elegance. For many nonslaveholding white women, the prevailing conventions did result in their performing different

---

1. Anne Firor Scott, *The Southern Lady: From Pedestal to Politics, 1830–1930* (Chicago: University of Chicago Press, 1970); Elizabeth Fox-Genovese, *Within the Plantation Household: Black and White Women of the Old South* (Chapel Hill: University of North Carolina Press, 1988).

kinds of work than men; for most black slave women, not even that distinction held.

The true burden of gender conventions for women can only be weighed through women's everyday responses to them. Southern women's personal narratives remain sparse, primarily because so many black slave and poor white women had neither the time nor the education to produce them, although some elite women left diaries, journals, and letters that grant us at least a glimpse of their personal responses. For these women, the burden of gender conventions weighed heavily and decisively shaped their experiences and expectations. Yeoman women of the southern heartland, to the extent that we can understand them, may also have experienced the influence of gender conventions directly, if only because their men and their ministers, not to mention the courts, supported such conventions. But the realities of yeoman women's lives did not necessarily afford the labor of servants and might necessitate their own labor in the fields, their traveling alone, or other activities that prevailing gender conventions did not countenance.[2] Black slave women, however, most forcefully experienced the gap between convention and reality. For them, the ubiquitous threat and frequent reality of rape, and of separation from their children, mocked the ideal of womanhood. No convention protected their sexuality or their motherhood, much less relieved them of an unending round of hard labor—frequently at tasks considered inappropriate for white women. And yet, even in reversal or nonobservance, the very existence of the conventions also impinged on the experience of poor white and black slave women, if only in shaping the ways in which those with power over such women perceived them.

The relations between yeoman and poor white women and gender conventions were governed by class, and those between slave women and gender conventions by race and class. And, in ambiguous cases, the tangle of race, class, and gender frequently defied disentangling. Thus, Kent Leslie argues that Amanda America Dickson, despite having been born a mulatto slave, lived the life of an elite lady in the house and under the protection of her wealthy, white, slaveholding father. Leslie presents Amanda America Dick-

2. Stephanie McCurry, "Defense of Their World: Gender, Class, and the Yeomanry of the South Carolina Low Country, 1820–1860" (Ph.D. diss., State University of New York, Binghamton, 1988).

son's story, recalled and retold by her granddaughter, as "a struggle to be outside the boundaries of racial categories by being inside the boundaries of an elite white family." In the end, Leslie reflects, the Amanda America Dickson of her granddaughter's recollection "sacrificed a chance for autonomy as a black woman and chose instead personal privilege 'in a make believe world.' "

Spanning the Civil War and the abolition of slavery, Amanda America Dickson's life encompassed radical changes in class and race relations, the contradictions and limitations of which she herself did her best to ignore, even as she clung to the ideology of elite womanhood. Her strategy in response to the harsh realities of her larger world had something in common with those adopted by some privileged free women of color who, living as the wives or concubines of white or free black men, themselves became slaveholding "ladies."[3] But the laws of Georgia prevented Amanda America Dickson's father from emancipating her, prevented her from becoming a free woman of color within the state. And not long after the laws of the nation freed her, the laws of Georgia prevented her from fully exercising her freedom because of her race.

If the histories and identities of antebellum southern women were preeminently shaped by slavery, and hence by class, those of postbellum southern women have preeminently been shaped by race. By freeing slaves, the Civil War transformed the experiences of and relations among black and white women. In the aftermath of the war, former slave women, together with their men, struggled to establish families and communities—to acquire property, establish schools and churches, and strengthen their people as a people. And, freedom notwithstanding, they struggled against formidable odds, notably the resistance of whites who, for their part, sought to restore something as close to the old order as possible. In the process, both black and white women sought to (re)construct their own identities in conformity with new circumstances, frequently on the basis of a reinterpretation of their separate and common histories.

3. Michael P. Johnson and James L. Roark, *Black Masters: A Free Family of Color in the Old South* (New York: W. W. Norton, 1984); L. Virginia Gould, "Urban Slavery, Urban Freedom: The Manumission of Jacqueline Lemelle," *Black Women and Slavery and Freedom in the Americas,* ed. D. Barry Gaspar and Darlene Clark Hine (Bloomington: Indiana University Press, 1992).

Scholars are beginning to explore the dimensions of the struggle for black women who sought to claim for themselves aspects of the ideology of domestic womanhood by affirming their identities as the wives of black men and the mothers of their own children. Resisting, to the extent possible, the pressures to labor in the fields and houses of whites, they turned to their families and their community organizations. Economic coercion rarely permitted them entirely to avoid laboring for whites, but they struggled mightily to subordinate that aspect of their roles to their identities as women among their people.

The war and its aftermath confronted many white women with a tension between the exigencies of labor and self-definition. Most white women, including those of the elite, confronted some measure of economic decline and the attendant obligation of undertaking more domestic labor than they had been accustomed to. Some white women had to work for wages to contribute to their families' support. Many turned, for the first time, to teaching, and thus followed the path previously followed by their northeastern and midwestern counterparts.[4] Altered circumstances and changing experiences did not, however, radically transform the ideology and conventions of gender. If anything, those circumstances and experiences prompted many white southerners to reaffirm rigidly the centrality of women's sheltered sexuality and domestic identity to a larger vision of social order, including domination over former slaves. White women did not immediately seize the new opportunities as openings to autonomy and independence but attempted to fit new forms of behavior into old gender conventions. Emancipation of the former slaves did, nonetheless, eventually force substantial reworking of those conventions.

The continuity between antebellum and postbellum southern society lay in the domination of whites over blacks; the rupture lay in the transformation of the terms of that domination. Where slavery had once permitted a conflation of class and racial domination that emphasized class, its abolition led whites to rely increasingly on a naked ideology of pure racial hierarchy. The consequences of this shift would gradually emerge as a central thread in the defini-

4. George C. Rable, *Civil Wars: Women and the Crisis of Southern Nationalism* (Urbana: University of Illinois Press, 1989); Mareva Layne McDaniel, "The Feminization of Teaching in South Carolina" (Ph.D. diss. in progress, Emory University).

tion of white and black southern women's identities. Class remained as important as ever but received less explicit attention as the justification for social relations. As white southerners engaged in a concerted effort, frequently laced with violence, to force black southerners into the lowest economic class, they justified their policies and actions in racial terms. The complex ideological transformations that accompanied this closing of racial lines along the single fault line of legal racial segregation still require attention, but Cheryl Thurber convincingly disentangles one important aspect of them.

Allowing that under slavery some black women may have assumed some, or even all, of the functions conventionally attributed to the "mammy," Thurber argues that the full-blown ideology of mammy, as represented in *Gone with the Wind*, emerged after the war and especially during the late nineteenth and early twentieth centuries. During the implementation of legal racial segregation, white southerners engaged in a rereading of their region's history, especially of slavery, in an effort to demonstrate the possibility for binding human relations within the context of stark social differentiation. For these southerners, it became compelling to demonstrate that at least some black women had lovingly and loyally served their "white folks" in that most sensitive of all roles, as the nurturers of their children. "Good" black women, in this vision, willingly accepted their own subordination.

The mammy in this interpretation figured as the embodiment of a collective myth—or better—fantasy of racial harmony at the core of racial hierarchy. Ironically, the image of the nurturing, asexual mammy enjoyed its widest popularity during the precise historical epoch in which the image of uncontrollable black male sexuality was being evoked as a screen for black social, political, and economic ambition and being taken to justify lynching. In this respect, the image of the mammy had less to do with the identities of black women than with those of white. As part of a complex and comprehensive ideology of racial domination, the mythological mammy contributed to the persisting southern commitment to confining white women within their "pure" domestic roles and excluding them from the corruption of public life. It is, as Mary Martha Thomas suggests, only within this general context that we can begin to understand the ways in which southern women responded to the campaign for woman suffrage at the end of the nineteenth and the beginning of the twentieth centuries.

Long alienated from the woman movement, which was understandably viewed as a staunch ally of the antislavery movement, some white southern women began during the 1890s to organize for woman suffrage. During this early phase, some at least embraced the argument that woman suffrage could be justified not by abstract ideas of justice but by the differences between women and men. Woman suffrage, in this view, posed no necessary challenge to white supremacy, which it could even serve. The early phase, however, resulted in no tangible victories. A second phase, between 1910 and 1917, scored considerably greater success, if only by recruiting substantially larger numbers of white women to the cause. Arguing both from justice and from women's special natures, this generation of Alabama suffragists generally avoided the issue of race, although they might easily have justified their goals with reference to white supremacy. Their opponents, however, raised race with a vengeance, effectively arguing that any move toward woman suffrage would irreparably jeopardize white supremacy. In the end, Thomas insists, notwithstanding fears of the black vote, "it would appear that the real objection to woman suffrage . . . was a perceived threat to gender roles." Most white southerners, and especially white southern men, resisted the fundamental implication of woman suffrage, namely that it recognized women as individuals outside the family and thus threatened that basic unit of social order.

Elizabeth Turner, looking at the specific case of Galveston, finds both illuminating similarities to and differences from the story Thomas tells for Alabama. Restoring class as a central analytic category, Turner closely investigates the responses of a pivotal group of Galveston women to the campaign for woman suffrage. Arguing, like Thomas, that most of them assimilated the main sensibilities of Progressivism and, on that basis, favored woman suffrage as the necessary arm of women's roles in social housekeeping, Turner demonstrates that the most sustained impulse for woman suffrage came not from WCTU members and other evangelical church women who sought to impose temperance, but from upper-class club women who simultaneously sought urban reform and careers for themselves and who worked with the men of their own class to force the modernization of the South. It is time, she concludes, "to look beyond filiopietistic notions of solidarity among white women and see the campaign for the vote as it was—a complex political movement destined to bulldoze aside forever the staid traditionalism of the nineteenth century."

With the unfolding of the twentieth century, the determination to topple the most constraining aspects of southern traditionalism moved increasing numbers of women to challenge the interlocking pieties of gender, race, and even class. Among the myriad of women, black and white, who organized against lynching and for the improvement of their communities, who worked for suffrage and the extension of women's rights, who participated in labor organizations and strikes, Lillian Smith has earned a special place as the outspoken critic of a racism that bolstered and masked all other forms of traditionalism, notably men's domination over women. But, Roseanne Camacho insists, even today, Smith remains insufficiently understood. For Smith, even as she linked race and gender in her comprehensive criticism of the South, also embraced her own generation's agenda of modernism and consequently retained a general humanist notion of "man" in which she wished to see women and blacks included. According to Camacho, recent theories of race and gender have promoted new agendas and strategies for the kind of social change that Smith favored, but such theories have also "undermined the validity of the many dualities Smith tried unsuccessfully to reconcile." Smith's ambiguities and silences all testified to her specific identity and history and to the relation between the two. A white, middle-class, southern woman, she sought simultaneously to realize and to transcend the categories that defined her and, like an intense Cassandra, to urge her region to realize and transcend its history.

The essays in this book represent a new generation's attempt to grasp the interconnections among southern women's identities and histories, and to penetrate the silences that still punctuate that common story. In her distinctively personal investigation, Darlene Clark Hine poignantly argues that southern black women, in response to their own vulnerability as victims of rape and domestic violence, have constructed a culture of dissemblance to protect their most intimate feelings and identities from the brutal scrutiny of a dangerous and hostile world. Given this history of dissemblance, reclaiming individual stories alone is not enough—indeed, for the majority of southern black women it may not even be possible. "In synchrony with the reclaiming and narrating," she insists, "must be the development of an array of analytical frameworks that allow us to understand why black women of all classes behave in certain ways and how they acquired agency."

In Toni Morrison's novel *Beloved*, Paul D. insists to Sethe: "Me and you, we got more yesterday than anybody. We need some kind of tomorrow." But tomorrows, Morrison suggests, depend upon reappropriating yesterdays. The character Beloved—ghost, memory, presence—herself embodies those yesterdays and their unutterable loneliness: "Everybody knew what she was called, but nobody anywhere knew her name. Disremembered and unaccounted for, she cannot be lost because no one is looking for her, and even if they were, how can they call her if they don't know her name? Although she has claim, she is not claimed." Beloved's was not, they had thought, a story to pass on. So, like an unpleasant dream, they forgot her. And their forgetting erased everything, even "the breath of the disremembered and unaccounted for."[5]

Today, as these essays demonstrate, southern women's historians are attempting to recover the "disremembered and unaccounted for." The discrete subjects of these essays constitute so many threads of the larger fabric that binds southern women, black and white, in an interlocking mesh. Jacquelyn Hall warns of the dangers of homogenizing the distinctiveness of southern women's experience and, especially, of overemphasizing southern racism, thereby implicitly minimizing racism throughout our society. Her plea to attend to the varieties of southern women's experience commands attention and is being met. Darlene Clark Hine enjoins us to recognize and rend the dissemblances behind which black women have concealed their identities, to develop an analytic framework that can help to account for those whom Morrison calls the disremembered. Between them, Hall and Hine remind us that if identities are always personal, they are also always historical. The legacy of slavery and a distinct form of racism bind southern women together in what Hall calls an "explosive intimacy" even as it divides them by an intimate antagonism. The gradual recovery of their interlocking stories, to which this volume contributes, is inescapably reshaping our understanding of American women's and southern history.

5. Toni Morrison, *Beloved* (New York: Random House, 1987), 273, 274, 275.

ᔥ Jacquelyn Dowd Hall

Partial Truths
Writing Southern Women's History

The First Southern Conference on Women's History had the feel of a historic occasion—a time to celebrate accomplishment, strengthen community, and acknowledge our good fortune in catching the wave of southern women's history just as the issues raised by our regional experience are moving from the periphery to the center of scholarly debate.[1] Yet the gathering also posed implicit questions. Why was this the "first" southern conference on women's history? Why now, in the late eighties, was silence giving way to initiative? What might account for the excitement in the air, the shared feeling that we were poised at last to write women into southern history and the South into the narrative of American women's past?

Southern women's history might have been written a long time ago if anyone had been listening in 1938 when Julia Cherry Spruill published *Women's Life and Work in the Southern Colonies*. But Spruill belonged to a generation of women's historians whose work fell into a void. Her successors, Gerda Lerner and Anne Firor Scott, launched our enterprise. In *The Grimké Sisters from South Carolina* (1967) and *Black Women in White America* (1972), Lerner made visible a pantheon of black and white southern heroines. Scott's *The Southern Lady* (1970) revised the myth of the ornamental plantation mistress and rescued foremothers whose battle for higher education and devotion to women's organizations erected the scaffolding on

1. For an insightful commentary on the conference, see Elsa Barkley Brown, "Open Letter about Issues Raised by 1988 Southern Conference," *Southern Association for Women Historians Newsletter* 19, no. 2 (May 1989): 3–7.

which Scott herself could stand. Together, Lerner and Scott helped inspire an upcoming generation whose energy and commitment quickly turned women's history into an astoundingly fast-growing field. Yet, by and large, these younger scholars took neither race nor region as their guiding themes. Fifteen years after the appearance of *The Southern Lady,* works on the South still constituted a tiny fraction of the outpouring of scholarship in American women's history.[2]

That neglect can be traced in part to the regional origins of the graduate students who comprised the first generation of women's historians. What gets written largely depends on who is doing the writing, and the South has not been notable for training and supporting female scholars. The region's poverty, together with its fierce resistance to coeducation and devotion to private, church-sponsored colleges, limited white women's opportunities. Black women were more likely to attend coeducational institutions, but these schools, which were founded for the most part by northern missionaries after the Civil War, concentrated on moral supervision and vocational training. Although both white women's colleges and coeducational black institutions nurtured autonomy, leadership, and social responsibility, they did not prepare women for scholarly careers, and research institutions such as the University of North Carolina and the University of Virginia did not fully open their doors to women until the 1970s.[3] Ambitious southern women left the re-

2. Spruill, *Women's Life and Work in the Southern Colonies* (Chapel Hill: University of North Carolina Press, 1938); Scott, *The Southern Lady: From Pedestal to Politics, 1830–1930* (Chicago: University of Chicago Press, 1970); Lerner, *The Grimké Sisters from South Carolina: Rebels against Slavery* (Boston: Houghton Mifflin, 1967); and Lerner, ed., *Black Women in White America: A Documentary History* (New York: Pantheon Books, 1972). For a survey of works on the South, see Jacquelyn Dowd Hall and Anne Firor Scott, "Women in the South," in *Interpreting Southern History: Historiographical Essays in Honor of Sanford W. Higginbotham,* ed. John B. Boles and Evelyn Thomas Nolen (Baton Rouge: Louisiana State University Press, 1987), 454–509.

3. For southern women's education, see Virginia Shadron et al., "The Historical Perspective: A Bibliographical Essay," in *Stepping Off the Pedestal: Academic Women in the South,* ed. Patricia A. Stringer and Irene Thompson for the Commission on the Status of Women in the Profession (New York: Modern Language Association of America, 1982), 145–68; and Pamela Dean, "Learning to Be New Women: Campus Culture at the North Carolina Normal and Industrial College," *North Carolina Historical Review* 68, no. 3 (July 1991): 286–306, and *Women on the Hill: A History of Women at the*

gion, and those who stayed seldom found jobs in major universities.[4] The expansion of higher education in the South after World War II has gradually altered this situation.[5] Yet few southerners figured among the students who launched women's history in the early 1970s, and those few usually did their graduate work in the Northeast or the Midwest. When the members of this pivotal generation began their research, they turned not to southern history but to topics that resonated with their own experience or that lay close at hand.[6]

The preoccupations of southern historiography also served to bury issues of gender. Until the 1950s most historians sang the praises of the Old South in order to vindicate the New. The publication of C. Vann Woodward's *Origins of the New South* in 1951 and the wholesale rewriting of the southern past sparked by the civil rights movement changed all that.[7] In the 1960s and 1970s no area of American history, save perhaps the study of colonial New England, exhibited such creativity. But race, not class or gender, was the new scholarship's obsession.

University of North Carolina (Chapel Hill: Division of Student Affairs, University of North Carolina, 1987). For insights into black women's educational experience, see Elsa Barkley Brown, "Educating Southern Black Women: Hartshorn Memorial and Spelman Colleges, 1881–1930" (paper presented at the Conference on Women in the Progressive Era, National Museum of American History, Smithsonian Institution, Washington, D.C., March 10–11, 1988).

4. Julia Cherry Spruill, who lived in Chapel Hill but was never offered an appointment at the University of North Carolina, is a case in point, as is another lifelong Chapel Hill resident, Guion Griffiths Johnson, author of *Ante-bellum North Carolina: A Social History* (Chapel Hill: University of North Carolina Press, 1937).

5. Between 1980–1983, 14 to 15 percent of historians employed in four-year institutions of higher learning in the South were women; this figure was essentially the same as the national average. However, the larger the department, the smaller the percentage of women employed (Ad Hoc Committee on the Status of Women in the SHA, "A Statistical Report on the Participation of Women in the Southern Historical Association, 1935–1985," *Journal of Southern History* 52, no. 2 [May 1986]: 282–88).

6. A distinguished exception was Sara M. Evans, author of *Personal Politics: The Roots of Women's Liberation in the Civil Rights Movement and the New Left* (New York: Alfred A. Knopf, 1979).

7. Woodward, *Origins of the New South, 1877–1913* (Baton Rouge: Louisiana State University Press, 1951). It should be noted, however, that Woodward built on a process of revisionism that began in the 1930s.

From the late nineteenth century onward, black women had artic-
ulated the links between racism and patriarchy.[8] But their insights
found voice primarily in fiction and women's organizations, not in
historical writing. Ignoring this black feminist tradition, the revi-
sionist historians of the 1960s collapsed the categories of race and
gender, using the struggle for "manhood" as the central metaphor
for their valorization of African-American culture. Only after the
triumph of the scholarship inspired by the civil rights movement
did feminist historians have room to maneuver. Only then could
black feminists make themselves heard when they rejected the monolithic, socially constructed category of race and asserted a more complex, if equally constructed, identity as southern African-American
women. Only after they had made *that* move could black and white
scholars join in the project of understanding how gender, class, and
race crosscut the history of the region.[9]

8. Among the scholars who have made this point is Hazel V. Carby, "'On
the Threshold of Woman's Era': Lynching, Empire, and Sexuality in Black
Feminist Theory," in *"Race" Writing and Difference*, ed. Henry Louis Gates
(Chicago: University of Chicago Press, 1986), 301–16, and *Reconstructing
Womanhood: The Emergence of the Afro-American Woman Novelist* (New York:
Oxford University Press, 1987).

9. For surveys of the new literature in black women's history, see Darlene
Clark Hine, "Lifting the Veil, Shattering the Silence: Black Women's His-
tory in Slavery and Freedom," in *The State of Afro-American History: Past,
Present, and Future*, ed. Darlene Clark Hine (Baton Rouge: Louisiana State
University Press, 1986), 223–49; Hall and Scott, "Women in the South";
Hall, "Partial Truths," in *Signs: Journal of Women in Culture and Society* 14,
no. 4 (Summer 1989): 900–911; Evelyn Brooks Higginbotham, "Beyond the
Sound of Silence: Afro-American Women's History," *Gender & History* 1,
no. 1 (Spring 1989): 50–67. A sixteen-volume series edited by Darlene Clark
Hine has now made hard-to-find texts widely available. See Hine, ed., *Black
Women in United States History: From Colonial Times to the Present* (New York:
Carlson Publishing, 1990). Studies focusing on the Indian and Hispanic
experience are beginning to reveal the multicultural nature of what has
usually been seen as a biracial society. See, for example, Theda Perdue,
"Southern Indians and the Cult of True Womanhood," in *The Web of South-
ern Social Relations: Women, Family, and Education*, ed. Walter J. Fraser, Jr.,
R. Frank Saunders, Jr., and Jon L. Wakelyn (Athens: University of Georgia
Press, 1985), 35–51, and "Cherokee Women and the Trail of Tears," *Journal of
Women's History* 1, no. 1 (Spring 1989): 14–30; Julia Kirk Blackwelder, *Women
of the Depression: Caste and Culture in San Antonio, 1929–1939* (College Sta-
tion: Texas A & M University Press, 1984); and Nancy Hewitt, "Politicizing
Domesticity: Anglo, Black, and Latin Women in Tampa's Progressive Move-

The final reason for the shortcircuiting of southern women's history was the very elegance and persuasiveness of an interpretive framework drawn from the experience of middle-class women in the Northeast. This rendition of women's history turned on the Industrial Revolution, which, beginning in the 1830s, severed work from life, the public from the private sphere, and transformed the household from a unit of production to a woman-dominated haven from a heartless world. Women lost their productive economic roles but gained access to education and a conviction of moral superiority. Above all, they acquired the sense of grievance and group identity that would inspire them to form voluntary associations, oppose slavery, and launch a movement for women's rights.

Much of the research done in women's history during the 1970s and early 1980s focused on the women's culture that flourished under this system of sex segregation. Carroll Smith-Rosenberg and Nancy F. Cott mapped the general terrain, and other historians have found one example after another of the values women shared.[10] Their work has had enormous influence, in part because it dovetailed with a more general current of cultural feminism, a move to claim the right of self-definition and to reevaluate the ascribed characteristics of womanhood in a positive light.

Cultural feminism made the important point that under conditions of oppression women developed strengths and attributes that ought to be valued and promoted. Yet like all interpretive frameworks it revealed only partial truths. The more thoroughly it was elaborated, the clearer its limitations became. It could not provide a long-term program for eliminating the conditions that nurtured the very qualities it praised. It was implicitly prescriptive, positing a model of womanhood to which all should adhere.[11]

In part because of the habits of our discipline—a concern for con-

ments," in *Gender, Class, Race, and Reform in the Progressive Era,* ed. Noralee Frankel and Nancy S. Dye (Lexington: University Press of Kentucky, 1991), 24–41.

10. Smith-Rosenberg, "Female World of Love and Ritual: Relations between Women in Nineteenth-Century America," *Signs* 1, no. 1 (Autumn 1975): 1–29; Cott, *The Bonds of Womanhood: "Woman's Sphere" in New England, 1780–1835* (New Haven: Yale University Press, 1977).

11. Linda Alcoff, "Cultural Feminism versus Post-Structuralism: The Identity Crisis in Feminist Theory," *Signs* 13, no. 3 (Spring 1988): 405–36, esp. 414.

text, a suspicion of general rules—and in part because socialist-feminist writers were careful to link domestic ideology to the logic of class formation, most historians of women's culture avoided the excesses of "essentialism" (the implication that the qualities we associate with femininity are fixed, timeless, and universal). Yet, taken as a whole, their work did tend to hide hierarchies among women and women's commonalities with men. Most important for our purposes, this literature had little to say about a region in which a slave labor system forestalled the Victorian separation of spheres. In the antebellum South, both black and white women continued to live in households that carried on basic economic production under the direct authority of a man. White women may have absorbed Victorian notions of female distinctiveness, but they did not translate that ideology into a feminist movement. Accordingly, the South made it into this literature mainly as a footnote or a mysterious exception to the rule. The result is what several scholars have termed the "New Englandization" of American women's history.[12]

If "sisterhood"—a group identity based on shared oppression and a shared culture—constituted the chief theme of the first wave of women's history, "difference"—among women as well as between men and women—has become the key word of the late 1980s. And it is no accident that studies of the South, by simultaneously refining and exploding women's history's dominant story, have helped to bring about this change.

Catherine Clinton, in *The Plantation Mistress*, was the first to decry the "New Englandization" of women's history. Dolores Janiewski's study of working-class women in Durham, North Carolina, anticipated the recent emphasis on race and class and argued against any notion of an interracial sisterhood "under the skin." Jean Friedman maintained that southern women *were* exceptions to the rule and traced their failure to achieve collective agency to the "enclosed garden" of kin-oriented evangelical communities.[13]

12. Elizabeth Fox-Genovese, *Within the Plantation Household: Black and White Women of the Old South* (Chapel Hill: University of North Carolina Press, 1988), 38–41; Catherine Clinton, *The Plantation Mistress: Woman's World in the Old South* (New York: Pantheon, 1982), xv–xvi. For the figurative and contested nature of the notion of "separate spheres," see Linda K. Kerber, "Separate Spheres, Female Worlds, Woman's Place: The Rhetoric of Women's History," *Journal of American History* 75, no. 1 (July 1988): 9–39.

13. Clinton, *Plantation Mistress*, xv–xvi; Janiewski, *Sisterhood Denied: Race,*

Suzanne Lebsock's *The Free Women of Petersburg* used a southern community study to illuminate global concerns. For the literary evidence on which most scholars have relied, she substituted legal records that allowed her to isolate moments of choice and thus to document the daily enactment of women's values. She challenged the notion of southern exceptionalism by showing how much urban women shared with their counterparts in other regions. And she demonstrated that the boundaries of "women's sphere" were far from static; on the contrary, even in a region untouched by organized feminism, those boundaries had been constantly renegotiated under the pressures of social and economic change. Like Friedman and Janiewski, Lebsock broke with the entrenched historiographical habit of separating blacks from whites and took free women of both races as the subject of her book.[14]

In contrast to Friedman and Lebsock, who attempted an integrated history yet focused primarily on white women, Deborah Gray White provided our first sustained look at black women's experience under slavery. *Ar'n't I a Woman?* constituted, among other things, a critical intervention in the "matriarchy debate." Where Daniel Patrick Moynihan had seen a female-dominated "tangle of pathology" and his liberal critics had found patriarchal two-parent households, White saw matrifocality and egalitarianism, born both of African antecedents and of creative adaptations to oppression. She also posited an African-American women's culture, a move that might be taken as an attempt to extend a New England model to the slave South. But White's description of female group identity in the slave quarters could also be seen as a strategic reversal in which the dominant story becomes the variant theme. Nancy Hewitt, for instance, used White's work to argue that slave women were typical rather than exceptional in developing female solidarity based on a sexual

---

Gender, and Class in a New South Community (Philadelphia: Temple University Press, 1985); Friedman, *The Enclosed Garden: Women and Community in the Evangelical South, 1830–1900* (Chapel Hill: University of North Carolina Press, 1985).

14. Lebsock, *The Free Women of Petersburg: Status and Culture in a Southern Town, 1784–1860* (New York: W. W. Norton, 1984). Among the early works in women's history, Mary Beth Norton's *Liberty's Daughters: The Revolutionary Experience of American Women, 1750–1800* (Boston: Little, Brown, 1980) was also notable for its racial and regional inclusiveness.

division of labor but wielding that identity in defense of same-class men and defiance of other-class women.[15]

Jacqueline Jones offered a panoramic view of black working women from the antebellum period through the late twentieth century. Her chapter on slavery stressed relations of domination and family ties rather than women's networks. But like White, she drew attention to the complexity of slave women's social identities, as expressed in the distinction they drew between the "labor of love" they performed within the slave community and the "labor of sorrow" expropriated by their masters.[16]

Elizabeth Fox-Genovese offered the strongest attack yet on "New Englandization." Southern women's history, she maintained, "does not constitute another regional variation on the main story; it constitutes another story." More systematically than any of her predecessors, Fox-Genovese delineated the "explosive intimacy" between plantation mistresses and their slaves. She rejected Anne Scott's stress on secret abolitionism among plantation mistresses and contended that women's class interests kept them loyal to the slave system. She painted a bleaker portrait of slave women's culture than that rendered by White and Jones. Where other scholars have seen black women buffered by African traditions, stable families, and women's networks, Fox-Genovese emphasized the damage wrought by the disruption of gender conventions within the slave community.[17]

15. White, *"Ar'n't I a Woman?" Female Slaves in the Plantation South* (New York: W. W. Norton, 1985); Hewitt, "Beyond the Search for Sisterhood: American Women's History in the 1980s," *Social History* 10, no. 3 (October 1985): 299–321. For other feminist contributions to the matriarchy debate, see Suzanne Lebsock, "Free Black Women and the Question of Matriarchy: Petersburg, Virginia, 1784–1820," *Feminist Studies* 8, no. 2 (Summer 1982): 271–92; Christie Farnham, "Sapphire? The Issue of Dominance in the Slave Family, 1830–1865," in *"To Toil the Livelong Day": America's Women at Work, 1780–1980,* ed. Carol Groneman and Mary Beth Norton (Ithaca: Cornell University Press, 1987), 68–83.

16. Jones, *Labor of Love, Labor of Sorrow: Black Women, Work, and the Family from Slavery to the Present* (New York: Basic Books, 1985).

17. Fox-Genovese, *Plantation Household,* 42, 315; Christine Stansell, "Explosive Intimacy," *The Nation* (March 27, 1989): 417–22. Stephanie McCurry, "Defense of Their World: Gender, Class, and the Yeomanry of the South Carolina Low Country, 1820–1860" (Ph.D. diss., State University of New York, Binghamton, 1988), makes a similar argument about the conservative implications of gender arrangements and household politics among the southern yeomanry. For assessments of antislavery sentiment among

These landmark books represent only a sampling of the research that is beginning to change the way we see both southern history and the history of American women. Much new work has yet to reach publication, and much continues to be published outside the mainstream scholarly presses and journals.[18] Thus far, the burden of most studies has been to challenge the New England paradigm by stressing regional differences. But as the outlines of southern women's history rise more clearly into view, the region may come to look less and less distinctive. Indeed, we may find ourselves regarding the South as in some ways more paradigmatic than peculiar. Better yet, attention to southern "difference" may expose other differences, thus undermining a habit of normative thinking that marginalizes the experience of "others" of every stripe.

Studies of emancipation and Reconstruction are a case in point. Stirred in part by the publication of the Freedmen's Bureau papers under the direction of Leslie Rowland and Ira Berlin, interest in this great turning point in the nation's history has intensified. New research has revealed a rural black culture in which men and women claimed the land as their due, viewed the franchise as a communal right, rejected the work ethic and possessive individualism in favor of an ethos of mutuality, and created self-help institutions that testify

---

white women, see Anne Firor Scott, "Women's Perspective on the Patriarchy in the 1850s," *Journal of American History* 61 (June 1974): 52–64; Drew Gilpin Faust, "In Search of the Real Mary Chesnut," *Reviews in American History* 10 (March 1982): 54–59. For the centrality of gender conventions in white plantation life, see Steven M. Stowe, *Intimacy and Power in the Old South: Ritual in the Lives of the Planters* (Baltimore: Johns Hopkins University Press, 1987); Bertram Wyatt-Brown, *Southern Honor: Ethics and Behavior in the Old South* (New York: Oxford University Press, 1982); and Orville Vernon Burton, *In My Father's House Are Many Mansions: Family and Community in Edgefield, South Carolina* (Chapel Hill: University of North Carolina Press, 1985).

18. See, for example, Suzanne Lebsock, *"A Share of Honour": Virginia Women 1600–1945* (Richmond: Virginia Women's Cultural History Project, 1984); Priscilla Cortelyou Little and Robert C. Vaughan, eds., *A New Perspective: Southern Women's Cultural History from the Civil War to Civil Rights* (Charlottesville: Virginia Foundation for the Humanities, 1989). Special issues on southern women have been compiled by *Southern Exposure* 4, no. 4 (1977); *Frontiers: A Journal of Women Studies* 9, no. 3 (1987); and *Helicon Nine: The Journal of Women's Arts and Letters*, no. 17/18 (1987). See also *Special Issue: Liberating Our Past, 400 Years of Southern History, Southern Exposure* 12, no. 6 (November/December 1984). For articles on black women, see *Sage: A Scholarly Journal of Black Women*.

to an autonomy in bondage and a process of rapid self-emancipation that we are just beginning to understand. Only a tiny proportion of the research in women's history has focused on this period.[19] But once we begin to think about the construction of gender among the ex-slaves not as an aberration but as the norm for many of the world's peoples, our conception of what constitutes the "master narrative" of women's history may be radically transformed.

The American Revolution has inspired some of the best of the new women's history, and in recent years historians have turned increasingly to the study of women and war. Yet George Rable's *Civil Wars*, published in 1989, constitutes the first sustained look at southern women and the crisis of southern nationalism. Anne Scott suggested that the war emancipated some white women even as it freed the slaves. Suzanne Lebsock, on the contrary, speculated that the experience of defeat gave rise to male backlash and a bunker mentality in men and women alike. Joel Williamson's argument about the psychological origins of racial extremism jibed with Lebsock's intuition. Rable concludes that southern white women, like their counterparts during the American Revolution, were politicized by war and drawn into non-traditional responsibilities. Yet these gains, if gains they were, were swept away by postwar reaction.[20] The work of these scholars, however, marks only the beginning of what looks to be an efflorescence of gender-conscious Civil War

19. See, however, Kathleen C. Berkeley, "'Colored Ladies Also Contributed': Black Women's Activities from Benevolence to Social Welfare, 1866–1896," in *Web of Southern Social Relations*, 181–203; Elsa Barkley Brown, "To Catch the Vision of Freedom: African-American Women Struggle for Peoplehood and Community" (paper presented at the Conference on Afro-American Women and the Vote, University of Massachusetts at Amherst, November 1987); Laura F. Edwards, "Sexual Violence, Gender, Reconstruction, and the Extension of Patriarchy in Granville County, North Carolina," *North Carolina Historical Review* 68, no. 3 (July 1991): 237–60.

20. Linda K. Kerber, *Women of the Republic: Intellect and Ideology in Revolutionary America* (Chapel Hill: University of North Carolina Press, 1980); Norton, *Liberty's Daughters*; Margaret Randolph Higonnet et al., eds., *Behind the Lines: Gender and the Two World Wars* (New Haven: Yale University Press, 1987); George C. Rable, *Civil Wars: Women and the Crisis of Southern Nationalism* (Urbana: University of Illinois Press, 1989); Scott, *The Southern Lady*, 105–33; Lebsock, *Free Women of Petersburg*, 237–49; Joel Williamson, *A Rage for Order: Black/White Relations in the American South since Emancipation* (New York: Oxford University Press, 1986), 78–86. For an earlier study, see Mary Elizabeth Massey, *Bonnet Brigades* (New York: Alfred A. Knopf, 1966).

scholarship. Studies that treat black women as well as whites, poor women as well as former plantation wives, may force us not only to rewrite the story of the Civil War but also to think about war itself in more nuanced terms.[21]

Whatever conclusions we reach about the impact of the conflict, the generation born after the Civil War and coming of age in the 1880s and 1890s broke with the past in significant ways. Southern historians have long squabbled over the question of continuity versus discontinuity. Woodward, the defender of discontinuity, has been challenged by what he calls "Continuarians" from the left and the right. But he has also received some strong recent support, most notably from Edward Ayers, whose forthcoming book argues that the New South was newer than even Woodward imagined. As evidence of change, Ayers cites the spread of railroads, towns, and factories, the pull of consumerism, black efforts to test the limits of segregation, Populist challenges to corporate power, and an outburst of cultural creativity that gave rise to the region's great popular music and distinctive religious forms.[22]

As we have seen, the dominant story in women's history was paced by the timing of capitalist development. What would happen to that story if it turned on this late nineteenth-century breakpoint in the nation's history: the proletarianization of the South's black slaves and white yeoman farmers and the emergence of a town-based middle class? And what would happen to our understanding of southern history if we saw class formation as a gendered process? What part did ideas about manhood and womanhood, intimacy and domesticity, play in the identity of the new middle class? What roles did women assume in a black community in which even the most prosperous men were denied economic and political power? How did white and black farm families renegotiate divisions of

21. See, for example, Drew Gilpin Faust, "Altars of Sacrifice: Confederate Women and the Narratives of War," *Journal of American History* 76, no. 4 (March 1990): 1200–228; Victoria Bynum, "'War Within a War': Women's Participation in the Revolt of the North Carolina Piedmont, 1863–1865," *Frontiers*, 43–49, 88, and "The Lowest Rung: Court Control over Free Black and Poor White Women," *Southern Exposure*, 40–44; LeeAnn Whites, *War, Industrialization, and Gender Reform: The Process of Feminization in the New South, Augusta, Georgia, 1860–1900* (forthcoming).

22. C. Vann Woodward, *Thinking Back: The Perils of Writing History* (Baton Rouge: Louisiana State University Press, 1986); Ayers, *The Promise of the New South, 1877–1906* (New York: Oxford University Press, forthcoming).

labor and sexual codes in response to the pressures and opportunities of a wage-based economy?[23]

We still have no general study of southern women's roles in the Progressive movement that was spawned by this economic transformation, notwithstanding Anne Scott's pathbreaking work and recent
attempts by feminist scholars to recast Progressivism as a women's
movement. Paula Baker and Nancy Hewitt, however, have suggested
strategies that may overcome this neglect: a renewed attention to politics, on the one hand, and a focus on community studies on the other.

Paula Baker has argued that nineteenth-century political culture
in fact consisted of two cultures. For men, participation in party
politics was a primary source of gender identity; issues themselves
were relatively unimportant. Women, on the other hand, joined
voluntary associations that were nonpartisan, highly programmatic,
and generally favorable to government action. These two cultures
converged in the early twentieth century, as women got the vote
and men fell away from partisan enthusiasm and looked more to
voluntarism and state intervention. Baker terms this development
the "domestication" of American politics. Others see it as the seed-
bed of the welfare state.[24]

Did such a convergence take place in the South? James Leloudis's
work on male educational reformers suggests that it did. So does
Glenda Gilmore's belief that the entry of white women and some black
women into party politics in North Carolina ushered in a "politics of
civility" that replaced the racial extremism of the 1890s and lasted until
the civil rights movement began.[25]

23. For attempts to address these issues, see Jacquelyn Dowd Hall et al.,
Like a Family: The Making of a Southern Cotton Mill World (Chapel Hill: Uni-
versity of North Carolina Press, 1987); Jacquelyn Dowd Hall, "Disorderly
Women: Gender and Labor Militancy in the Appalachian South," *Journal of
American History* 73, no. 2 (September 1986): 354–82; Janette Greenwood,
"New South Middle Class: Race and Class in Charlotte, North Carolina,
1852–1920" (Ph.D. diss. in progress, University of Virginia).

24. Baker, "The Domestication of Politics: Women and American Political
Society, 1780–1920," *American Historical Review* 89, no. 3 (June 1984): 620–47.

25. Leloudis, "'A More Certain Means of Grace': Pedagogy, Self, and
Society in North Carolina, 1880–1920" (Ph.D. diss., University of North
Carolina, 1989); Gilmore, "Finding the Fault Line of White Supremacy:
Black Women and Ballots in North Carolina, 1920" (paper presented at the
First Southern Conference on Women's History, Converse College, Spar-
tanburg, S.C., June 11, 1988).

Nancy Hewitt has made a strong case for the use of community studies to explore these and other issues. Hewitt believes that an emphasis on national women's groups privileges permanent, same-sex organizations as a vehicle for female activism over the spontaneous mobilizations more characteristic of the working class. She argues that we should stand in the local community looking out, for that perspective includes larger movements and global forces, even as it reveals the contradictions and complexities that push us to new levels of analysis.[26]

Nancy Schrom Dye argues for reinterpreting Progressivism from exactly this community-based point of view. She believes that early Progressivism was a broad-based democratic movement. Its typical local leader was a married woman with children, not an educated single woman like Jane Addams who personified the movement at the national level. Such women erased the line between public and private in a fight against the dangers industrialization posed.[27]

The turn-of-the-century South held its own peculiar dangers. Lee-Ann Whites's rendition of an intriguing debate between two of Georgia's leading Progressives, Clare DeGraffenried and Rebecca Latimer Felton, illustrates one form women's fear took. Both DeGraffenried and Felton were preoccupied with the suffering of white farm women and widowed textile workers who could no longer count on male protection and support. But DeGraffenried advocated protective legislation, while Felton gained notoriety as an advocate of lynching as a means of shielding isolated rural women from sexual assault. Tellingly, when another reformer, Jessie Daniel Ames, sought to revise and extend female Progressivism in the 1920s and 1930s, she turned Felton's solution on its head. She rejected chivalry in the name of autonomy, picturing women not as dependent members of households but as individual citizens who needed only the equal protection of the law.[28]

26. Nancy Hewitt, "The Feminist Frontier: Women and Community Activism" (Diane Weiss Memorial Lecture, The Center for the Humanities, Wesleyan University, Middletown, Conn., October 1987).

27. Dye, "Reform at the Grassroots: Women, Family and Community in the Progressive Era" (paper presented at the Conference on Women in the Progressive Era).

28. Whites, "The De Graffenried Controversy: Class, Race, and Gender in the New South," *Journal of Southern History* 54, no. 3 (August 1988): 449–78; Jacquelyn Dowd Hall, *Revolt against Chivalry: Jessie Daniel Ames and the Women's Campaign against Lynching* (New York: Columbia University Press, 1979), and "'The Mind That Burns in Each Body': Women, Rape and

Black women were, if anything, even more preoccupied with racial violence and sexual exploitation. From the late nineteenth century onward, rape has been a central theme in black women's literature, while black women reformers have consistently linked the lynching of black men with the violation of black women. As Hazel Carby has argued, the "analysis of the relation between political terrorism, economic oppression, and conventional codes of sexuality" put forward by the antilynching reformer Ida B. Wells at the turn of the century "has still to be surpassed." Elsa Barkley Brown has suggested that "womanism" best describes the stance of such activists, who drew no distinction between race progress and the defense of black womanhood and fought simultaneously for sexual equality in the black community and racial equality in the society at large.[29]

Darlene Clark Hine and Deborah White have underlined the costs of this struggle. Victimized by black men as well as whites, black women sought to shield themselves from negative stereotypes about their sexuality. In so doing, they created a "culture of dissemblance" that masked their private lives and contributed to their historical invisibility. Moreover, clubwomen who made chastity the "litmus test of middle-class respectability" drove a wedge between themselves and the masses of black women.[30]

Racial Violence," in *Powers of Desire: The Politics of Sexuality,* ed. Ann Snitow, Christine Stansell, and Sharon Thompson (New York: Monthly Review Press, 1983), 328–49.

29. Carby, "'On the Threshold of Woman's Era,'" 307; Elsa Barkley Brown, "Womanist Consciousness: Maggie Lena Walker and the Independent Order of Saint Luke," *Signs* 14, no. 3 (Spring 1989): 610–33. Other important studies of black women activists include Jacqueline Anne Rouse, *Lugenia Burns Hope: Black Southern Reformer* (Athens: University of Georgia Press, 1989); Dorothy Salem, *To Better Our World: Black Women in Organized Reform, 1890–1920* (Brooklyn: Carlson Publishing, 1990); Rosalyn Terborg-Penn, "African-American Women's Networks in the Anti-Lynching Crusade," in Frankel and Dye, eds., *Gender, Class, Race, and Reform,* 148–61; and Glenda Elizabeth Gilmore, "Gender and Jim Crow: Sarah Dudley Pettey's Vision of the New South," *North Carolina Historical Review* 68, no. 3 (July 1991): 261–85.

30. Hine, "Rape and the Inner Lives of Black Women in the Middle West: Preliminary Thoughts on the Culture of Dissemblance," *Signs* 14, no. 4 (Summer 1989): 912–20; White, "Fettered Sisterhood: Class and Classism in Early Twentieth-Century Black Women's History" (paper presented at the American Studies Association Meeting, Toronto, Canada, November 5, 1989).

The women's interracial movement that emerged in the South in the 1920s demonstrated the salience of this issue for black and white southern women alike. Addressing the founding meeting of the Woman's Committee of the Commission on Interracial Cooperation in 1920, the North Carolina educator Charlotte Hawkins Brown protested against the racial-sexual ideology that made protection of white women the excuse for lynching and cast all black women as willing participants in interracial sex. Subsequently, the Woman's Committee took as its central concern the integrity and well-being of "the Negro home" and attacked the sexual exploitation of black women that, in its view, constituted the chief threat to that well-being. The committee's successor, the Association of Southern Women for the Prevention of Lynching, focused on combating violence against black men, but it also grappled with the issues of rape and interracial sex. Jessie Daniel Ames, the group's director, was a passionate critic of the double standard that "considers an assault by a white man as a moral lapse upon his part, better ignored and forgotten, while an assault by a Negro against a white woman is a hideous crime punishable with death by law or lynching."[31]

In "Seeking Ecstasy on the Battlefield: Danger and Pleasure in Nineteenth-Century Feminist Sexual Thought," Ellen C. DuBois and Linda Gordon sought to understand "how feminists conceptualized different sexual dangers, as a means of organizing *resistance* to sexual oppression." The new studies of black and white southern women show how race and region complicate the question. At the same time, these studies avoid treating either group monolithically by dealing openly and empathetically with its limitations and internal divisions.[32]

Rosalyn Terborg-Penn, Marjorie Spruill Wheeler, Dolores Janiewski, Suzanne Lebsock, Mary Martha Thomas, and others are similarly complicating our understanding of the southern suffrage move-

31. Hall, *Revolt against Chivalry,* 93–94, 98–100, 201–6. See also Hall, "'The Mind That Burns,'" and "A Bond of Common Womanhood? Building a Women's Interracial Community in the Jim Crow South," in *Women, Families and Communities: Readings in American History,* ed. Nancy Hewitt, 2 vols. (Glenview, Ill.: Scott, Foresman, 1990), 2:99–114.

32. Linda Gordon and Ellen Carol DuBois, "Seeking Ecstasy on the Battlefield: Danger and Pleasure in Nineteenth-Century Feminist Sexual Thought," *Feminist Studies* 9, no. 1 (Spring 1983): 9.

ment. Building on the foundation laid by A. Elizabeth Taylor, these studies underline the significance of white (and some black) women's acquiring the vote during a period in which black people as a group were disfranchised and the vote itself lost importance as an avenue and index of political participation.[33]

Lebsock has suggested that our investigation of this issue has been stymied in part by the influence of Aileen S. Kraditor's powerful 1965 study, *The Ideas of the Woman Suffrage Movement, 1890–1920*. Kraditor argued that southern suffragists sought the franchise primarily in order to increase the white electorate and counter the black vote. Lebsock believes that Kraditor was right in pinpointing race as a central theme but that she underestimated the salience of gender issues in southern political culture; obscured changes in southern suffragist strategies over time; diverted attention from the antisuffragists who took the race-baiting offensive; and ignored the activists who went on to participate in interracial coalitions.[34]

Other students of southern suffragism take a different tack. Marjorie Spruill Wheeler argues that race was the key to the timing and the changing strategies of the southern movement but that the calculations of national leaders were as important as the attitudes of southern women in determining the ways in which the race issue was framed and used. Rosalyn Terborg-Penn has shown in detail how discrimination against black women pervaded the feminist movement, North and South.[35]

It has become a truism that the Progressive movement did not end in 1920. In the South in particular, women's reform efforts in some ways intensified after World War I, as activists began building alliances across class and racial lines. Indeed, the 1920s, like the 1890s, may have constituted a breakpoint that brought a new political generation

33. Among Taylor's many studies of the southern suffrage movement is *The Woman Suffrage Movement in Tennessee* (New York: Bookman, 1957).

34. Kraditor, *The Ideas of the Woman Suffrage Movement, 1890–1920* (New York: Columbia University Press, 1965); Suzanne Lebsock, "Woman Suffrage and White Supremacy: A Virginia Case Study," in *Visible Women: An Anthology*, ed. Nancy Hewitt and Suzanne Lebsock (Urbana: University of Illinois Press, forthcoming).

35. Wheeler, "New Women of the New South: The Leaders of the Woman Suffrage Movement in the Southern States" (Ph.D. diss., University of Virginia, 1989); Terborg-Penn, "Discontented Black Feminists: Prelude and Postscript to the Passage of the Nineteenth Amendment," in *Decades of Discontent: The Women's Movement, 1920–1940*, ed. Lois Scharf and Joan M. Jensen (Westport, Conn.: Greenwood Press, 1983), 261–78.

to the fore. Certainly, the 1920s generation rapidly assimilated modernist thought. During the interwar period, the South's writers, artists, social scientists, and political activists (followed belatedly by its historians) abandoned regional self-congratulation for lacerating self-criticism. Nowhere in the Western world was this change more concentrated and more dramatic. And its chief product—the southern literary renaissance—has received a great deal of scholarly attention.

Yet in all these studies, the southerners who struggle to "tell about the South," to question traditional boundaries and hierarchies and come to terms with the dark side of the region's psyche, turn out, for the most part, to be white men.[36] This blind spot is indefensible on two counts. First, it ignores the great achievements of black southern writers during this period. Second, it entirely overlooks the centrality of women and of gender issues to the modernist movement.

In their trilogy, *No Man's Land*, Sandra Gilbert and Susan Gubar argue that the entire movement of literary modernism developed as a response to the emergence of women into public and literary life. Male writers wrestled with anxieties about the castrating effects of female creativity while women celebrated their newfound power. If, until recently, the South has produced few women historians, the same cannot be said about its writers. Anne Loveland's and Roseanne Camacho's research on Lillian Smith; Anne Goodwyn Jones's book on southern women writers and her work-in-progress on "Faulkner's Daughters"; Alice Walker's recovery of Zora Neal Hurston; Louise Westling's study of Carson McCullers, Eudora Welty, and Flannery O'Connor; and Darden Asbury Pyron's research on Margaret Mitchell: these and other studies have uncovered women's unique contributions to southern modernism and the particularly intense form that the questioning of gender boundaries assumed in the region.[37]

36. Lillian Smith is among the most notable exceptions to this rule. Fred C. Hobson, *Tell About the South: The Southern Rage to Explain* (Baton Rouge: Louisiana State University Press, 1983); Richard H. King, *A Southern Renaissance: The Cultural Awakening of the American South* (New York: Oxford University Press, 1980); Daniel Joseph Singal, *The War Within: From Victorian to Modernist Thought in the South, 1919–1945* (Chapel Hill: University of North Carolina Press, 1982).

37. Sandra M. Gilbert and Susan Gubar, *The War of the Words*, vol. 1 of *No Man's Land: The Place of the Woman Writer in the Twentieth Century* (New Haven: Yale University Press, 1988). Anne C. Loveland, *Lillian Smith, a Southerner Confronting the South: A Biography* (Baton Rouge: Louisiana State University Press, 1986); Roseanne V. Camacho, "Race, Region, and Gender

The emergence of southern women's history, whose contours I have outlined above, comes at a moment of reevaluation and self-criticism in American women's history, a moment in which many voices are calling for revision of the dominant story. There are dangers in this rewriting. Studies of the South may posit a falsely unified "North," overlooking the ways in which the concepts of "North" and "South" are culturally—and mutually—constructed. We may equate "race" with "blacks," forgetting how racial identity shapes "white" lives. Above all, we may succumb to a male model of creativity in which each generation of hungry young writers, beset by the "anxiety of authorship," seeks to overthrow its literary fathers.[38]

The search for sisterhood that grew from the optimism of the early women's movement revealed a partial truth, but so does the emphasis on conflict and "difference" that marks our more chastened times. Indeed, if women's experience in the South teaches us anything, it is the destructive power of ideologies that draw invidious distinctions between women, thus obscuring their interrelationships and undercutting their alliances.

Our purpose, in any case, should not be to replace one model or agreed-upon fiction with another. Rather than seeking some new "centered structure," we need a historical practice that turns on partiality, that is self-conscious about perspective, that releases multiple voices rather than competing orthodoxies, and that, above all, nurtures an "internally differing but united political community."

in a Reassessment of Lillian Smith," 157–76 in this volume; Anne Goodwyn Jones, *Tomorrow Is Another Day: The Woman Writer in the South, 1859–1936* (Baton Rouge: Louisiana State University Press, 1981); Alice Walker, *In Search of Our Mothers' Gardens: Womanist Prose* (New York: Harcourt Brace Jovanovich, 1983); Louise Westling, *Sacred Groves and Ravaged Gardens: The Fiction of Eudora Welty, Carson McCullers, and Flannery O'Connor* (Athens: University of Georgia Press, 1985); Darden Asbury Pyron, ed., *Recasting: Gone with the Wind in American Culture* (Miami: University Presses of Florida, 1983), and *Southern Daughter: The Life of Margaret Mitchell* (New York: Oxford University Press, 1991). Thadious M. Davis, "Lumina Silvervale Wrote: Women's Art and Authorship in the Southern Region," *A New Perspective*, 53–64, offers a brilliant cross-class, cross-race overview of women's writing in a diverse region.

38. For contrasting models of creativity, see Harold Bloom, *The Anxiety of Influence: A Theory of Poetry* (New York: Oxford University Press, 1973); and Ruth Perry and Martine Watson Brownley, eds., *Mothering the Mind: Twelve Studies of Writers and Their Silent Partners* (New York: Holmes & Meier, 1984).

Only such a community of feminist scholars can realize what Ellen Carol DuBois and Vickie L. Ruiz have termed "an old populist dream and a postmodern challenge": a truly multicultural and thus a truly inclusive history of American women.[39]

39. Judith Newton and Nancy Hoffman, "Preface," *Feminist Studies* 14, no. 1 (Spring 1988): 3–9. For a critique of "centered structures," see Leslie Wahl Rabine, "A Feminist Politics of Non-Identity," *Feminist Studies* 14, no. 1 (Spring 1988): 11–31, esp. 23; and Jane Flax, "Postmodernism and Gender Relations in Feminist Theory," *Signs* 12, no. 4 (Summer 1987): 621–43. "Introduction," in *Unequal Sisters: A Multicultural Reader in U.S. Women's History*, ed. DuBois and Ruiz (New York: Routledge, 1990), xiii.

❧ Susan Westbury

Women in Bacon's Rebellion

As colonial historians try to write more inclusive histories, they are challenged by what we might call the great canonical events, such as wars and revolutions. In them the actions of white males, as distinguished from those of black males, Indians, or females of all races, seem to be decisive. As historians of women try to uncover the realities of women's lives, they too must confront wars and revolutions; in so doing, they force us to listen for what Jacquelyn Hall calls "multiple voices," and thus to think of war in "more nuanced terms." Only slowly are we gaining a point of view that sets leaders in their contexts, restores the minor players' parts, and declines interpretations that center on great men alone. And only recently have we begun to consider region as well as class and race in the history of women's experience. From these newer points of view, then, this paper looks at a familiar event—Bacon's Rebellion, the firestorm that hit Virginia in 1676 and usually considered to be an all-male affair.

At first glance, even the name of the Rebellion attests to its domination by one man, but contemporary sources acknowledge the roles of other actors—both male and female. Moreover, careful reading of seventeenth-century narratives (one of which was written by Virginia woman Ann Cotton) shows that women as well as men participated actively, although the women's contributions have gone largely unnoticed beside the doings of Bacon and the other men.[1]

1. One account is called "The History of Bacon's and Ingram's Rebellion, 1676," thus giving some credit to Laurence Ingram who took command of the rebels after Bacon's death (Charles McLean Andrews, ed., *Narratives of the Insurrections 1675–1690* [New York: Scribner's, 1915], 47–98). "A True Narrative of the Late Rebellion in Virginia, by the Royal Commissioners, 1677" omits Bacon's name altogether and suggests he was the pawn of other

Yet specific attention to women's participation throws new light on the history of that uprising. Politics crossed gender as well as class lines, and rebel and loyalist women responded differently to the turmoil that engulfed them in 1676.

Twentieth-century histories of Bacon's Rebellion have focused on the personalities of the leaders, or on the political, economic, and military circumstances of the uprising, but almost none mention women, apparently on the grounds that women's actions counted for little in the history of the Rebellion, or for that matter, in the history of women.[2] This view derives from the assumption that

---

planters (Andrews, *Narratives*, 105–41, 110–11). Although Andrews was unable to identify the author of the "History," the first-mentioned work has since been attributed to Virginia planter John Cotton. See also Jay B. Hubbell, "John and Ann Cotton of 'Queen's Creek,' Virginia," *American Literature* 10 (1938): 179–201. For the part played by an Indian woman see Mary W. McCartney, "Cockacoeske, Queen of Pamunkey: Diplomat and Suzeraine," in Peter H. Wood et al., eds., *Powhatan's Mantle: Indians in the Colonial South* (Lincoln: University of Nebraska Press, 1989), 173–95. Mrs. Ann Cotton, "An Account of Our Late Troubles in Virginia," in Peter Force, comp., *Tracts and other Papers . . . North America* (1836–1846; reprint, Gloucester, Mass.: Peter Smith, 1963), 1 no. 9.

2. Thomas Jefferson Wertenbaker, *Torchbearer of the Revolution: The Story of Bacon's Rebellion and Its Leader* (Princeton: Princeton University Press, 1940), portrays Bacon as a martyr who died for American freedom, while Governor Berkeley embodies English oppression. As a corrective, Wilcomb E. Washburn's *The Governor and the Rebel: A History of Bacon's Rebellion in Virginia* (New York: W. W. Norton, 1957) presents Bacon as the leader of a mob of aggressive, unprincipled frontiersmen and William Berkeley as a sensible, loyal governor. Other accounts have focused less on leaders and more on political and economic circumstances. Bernard Bailyn, "Politics and Social Structure in Virginia," in James Morton Smith, ed., *Seventeenth-Century America: Essays in Colonial History* (Chapel Hill: University of North Carolina Press for the Institute of Early American History and Culture, 1959), 90–115, sees struggles between competing elites as the main cause of the troubles in Virginia. Warren M. Billings, "The Causes of Bacon's Rebellion: Some Suggestions," *Virginia Magazine of History and Biography* (hereafter cited as *VMHB*) 78 (1970): 409–35, analyzes the fifteen years before the conflict broke out. Stephen Saunders Webb, *1676: The End of American Independence* (New York: Alfred A. Knopf, 1984), makes some token references to women (5–6, 20–21, for example) but concentrates mostly on the larger imperial system and the men who ran it. Edmund S. Morgan, *American Slavery, American Freedom: The Ordeal of Colonial Virginia* (New York: Oxford University Press, 1975), connects the rebellion to the planters' decision to switch to slave labor, while T. H. Breen, "A Changing

women were apathetic politically before the suffrage movements of the nineteenth and twentieth centuries; that political behavior in earlier centuries was restricted to male leaders, voters, or members of mobs; and that war is restricted to the actions of males in military engagements. It is true that women had no role in formal military organizations in America until the twentieth century and none in Europe until the time of the Commune of 1871 in France. But if we hold to these rather limited definitions of political behavior and military participation, we miss significant aspects of women's lives as well as an important dimension of Bacon's Rebellion. As it happens, several women are mentioned by name as taking what should be construed as political roles in the Rebellion. Moreover, it should puzzle us to note that women (apart from the heroic captive Mary Rowlandson) apparently played no analogous political roles in King Philip's War (1675), although Indian attacks on the New England colonies were so severe as to threaten their existence.[3] To understand women's actions in Bacon's Rebellion, we need to consider two perspectives. First, the conflict was a civil war on a small scale, so women were involved willy-nilly. Second, to ignore their part is to misunderstand the very nature of the Rebellion within the reality of a Virginia society in which, for all women and those men lucky enough to marry them, family constituted the fundamental social unit.

The social reality of women's lives on the Chesapeake departed significantly from the demographic generalizations that historians have correctly made about the society as a whole.[4] In the first three-

Labor Force and Race Relations in Virginia, 1660–1710," in *Puritans and Adventurers: Change and Persistence in Early America* (New York: Oxford University Press, 1980), shows how alliances between poor whites, servants, and slaves marked the conflict.

3. See "Women in Arms," *Times Literary Supplement*, January 14, 1965; Douglas E. Leach, *Flintlock and Tomahawk: New England in King Philip's War* (New York: Macmillan, 1958); Mary White Rowlandson, *The Soveraignty & Goodness of God . . . Being a Narrative of the Captivity and Restauration of Mrs. Mary Rowlandson* (Cambridge, Mass.: Samuel Green, 1682).

4. On Chesapeake society and demography see Lois Green Carr and Lorena S. Walsh, "The Planter's Wife: The Experience of White Women in Seventeenth-Century Maryland," *William and Mary Quarterly* (hereafter cited as *WMQ*) 3d ser., 34 (October 1977): 542–71; Darrett B. Rutman and Anita H. Rutman, "'Now-Wives and Sons-in Law': Parental Death in a Seventeenth-Century Virginia County," in Thad W. Tate and David L. Am-

quarters of the seventeenth century, most people came as servants, and of these about two-thirds were men. Such an unequal sex ratio set this area of the South apart from other regions and had well-documented effects on the whole society, particularly the failure of both Virginia and Maryland to generate a natural population increase until the last quarter of the seventeenth century. Also, short life expectancy made family formation difficult. But those women who survived the seasoning period, and, in the case of servants, the period of their indentures, married: "Comely or homely, strong or weak, any young woman was too valuable to be overlooked, and most could find a man with prospects."[5] Widows remarried quickly. Widowers, given the shortage of women, might wait longer. But marriage was a popular institution on the Chesapeake, and most of the male leaders of the Rebellion were married, though this fact indicates their social standing as much as Virginia's demographic conditions.

Married couples in early Virginia, if Darrett and Anita Rutman's study of Middlesex County is a guide, tried to settle near relatives who would provide support and companionship. Once settled, people tried to reestablish, to the extent possible, the patterns of community they had known in England. Since Virginia was an immigrant society throughout the seventeenth century, the force of these patterns was constantly renewed by a stream of newcomers from England. For the Virginia gentry especially, Chesapeake society accordingly took shape as a kind of imperfect mirror of English society. And English society, as Peter Laslett has shown, was one in which families were arranged in hierarchical order and in which political action was the sole prerogative of men who were heads of families.[6] To the extent that adverse frontier conditions and demographic circumstances permitted, Virginia conformed to the English pattern. And Virginia women of the gentry class lived within

---

merman, eds., *The Chesapeake in the Seventeenth Century: Essays on Anglo-American Society* (Chapel Hill: University of North Carolina Press, 1979), 153–82; Russell R. Menard, "Immigrants and Their Increase: The Process of Population Growth in Early Maryland," in Aubrey C. Land, Lois Green Carr, and Edward C. Papenfuse, eds., *Law, Society, and Politics in Early Maryland* (Baltimore: Johns Hopkins University Press, 1977), 88–110.

5. Carr and Walsh, "The Planter's Wife," 550.

6. See Darrett and Anita Rutman, *A Place in Time: Middlesex County, Virginia 1650–1750* (New York: W. W. Norton, 1984), 47–52; Laslett, *The World We Have Lost* (New York: Scribner's, 1965), 19, 22–52.

the same restrictive norms, or gender conventions, that were imposed on women of their status in seventeenth-century England. What is surprising is that when Bacon's Rebellion began, some women broke with those expectations, committed themselves to the rebel cause, and thereby placed themselves in danger of losing both their husbands and their property.

At the beginning of the conflict, the norms of seventeenth-century female behavior were not at issue, but the physical safety of all white Virginians living in the outlying areas of the colony was. The Indian troubles that precipitated Bacon's Rebellion began in the summer of 1675 in northern Stafford County beside the Potomac River. A petty feud between a plantation owner and a group of Indians led to the killing of a white herdsman. The local militia twice crossed into Maryland to avenge the murder. The first time they attacked the wrong Indians; the second time they violated a truce by murdering Indian envoys; and finally, through carelessness, they allowed the besieged Indian men, women, and children to escape. The Susquehannock Indians then fled southward across the heads of the Rappahannock and York rivers, attacking outlying plantations and killing, according to the royal commissioners' report, as many as three hundred people.[7] Thomas Mathew, the planter whose herdsman had been killed, described the terror on the frontier: "In these frightfull times the most Exposed small families withdrew into our houses of better Numbers. . . . Neighbours in Bodies Joined their Labours from each Plantation to others Alternately, taking their Arms into the Fields, and Setting Centinels; no Man Stirrd out of Door unarm'd."[8]

In response to this emergency, Governor William Berkeley and

7. "A True Narrative of the Late Rebellion in Virginia, by the Royal Commissioners, 1677," in Charles McLean Andrews, ed., *Narratives of the Insurrections 1675–1690* (New York: Scribner's, 1915), 106–8. The Royal Commissioners' narrative is the official account, but the commissioners, like everyone else involved, were not objective. One of them, Francis Moryson, had lived in Virginia since 1649 and had held various official posts there. The other two, as loyal Stuart servants, were more distanced; they were anxious to calm things down and so secure the king's revenues. See John W. Raimo, *Biographical Dictionary of American Colonial and Revolutionary Governors 1607–1789* (Westport, Conn.: Meckler Books, 1980), 476–77.

8. Thomas Mathew, "The Beginning, Progress and Conclusion of Bacon's Rebellion, 1675–1676," in Andrews, *Narratives*, 20. On Mathew's authorship of this narrative see pp. 12–14.

the Assembly ordered forts to be built and manned with soldiers who were to use them as bases for punishing Indian attacks. But nothing the authorities could do convinced the frontier planters that they were safe in the face of continuing warfare. They feared for themselves and for their families, and that fear, by their own accounts, drove them to defy Governor Berkeley and fight their Indian attackers. The "dayely cryes" of their women and children emboldened the men of Charles City County to take up arms against a government that they believed came too slowly to their rescue with preposterous and useless remedies. The royal commissioners' report repeated the claim: "The unsatisfied People finding themselves still lyable to the Indian Crueltyes, and the cryes of their wives and children growing grievous and intollerable to them" became convinced that the governor and the grandees were unwilling to protect them.[9]

Such appeals on behalf of the sufferings of women and children had their political uses in the seventeenth century. They were a standard device for justifying unlawful actions or for calling attention to social chaos. In 1651, for example, Governor Berkeley had used such an appeal when describing the condition of England under the Protectorate: "the wifes pray for barreness and their husbands deafness to exclude the cryes of their succourles, starving children."[10] Living in Virginia, Berkeley knew nothing firsthand of the scenes he was writing about, but he believed that political disorder must necessarily entail social disorder. In 1676 the rebels in frontier Charles City County, where unauthorized resistance to the Indians began, invoked the same political truth by claiming that Berkeley's regime endangered their wives and children. But, in this case, what the rebels were saying appears to have been true. There is other evidence that women were deeply affected by the social disorder caused by the Indian attacks and the small-scale civil war that followed when Bacon assumed leadership of the anti-Indian forces.

The charges and countercharges made by rebels and loyalists in Charles City County after the Rebellion testify to the disorder

9. "Charles City County Grievances 1676," *VMHB* 3, no. 2 (October 1985): 137; "True Narrative," 108; Washburn, *The Governor and the Rebel,* 25–27.

10. "Speech of Sir Wm. Berkeley, and Declaration of the Assembly, March, 1651," *VMHB* 1, no. 1 (June 1894): 76.

there.[11] Colonel Edward Hill, a member of the Council and an ardent supporter of Berkeley, figures largely in the formal complaints that local people made to the royal commissioners, who arrived early in 1677. After Bacon's death and the collapse of the Rebellion, Hill, like other loyalists, went around the county exacting payments, or compositions, from known rebels as the price of their pardons. Sometimes his actions resembled robbery. Hill tried to cajole the widowed Mrs. Hunt's one hogshead of tobacco away from her; when she refused to surrender it, he "wrongfully tooke and carried [it] away." Mrs. Hunt apparently did not seek formal redress, but of the nine people named as having grievances against Hill, two were women: Sara Weekes and Mrs. John Baxter.

In answer to these complaints, Hill made his own reply to the charges against him, which he in turn sent to the commissioners. He was quite frank about his treatment of the rebel women: Yes, he had put Sara Weekes under guard for a time, "idle, infamous slutt to the highest degrees of robing, thieving and whooreing, &c.," that she was. Hill did not give Weekes a title, which indicates that she was a servant. The string of abusive charges heaped on her reflects the common assessment of the behavior of serving women.[12] As to the Baxters, who were apparently more respectable people: yes, he had put them under guard and later had sent them both to prison. To justify his actions, Hill pointed to the sufferings of his own wife at the hands of the rebels. While her husband was away fighting for the governor, the rebels took over Shirley Hill's plantation, drank up all the liquor, and then turned their wrath on the pregnant Mrs. Hill. According to Hill, they beat her with Hill's own cane, tore her childbirth linen from her hands, drove her from the house, "and with her ledd away my children where they must live on corne and water and lye on the ground, had it not been for the charity of good people, and would not suffer them to feed on my own provisions or have a bed to lye on." Later, in 1680, Hill was again driven to defend himself against the reputation his rapacious behavior had earned him during and after the Rebellion; he claimed that his wife and children had also been imprisoned for a time during the troubles.

11. For the charges see "Charles City County Grievances, 1676," *VMHB* 3, no. 2 (October 1895), 132–60, esp. 137, 145; for the countercharges, see "The Defense of Colonel Edward Hill," *VMHB* 3, no. 3 (January 1896): 239–52, and no. 4 (April 1896): 341–49.

12. See, for example, Rutman and Rutman, *A Place in Time*, 130.

The Hills and the Baxters were not the only families to suffer at the hands of partisans on both sides. Writing to the English Secretary of State, Philip Ludwell, a Virginia councilor, reported the "ravishing of women and children from their homes," their imprisonment in the rebels' camp, and their being threatened with death.[13]

During Bacon's ascendancy, the wives of loyalist leaders were in particular danger. As the tide of battle turned, Governor Berkeley returned from the Eastern Shore, where he had been driven by the Baconians, and occupied Jamestown. The town was strongly manned, and Bacon, hurrying to the scene, feared an attack from the loyalists inside. Therefore, he sent out parties of soldiers to capture and bring in the wives of the loyalist leaders holding the town. Then he sent one of these women to warn the loyalists that their wives, now Bacon's hostages, would be placed in the line of fire in the event of any attack from inside the fortified town. John Cotton, a planter living at Queens' Creek near Williamsburg, observed that the loyalists considered Bacon's employment of women hostages foul play: "A Method, in war, that they were not well aquainted with (no not those the best inform'd in millitary affaires) that before they could com to pearce their enimies sides, they must be obliged to dart there wepons through there wives brest." The story of the hostages illustrates that Bacon's Rebellion respected neither gender nor class: the wives of gentlemen, like the wives of ordinary men, were vulnerable in the conflict. The foregoing incidents, if they are representative of others that have gone unrecorded, speak for the silenced voices of countless Virginia women, and they definitely indicate the extent of social disorder as well as political upheaval during the Rebellion. As for the social upheaval, Alice Creyke, a member of one of the elite families loyal to Governor Berkeley, remarked that the conflicts among the Virginia colonists themselves were greater than those with the Indians. "Ye differences with in our selves being far greater then those without," she wrote, "and a reason why the other was not before remedyed." Even though the Rutmans, noting the swift restoration of social order in Middlesex County after the Rebellion, have suggested that it was therefore a superficial conflict,

13. "Defense," 344, 250; Ludwell to Henry Coventry, April 14, 1677, Coventry Papers, Great Britain, Public Record Office, C.O. 5/1355, fol. 155. Both sides apparently involved women and children in their struggles. Mrs. Sarah Drummond, wife of a rebel leader, claimed that loyalists drove her and her children from the family's plantation (fol. 187).

the mistreatment of women and children by both sides can hardly have been quickly forgotten or forgiven.[14]

Not all women were willing to suffer passively. A terse but telling comment in the royal commissioners' narrative reveals that some women participated in the Rebellion directly. As Bacon and his troops passed by on their way to Jamestown, some rebel women offered them food and volunteered to fight alongside the men, saying "if hee [Bacon] wanted assistance they would come themselves after him." Bacon's own wife, Elizabeth, remained at Curles, the family plantation, during the fighting, almost certainly constrained by one of her two pregnancies between 1674 and 1676. There she was exposed both to the wrath of Indians and the governor. When Berkeley came to Curles in search of the rebel leader, he promised Mrs. Bacon that he would hang her husband when the latter returned home. Another rebel's wife, Mrs. Anthony Haviland, was "an excellent divulger of news" and according to Colonel Hill, often acted as Bacon's emissary, carrying his papers and declarations up and down the country. The governor's pardon of February 1677 named Sarah Grendon of Charles City County as a "great encourager and assister in the late horrid Rebellion" and excepted her from the pardon. Governor Berkeley wrote ruefully to England that Mrs. Grendon had told hundreds that he "was a greater frend to the Indians than to the English."[15]

Assistance like Mrs. Haviland's and Sarah Grendon's was important to Bacon. With such help, support for his determination to fight the Indians with or without the governor's commission spread widely after he took command of the irregular forces collected at Jordan's Point. The royal commissioners said that Bacon had "insinuated his instruments" to preach Rebellion, and clearly Mrs. Haviland and

14. "Bacon's and Ingram's Rebellion," 68–69. This harsh treatment of loyalists' wives is also mentioned in "True Narrative," 135. Creyke, alias Corbyn, to Thomas Corbyn, April 22, 1677, in "The Corbin Family," *VMHB* 29, no. 3 (July 1921): 379; Rutman and Rutman, *A Place in Time*, 86–87.

15. "True Narrative," 130; Elizabeth Bacon's letter to her sister, June 29, 1676, is reprinted in "Bacon's Rebellion," *WMQ* 1st ser., 9, no. 1 (July 1900): 4–5; see also 6 n. "Defense," 345; "An act of Indemitie and free pardon," in William Waller Hening, ed., *The Statutes at Large . . . of Virginia*, 13 vols. (New York: Bartow, 1823), 2:371; Berkeley to Henry Coventry, July 1, 1676, Coventry Papers, vol. 77, fol. 144, Papers of the Marquess of Bath, Longleat House, Wiltshire, England.

Sarah Grendon were two such instruments. Mrs. Haviland had good reason: her husband went with Bacon on the Occaneechee campaign, an illegal foray against the Indians, and was therefore deeply involved in the Rebellion. But Sarah Grendon, defying gender conventions, acted on her own initiative. When the Rebellion started, her husband, Thomas Grendon, was away from Virginia. She, however, was deeply committed to the rebels' cause. After Bacon had died and the Rebellion was over, Sarah Grendon admitted that she had given gunpowder to Bacon's forces but claimed she believed it would only be used against the Indians. Forced to beg a pardon from the royal commissioners, she belittled what she had done, saying that her actions amounted only to foolish words, spoken by "an ignorant woman."[16] Here was a woman, far from ignorant, who not only defied the gender conventions of her society but invoked the same conventions—those that assumed the ignorance and passivity of women in wartime—to her own defense. We know frustratingly little about her.

Sarah Grendon had been married three times when the Rebellion began in 1676. The date of her birth is unknown, but her first husband, Thomas Stegge, died in 1670, her second, George Harris, in 1672, and her third, Thomas Grendon, in 1685. Strangely for a much-married woman, she had no children. The wills of her first three husbands made provision only for a widow. Thomas Stegge made her the executrix of his substantial estate and instructed his heir, his nephew William Byrd I, to pay careful attention to Sarah's "prudent and provident" advice. Stegge's will left Sarah a generous gift and acknowledged her "affectionate and tender care" during his last illness. Byrd was young and new to the country, but apparently Sarah, even at the time of her first marriage, was sufficiently competent to be useful to him. George Harris, her short-lived second husband, left her £1,600, "with all her Clothes, Rings, Jewell's and plate." After the Rebellion her third husband, Thomas Grendon, made her a handsome provision in his will—either personal estate in Virginia or real estate in England—thus indicating that he bore her no ill will for her part in the Rebellion. During the altercations in Charles City County after the Rebellion, Colonel Hill tried to claim

16. "True Narrative," 111; Sarah Grendon to Herbert Jeffries, n.d., Coventry Papers, vol. 78, fols. 5, 6.

that even though Thomas Grendon was out of the country he was responsible for his wife's rebelliousness, a claim probably intended as an excuse for confiscating Grendon's property, although the subterfuge was hardly necessary. When Hill visited the Grendon plantation in February 1677, he came armed with a warrant from the governor to arrest Sarah Grendon and seize her husband's property. For some reason he was satisfied with a great deal of moveable property and left Mrs. Grendon in peace.[17]

With the Rebellion quelled, there ensued a period of repression and violence on the part of the victorious loyalists. The new Assembly, which met at Green Spring, the governor's plantation, in February 1677, followed up with vindictive legislation. The legislators drew up an omnibus act partially intended to prevent seditious and scandalous libels, which they called "the fore runners of tumult and rebellion." They especially targeted women offenders like Sarah Grendon and Mrs. Haviland. As the common law stood in the seventeenth century, most crimes a married woman committed could not be held to her account, since it was assumed that she had acted at her husband's command. The exceptions were treason, murder, and keeping a brothel. The Virginia Assembly must have thought that the women involved in the Rebellion would slip through its fingers because of these provisions and accordingly tried to make married women liable for their seditious libels.[18]

The new law exacted specific penalties from women. For a first offense men would pay a fine of one thousand pounds of tobacco and cask, and double the amount for a second offense, as well as standing at the pillory for two hours. But married women could expect a different fate: for a first offense, twenty lashes; thirty for a second, unless they could pay the same fine as the men. Julia Cherry

17. On Grendon's first three marriages, see *VMHB* 24, no. 3 (July 1916): 255; 35, no. 3 (July 1927): 227–29 (Thomas Stegge); 12, no. 4 (April 1904): 404–5 (George Harris); and 1, no. 4 (April 1894): 441 (Thomas Grendon); "Defense," 250. See also "Personal Grievances of Certain Inhabitants of Virginia," in Samuel Wiseman's Book of Record 1676–1677, Pepysian Library 2582, Magdalene College, Cambridge, abstracted in John D. Neville, *Bacon's Rebellion* (Jamestown Foundation, n.d.), 369–70.

18. See "An Act for the releife of such loyall persons as have suffered losse by the late rebells," Hening, *Statutes* 2:385. Sir William Blackstone, *Commentaries on the Laws of England in Four Books* (Chicago: Callaghan and Co., 1899), 4:28–29.

Spruill, in her classic study *Women's Life and Work in the Southern Colonies* (1938), notes that colonial women sometimes endured the harsh physical punishments set by law because they could not pay their fines.[19] But this Act of 1677 invited husbands to maintain social order by not paying their wives' fines and therefore subjecting them to flogging. Perhaps the Assembly was also trying, as a sort of second shot, to intimidate married women with the possibility of humiliating punishment for future misbehavior.

As for Sarah Grendon, she still had the governor's warrant hanging over her. To free his wife from the accusation of treason, Thomas Grendon asked the royal commissioners to try her themselves. On May 10, 1677, they visited Charles City County, heard allegations against Mrs. Grendon, and dismissed them. On the same day both the governor and the attorney general of the colony held court in the county and found no evidence to try Mrs. Grendon for her life because, they said, she had done nothing more than many others during the Rebellion. In 1685, Thomas Grendon died, and, of course, Sarah Grendon married again.[20]

Another participant who stepped outside prescribed gender roles to challenge Governor Berkeley directly was Lydia Chisman. Born in Virginia, she was a woman with Quaker connections—her Quaker stepfather had refused to have the Book of Common Prayer used at his funeral, and Lydia herself married into a Quaker family.[21] Her husband, Edmund Chisman, was one of Bacon's commanders. When the Rebellion ended, he was captured and brought before the governor for one of the summary trials and quick trips to the scaffold for which Berkeley became known in the days of his triumph. Lydia Chisman, present at her husband's trial, unexpectedly made an eloquent and touching plea for him. If the Chismans moved in Quaker circles and Lydia took part in religious meetings where she

19. Spruill, *Women's Life and Work in the Southern Colonies* (Chapel Hill: University of North Carolina Press, 1938), 320, 339.

20. "Personal Grievances," 370. Sarah's fourth husband was Edward Braine. See *VMHB* 24 (1916): 351.

21. "Notes on Cole-Scasbrook-Wills," *WMQ* 1st ser., 24, no. 3 (January 1915): 200; "Major Edmund Cheeseman, Jr.," *WMQ* 1st ser., 1, no. 1 (July 1892): 30–35; Keith Thomas, "Women in the Civil War Sects," in Trevor Aston, ed., *Crisis in Europe: 1560–1660* (New York: Basic Books, 1965), 317–40.

had the right to speak, that behavior might have transferred in this crisis into political life. The scene is recorded in John Cotton's narrative of the Rebellion. When Berkeley asked Chisman why he had supported Bacon,

> his Wife steps in and tould his honour that it was her provocations that made her Husband joyne in the Cause that Bacon contended for; ading, that if he had not bin influenc'd by her instigations, he had never don that which he had don. Therefore (upon her bended knees) she desired of his honour, that since what her Husband had don was by heer meanes, and so, by Consequence, she most guilty, that she might be hang'd, and he pardon'd.[22]

In the course of Chisman's trial, Governor Berkeley called Lydia Chisman a whore, but John Cotton, in his account of the case, pronounced the governor irrational in this judgment, because a woman who was a whore could not love her husband enough to sacrifice her life for him. According to John Cotton, what Lydia Chisman said about her influence over her husband was true, and Governor Berkeley knew it. Yet she was not punished.

Lydia Chisman's unusual actions attest to her involvement and her extraordinary bravery. Not only did she encourage her husband in the Rebellion, but, when pressed, she declined to take refuge in the gender role ascribed to wives in such cases. Instead, she voluntarily confessed and was willing to suffer the death penalty in order to save her husband. Her plea went unheeded, and Chisman died in prison awaiting execution. His estate was confiscated, but Lydia Chisman seems to have regained it in 1678. And, of course, she married again.[23]

In this case it was not Lydia, but Governor Berkeley (and the chronicler John Cotton) who let gender conventions shape their responses to her behavior. The connection that Berkeley and Cotton made between unfeminine behavior and sexual promiscuity is straight out of the conduct books of the seventeenth century, which prescribed proper female behavior. In her study of these books, Angeline Goreau notes that sexual chastity, called "honesty," was set up as the chief goal of women's lives. To ensure chastity the prescriptive literature recommended severe limitations on female behavior: special ways of walking and talking, for example. As Richard Braith-

22. "Bacon's and Ingram's Rebellion," 81–82.
23. "Major Edmund Cheeseman, Jr.," 33–34.

waite in *The English Gentlewoman* (1631) suggested, "In your very motion, gesture, and gate [gait], observe modesty, it will infinitely become you, and attract a kind of reverent esteem in those who eye you." As if to reinforce the lesson he warned, "It is no hard thing to gather the deposition of our heart, by the dimension of our gate [gait]."[24] These admonitions were directed at English gentlewomen as a precaution against their suspected lasciviousness. John Cotton's as well as Governor Berkeley's comments on Lydia Chisman's behavior indicate that they held women to similar standards of decorum, even in the wilds of Virginia.

Mrs. Haviland, Sarah Grendon, and Lydia Chisman were all rebel women, but the narratives of the Rebellion have something to say about loyalist women, too. Mrs. Hill, the wife of Colonel Edward Hill, we have already met. In the hands of a merciless mob, according to her husband, she did nothing in her own defense; she merely suffered. In contrast to the rebel women who were willing to flout gender conventions to take active roles on their own behalf, Mrs. Hill's role in Bacon's Rebellion was apparently limited to passive suffering and procreation—well within the bounds of perceived roles for women. The same is true of the "White Aprons," the loyalist women Bacon took hostage to prevent their husbands' attacking him from inside Jamestown. They, too, followed gender prescriptions, behaving like the hapless victims women were supposed to be in wartime. Another loyalist wife, Mrs. George Mason, whose husband commanded the militia regiment in Stafford County, was somewhat more active, but only in the traditional feminine role of nurse. When the Rebellion began, her husband and his men attacked a party of Doeg Indians in Maryland, murdered the Doeg leader during a parley, and took captive his eight-year-old son. The Indian boy sank into a coma in Colonel Mason's house and Mrs. Mason nursed him. For ten days the boy was almost lifeless. Mason and a fellow militia captain decided that the Indian child was bewitched, and that baptism was the cure. They summoned Mason's clerk to read the Church of England rite and became the boy's godfathers. This done, the men returned to drinking punch while Mrs. Mason stayed with the child. After a while, the boy woke, and she spoon-

24. See Angeline Goreau, *The Whole Duty of Woman* (New York: Dial, 1985), 10, 36–37.

fed him a "Cordial."[25] Mrs. Mason's role may well have been the crucial one, but John Cotton, the narrator, ignores it and implies that the men's role was to effect the "bewitched" boy's recovery by calling up the stronger power of the sacrament.

With one notable exception it appears that most loyalist women, like Mrs. Mason, were meek helpmates or helpless victims, or like Alice Creyke, confined their activities to letter writing and sour comments. At the close of the Rebellion, Alice Creyke wrote sanctimoniously to a relative in England how glad she was that the rebels had arrived "at that ignoble port the Gallows, where a Rebellion always leads its followers."[26]

Lady Frances Berkeley, the governor's wife, proved a notable exception to loyalist women's passivity. At the beginning of the conflict, Berkeley sent Lady Frances to England to present his side of the story to the authorities. No inexperienced provincial matron, she had useful connections in England. When she arrived, she sent Secretary of State Henry Coventry a curious letter, witnessed by her husband and some of his supporters, describing her behavior toward Nathaniel Bacon.[27] She had, she wrote, taken it upon herself to counter the widespread belief in Virginia that Bacon was rich enough to pay the expenses of the families of men involved in his unauthorized fight against the Indians. To quell this rumor, she announced far and wide the exact extent of his substantial debts, based on information she collected from his creditors. On the other hand, she denied that she stooped to slander, saying that she did not call Bacon a "parliament captain" a term which, by its reference to the losing side in the Civil War, would have amounted to a charge of intense disloyalty. Her defensiveness is odd and may indicate the Berkeleys' fear that the King and the Privy Council would blame the governor rather than the rebels for the breakdown of order in Virginia.

Lady Frances returned to Virginia triumphant, escorted by one of the royal commissioners and a thousand troops to put down the Rebellion. But if she thought that the commissioners would take her husband's side, either by corroborating his account of the Rebellion or by vindicating his harshness when it was over, she was soon

25. This entire episode is recorded in Mathew, "The Beginning . . . of Bacon's Rebellion," 18.

26. "The Corbin Family," 379.

27. "Declaration of Lady Frances Berkeley," n.d., Coventry Papers, vol. 77, fol. 41; see also "Lady Frances Berkeley," *Notable American Women* (Cambridge: Belknap Press of Harvard University Press, 1971), 1, 135–36.

disillusioned. Disagreements broke out between the Berkeleys and the commissioners. Not only did the king's charge to the commissioners that they were to hear the people's grievances imply royal criticism of the governor, but the king also named one of them, Colonel Herbert Jeffreys, governor and summoned Berkeley back to England. Berkeley died there in July 1677, leaving all his property as well as a handsome testimonial to his wife. In his will he wrote, "And I doe further make this declaration, that if God had blest me with a far greater estate, I would have given it all to my Most Dearly beloved wife."[28] Lady Frances remarried, this time choosing Philip Ludwell, one of Berkeley's loyal supporters. Ludwell became a leader of the Green Spring faction, which in post-Rebellion Virginia opposed efforts to bring the colony under stricter imperial control. Lady Frances joined in her new husband's struggle and, unlike most women of her class, continued to lead an intensely political life in faction-ridden Virginia.[29]

Virginia women as well as Virginia men were deeply engaged in Bacon's Rebellion, and women as well as men suffered in the civil strife that followed. But it is the women's story that has been left out. Most of the women described here belonged to the literate gentry whose history tends to be preserved. In this case the women themselves contributed to the writing of that history, but their words as well as their actions have been largely ignored. Nevertheless, their part is important for a fuller understanding of Bacon's Rebellion. That both rebels and loyalists attacked women and children indicates that the conflict was not a matter of soldierly skirmishes, but one of acute social disorder that cannot be explained adequately by describing it in terms of elites maneuvering for political position. Moreover, a careful reading of the seventeenth-century sources reveals that there was a distinct difference between the participation of loyalist women and those women who chose the rebel side.

Except for Lady Frances Berkeley, female loyalists in their passivity seem to have abided by the restrictive standards of feminine behavior prescribed by English society. In that society, political action was almost inconceivable for women. These Virginia women were limited and directed by the mores of that larger society, even if they lived on its wild peripheries. That some women of the same

28. Hening, *Statutes* 2:559.
29. Warren M. Billings, John E. Selby, and Thad W. Tate, *Colonial Virginia: A History* (New York: KTO Press, 1986), 101.

status felt obliged to flout traditional mores and take part in the Rebellion indicates the deep and decisive nature of the crisis in Virginia society in 1676–1677. In that crisis rebel women stood side by side with their husbands in very dangerous and treasonous proceedings. The home authorities came down, somewhat ambiguously, on the governor's side, and in Virginia it was a brave man or woman who stood against Berkeley's wrath. Seeing the women's part gives Bacon's Rebellion another dimension, one different from those that focus on leaders and elites, on imperial relations, or on the origins of an American revolutionary tradition. The experience of these Virginia women suggests that the woman's part may have been left out of other colonial conflicts. Certainly gender can no longer be ignored in the study of even such traditionally male theaters of action as wars and revolutions.

ℬ Kathy Roe Coker

The Calamities of War
Loyalism and Women in South Carolina

By the summer of 1781, long before the surrender of British forces at Yorktown in October, the patriots were almost in complete control of South Carolina. As the months passed, the problem of what to do with the loyalists and their families weighed heavily on Governor John Rutledge's mind. He put the matter clearly in his address to the legislature when it met on January 8, 1782, at Jacksonborough. He lamented that the people had not only suffered from the "Common Calamities of War" but also from "the Wanton and Savage manner" in which the British had conducted it, subjecting their enemies to "such severities as are unpracticed, and will Scarcely be Credited by Civilized Nations." Many of South Carolina's "worthiest citizens were, without cause long and closely confined, some on board of prison-ships, and others in the town and castle of St. Augustine." They and their families "were victims to the inveterate malice of an unrelenting foe. Neither the tears of mothers, nor the cries of infants, could excite . . . pity or compassion."[1]

In South Carolina as in other states, women—both loyalist and patriot—were victims in the American Revolution. Although some women may have gained their own measure of independence through

1. Edward McCrady, *The History of South Carolina in the Revolution, 1780–1783* (New York: Macmillan Company, 1902), 521, 563–74; A. S. Salley, ed., *Journal of the House of Representatives of South Carolina, January 8, 1782–February 26, 1782* (Columbia: University of South Carolina Press, 1916), 3, 12–13; and David Duncan Wallace, *The History of South Carolina*, 4 vols. (New York: The American Historical Society, 1934), 2:299–300. For Rutledge's views see Jerome Nadelhaft, *The Disorders of War: The Revolution in South Carolina* (Orono: University of Maine at Orono Press, 1981), 75.

having to manage farms and families while their husbands were absent during the war, and many widows were forced to become knowledgeable about their husbands' property after the war, South Carolina's loyalist women, especially the wives and widows of men with substantial property, clung to traditional views of women as passive, helpless casualties of war, even while actively seeking redress from the courts.

In his address Rutledge observed that South Carolina had "been remarkably conspicuous" in its leniency toward the loyalists, compared with other states, which had appropriated the property of loyal British subjects to the "publick use." The loyalists' behavior when they were in power, said the governor, was "so reprehensible that Justice and policy forbid their free readmission to the right and privileges of Citizens." Rutledge told the legislators that it was their responsibility "to determine, whether the forfeiture and appropriation of . . . Property should now take place." If they did decide to act in this direction, the governor asked them to remember the state's reputation by providing "support, for the families of those whom you may deprive of their Property."[2]

Would South Carolina follow other states and punish the loyalists by seizing their property? The answer was a resolute yes. On February 26, 1782, the legislature passed *Act Number 1153*, which confiscated the property of 238 individuals identified as loyalists. And, in addition to confiscation, many suffered banishment. Most people named in the Confiscation Act would have to leave the state.[3]

No sooner had the Jacksonborough Assembly passed the Confiscation Act and adjourned than the loyalist subjects of these punitive measures began attempts to secure their pardon. The Fifth General Assembly received over 250 petitions for relief from loyalists, individuals acting on behalf of the loyalists, or both.[4] Among

2. Salley, *Journal of the House*, 9–13; McCrady, *The History of South Carolina*, 563–67; and Nadelhaft, *Disorders of War*, 75.

3. A. S. Salley, ed., *Journal of the Senate of South Carolina, January 8, 1782–February 26, 1782* (Columbia, S.C.: The State Company, 1941), 54, 72, 73–80; Thomas Cooper and David J. McCord, eds., *The Statutes at Large of South Carolina*, 10 vols. (Columbia, S.C.: A. S. Johnston, 1836–1841), 4:516–26, 6:629–33, 634–35; Nadelhaft, *Disorders of War*, 77, 81, 83; and McCrady, *History of South Carolina*, 576–78. The Confiscation Act actually divided the loyalists into six classes depending upon their actions against the state.

4. Theodora Thompson and Rosa Lumpkin, eds., *Journals of the House of Representatives 1783–1784* (Columbia: University of South Carolina Press,

those petitions were more than sixty appeals from women or their representatives.

Although the Jacksonborough Assembly punished loyalists, the legislators were mindful of Governor Rutledge's concern for the loyalists' families. That concern was evident in Article 10 of the Confiscation Act, which authorized the Commissioners of Forfeited Estates to provide, as necessary, for the "temporary support" of the families of those persons identified on the lists. After the Assembly determined the value of the confiscated property, the legislators intended to decide "what final provision . . . [was to] be made for the said families."[5]

The following year on March 16, 1783, the Assembly amended the Confiscation Act to provide for the disposition of all the personal property belonging to the confiscated estates, but there were exceptions: "the household furniture, plate, linen, apparel, carriages, and carriage-horses, with such negroes as are generally attendant upon the families of those persons who are described in the Confiscation Act, shall be allowed to them."[6] Perhaps the legislature recognized that women traditionally were in charge of the household and would be most affected by the confiscation of family possessions.

Two years later on March 17, 1785, the Assembly passed "An Act To Afford A Maintenance To The Persons Therein Mentioned." The preamble testifies to the legislators' motivation: "it is but consistent with justice and humanity that a suitable maintenance should be made to the widows and orphans of the following persons, whose whole estates are under confiscation."[7] Although this act addressed the cases of a few, it evidenced the sympathetic attitude of the Carolina legislature toward the wives, widows, other female relatives, and children of loyalists. The legislators obviously believed the state had an obligation to provide for such people—as long as these women's and children's interests did not conflict with those of the state.

Although the only woman specifically named in the Confiscation Act was Margaret Colleton, an absentee landowner in London, at

1977), ix–x. Hereafter, cited as *JHR* with the applicable dates of the legislative session.

5. Cooper and McCord, *Statutes* 4:521.

6. Ibid., 555–57. On attitudes toward the wives of loyalists see Linda Kerber, *Women of the Republic: Intellect and Ideology in Revolutionary America* (Chapel Hill: University of North Carolina Press, 1980), 9.

7. Cooper and McCord, *Statutes* 4:666–67.

least sixty-five cases concerned women who, as so many of them pointed out in their petitions to the Assembly, were the innocent victims of the "calamities of war." Colleton had echoed this viewpoint in a letter of July 13, 1778, to her Charleston attorneys. She told them that "owing to the Calamity of War, with which it has pleased God to afflict both Countries," which she had "born . . . with resignation," she had been unable to receive any "remittance" from her property. She trusted "that a helpless woman in the 76th year of her age, not native, nor even an Inhabitant, and therefore certainly as little obnoxious, as she can be serviceable" would not be penalized as an absentee landlord by the loss of some or all of her property. Margaret Colleton was dead by the time of the Confiscation Act, but her heir, James Nassau Colleton, sued for and won redress.[8]

At no time did the Jacksonborough Assembly ever assume that women could have played any other than a passive role in the conflict between Britain and the colonies. Even during the war, as Linda Kerber notes, it was generally assumed that "married women could make no political choices of their own. . . . The wife of a tory was judged to be under such clear control of her husband that she perforce became a tory herself." And once the war was over, "Americans permitted themselves to be even more sympathetic to the awkward position of the married woman and assumed she had been apolitical unless proven otherwise."[9]

South Carolina attorney John Deas typified this view of women when he represented Jane Linwood, widow of Nicholas Linwood, and William Baker, son of the late Sir William Baker, before the General Assembly in 1783. Sir William Baker was an absentee landlord and a London merchant who had formed a partnership with Nicholas Linwood, a London wine merchant and member of Parlia-

8. Cooper and McCord, *Statutes* 6:629, and James Nassau Colleton, June 2, 1783, Letters to the Commissioners of Forfeited Estates (CFE), Records of the Comptroller General (CG), South Carolina Department of Archives and History (SCDAH).

9. A number of states safeguarded a woman's property interests in her loyalist husband's estate if she declared her political allegiance. See Kerber, *Women of the Republic,* 124–25, and Jane Rendall, "Feminism and Republicanism, American Motherhood," *History Today* 34 (December 1984): 31.

ment from 1761 to 1773. At one time they owned several baronies in South Carolina.

By 1782 Sir William Baker's son, William, and Nicholas Linwood's widow, Jane, owned at least 40,333 acres in South Carolina, including Purrsyburg Barony of 12,600 acres, Black River Barony totaling 11,528 acres, Saltcatchers Barony of 11,679 acres, and Peedee Barony of 12,000 acres. All of this property was subject to confiscation in February 1782 when Sir William Baker's and Nicholas Linwood's names appeared on the confiscation lists.[10]

On February 3, 1783, the Senate and the House considered two petitions from John Deas on behalf of Jane Linwood and William Baker, trying to recover their inheritance. Attorney Deas began his plea by stating, "Mrs: Linwood as a Lady cannot be deemed Guilty of any Act inimical to the American Cause." That was the only mention he made of Jane Linwood. As for William Baker, Deas attested that his client, though a member of the House of Commons, was a "warm advocate for the Rights of America," and "in the house of Commons ever reprobated the Conduct of the British Ministry." In addition, Baker had made "liberal Contributions for the relief of American prisoners," and he and his father had paid a "double Tax for nonresidence." Accompanying the petition to the Senate were excerpts from Baker's speeches in the House of Commons in support of the American cause. In one speech Baker had referred to the "measures of a weak and wicked Administration whose injustices, obstinacy, and folly" cost the Empire her possessions in America.[11]

From the Senate and House floors the case of Baker and Linwood went to the Free Conference Committee. That committee considered Deas's evidence as well as testimony from two of William Baker's acquaintances, James Motte and George Miller. Motte believed Baker was a "very great friend to America." Miller remarked, "As a man," Baker was "an honour to human nature, and for eight years past he was decided in favor of America." After hearing this testi-

10. Cooper and McCord, *Statutes* 6:629, and Return of Estates, CFE, Records of the CG, SCDAH.

11. On William Baker, see Sir Lewis Namier and John Brooke, *The House of Commons 1754–1790*, 3 vols. (New York: Oxford University Press, 1964), 2:42. For the quotations of Baker's speeches see the petitions by John Deas, February 1 and 3, 1783, Petitions to the General Assembly (GA), Records of the General Assembly (GA), SCDAH, and Thompson and Lumpkin, *JHR 1783–1784*, 82–83.

mony, the committee voted to rescind the Confiscation Act for Baker and Linwood, "in consideration of his [Baker's] being a warm friend to America since the commencement of the war."[12] Jane Linwood's political sentiments apparently did not matter.

The General Assembly took the committee's advice and on March 26, 1784, removed the names of Sir William Baker and Nicholas Linwood from the confiscation list but levied an amercement, or punitive tax, on their property. Two years later Act Number 1338 lifted the amercement. William Baker and Jane Linwood agreed to accept the earlier sale by the Commissioners of Forfeited Estates of 7,474 acres of their property in Saltcatchers Barony in lieu of further amercement.[13] In all of these transactions the only mention of Jane Linwood was Deas's reference to her apolitical nature in his 1783 petition. She was guiltless of any political wrongdoing, but she and other loyalist women or their representatives nonetheless had to petition the legislature or the courts or both in order to establish their claims and protect their property rights.

The majority of the cases falling within the scope of this study support the Linwood case's apolitical view of women. The woman's petitions have what Mary Beth Norton, in *Liberty's Daughters: The Revolutionary Experience of American Women, 1750–1800*, refers to as a "domestic flavor." That is, to these women the home and family, not the Revolution, were the primary concerns. These South Carolina women had not taken and now did not seek a public or political role. Their households and family concerns, as evidenced in their petitions, were the cornerstones of their lives. They were, however, stepping beyond the domestic realm in publicly seeking relief from confiscation.[14]

In case after case, these South Carolina women described what confiscation meant to them in terms such as a "calamitous condi-

12. Minutes, 1783–1784, Free Conference Committee, Records of the GA, SCDAH.

13. Cooper and McCord, *Statutes* 6:634, 758.

14. See Norton, *Liberty's Daughters: The Revolutionary Experience of American Women 1750–1800* (Boston: Little, Brown, 1980), 176, 177. Norton's claim that after the Revolution "those [women] who adhered wholly to the traditional domestic realm were anomalous," does not apply to most of these women. See also Norton's "Eighteenth-Century American Women in Peace and War: The Case of the Loyalists," *William and Mary Quarterly* 3d ser., 33 (July 1976): 386–409.

tion," "great misfortune," a "deplorable situation," "helpless and distressed situation," "calamity of war," and "destitute of support." They described themselves as "objects of pitty and compassion." Mary Broun petitioned "out of Duty and Regard" for her husband, adding that she and "an innocent Babe" depended on him for support. Sarah Glen told the legislature that she and six children depended on her husband for their support. If her husband were not relieved, she was "utterly unequal to the task; And They must turn out an incumbrance to the community instead of being of service to it." Eleanor Mackie pleaded, "If the terms of the Sale be exacted, she must be compleatly wretched & deplorable cast forlorn on the wide World, friendless & hopeless destitute of all resource & Subsistence with a mind preyed upon by Sorrow and a Body weaken'd by care and the approaches of Age." Ann Legge prayed for her husband Edward's pardon, but realizing that "policy [might] dictate a refusal to this part of her prayer," she "Humbly Intreat[ed] . . . [the] Honorable House to prevent her & her three poor inscent [sic] children from experiencing those Calamities which a total Loss of her little remaining property must eventually produce, by Vesting that property in her or her children."[15]

Some women, however, ignored the plight of their husbands and pleaded only for themselves and their children. Elizabeth Atkins believed "it never was the Intention of the Legislature to reduce to abject Poverty" the family "for the Conduct of a Husband, or a Father." Similarly, Margaret Brisbane, wife of loyalist James Brisbane, a native Carolinian, Charleston planter, and member of Charleston's gentry, sought relief only for herself and her children. In her petition of February 22, 1783, Brisbane described her husband as "a gentleman, whose political Sentiments differed from those of his fellow Citizens, which induced him to quit this Country, at a very

15. Glen, January 24, 1783; Mackie, February 5, 1784; Legge, January 17, 1783, in Petitions to the GA, Records of the GA, SCDAH. The other two women were Isabella Kingsley and Elizabeth Colles. See Isabella Kingsley, January 28, 1783, and Elizabeth Colles, January 25, 1783. The 1784 legislature granted a partial reprieve to Edward Legge and Robert Beard. Isabella Kingsley and her husband were not so fortunate. For other examples, see the following Petitions to the GA in Records of the GA, SCDAH: Sarah Capers, February 22, 1783; Judith Gaillard, February 22, 1783; Ellinor Gaillard, February 22, 1783; Margaret Cunningham, January 20, 1785; Elizabeth Atkins, January 31, 1783; Mary Anderson, January 8, 1785; Ann Legge, January 17, 1783; and James Colleton, June 2, 1783.

early period, in this unhappy Contest." She was fearful that the legislature "under an Idea of Retaliation, or from political Motives" would also banish the "unfortunate & distressed Wives & Children, of those persons who have become so obnoxious." She, therefore, took "the Liberty" of asking the Assembly to consider her both as a wife and as a mother—"a Mother who must be parted" from her children by a former marriage in the event her fear of banishment was realized. She wanted to remain in South Carolina with all her children. If the Assembly did not grant a portion of Brisbane's estate to the support and maintenance of her and her children, they would surely suffer. Margaret Brisbane concluded her petition with a moving appeal:

> Called on, as she is, by Humanity, towards her offspring, she finds herself *impelled* to make this Request, & flatters herself with Hopes, That when the House reflects on the Weak and Defenceless Situation of Woman & Children, who are not the promoters of the War, nor, from their Sphere in Life, can possibly be disadvantageous to the Contest, and whose Opinions seldom avail, and do not frequently operate, on the Judgement of Men; when they recollect this, and are informed that her Sentiments with *regards to the present Contest* never coincided with, but were always contrary to her Husbands That they will take into Consideration, the facts above set forth, and extend in Benevolence, towards her, by permitting her to remain in this Country, and towards her Children jointly with herself, by granting some part of that Property which she *once considered*, as, in some degree, her own, and Ultimately, as the Inheritance of her now destitute Children; and thereby enable them, to go through Life, without the prospect of penury & want.[16]

Margaret Brisbane had stepped beyond a woman's sphere not only in professing a political position, but in daring to take one contrary to her husband's. She also considered his property her own. Yet she was still cognizant of and restricted by (at least in her public statement) the traditional female role. Here was a woman obviously torn between her private and public self. But the state, unmoved, took no action on her appeal. Nor was she successful in

16. Elizabeth Atkins, March 1, 1785, Petitions to the GA, Records of the GA, SCDAH, and Lark Adams and Rosa Lumpkin, eds., *Journals of the House of Representatives, 1785–1786* (Columbia: University of South Carolina Press, 1979), 158, 248, 252. On March 18, 1785, the House agreed to a settlement in favor of Atkins. E. Haviland Hillman, "The Brisbanes," *South Carolina Historical and Genealogical Magazine* 14 (July 1913): 124–27, 129–30.

fulfilling her desire to remain in South Carolina. She was finally obliged to join her husband in his exile.

Margaret Brisbane could at least rejoin her husband, but what was a loyalist's widow to do? The Confiscation Act was silent on whether the seizure of an estate affected dower rights. According to common law, the right to dower assured a widow a life interest in one-third of any real property her husband owned during the marriage. The widow was given the use of the property during her life as a means of support, and when she died her husband's heirs became the owners of the property. The Jacksonborough Assembly's failure specifically to reserve dower rights deviated from confiscation acts in some other states, which excluded dower portions from seizure. North Carolina, for example, set aside for the wives and children of absentees (loyalists who had left the state) a portion of the estate equaling the amount they may have been granted had the absentee died intestate. A Virginia law reserved dower rights only to those wives and widows who lived in the state. The dower rights in the estates of executed traitors also were preserved in a Massachusetts treason statute passed in 1779. But in South Carolina, loyalists' wives, widows, or their representatives were forced to address dower rights in their petitions to the legislature or the courts or both.[17]

Asserting her right to the contested property, Elizabeth Mitchel, wife of John Mitchel, informed the Assembly in February 1783 that her husband "seized in his life time and at the time of his death of a comfortable inheritance real and personal" and had willed his estate to her and her children. She explained that at the time of his death, John Mitchel was "a man of a very distracted mind" and, in fact, for the "last few years of his life was not generally considered as a man of sound mind." His widow argued that any "misconduct" on his part must have resulted from "insanity only." Indeed, the British had confined him "as an absolute madman." Nevertheless, Elizabeth

17. Cooper and McCord, *Statutes* 6:631; Margaret Brisbane, February 22, 1783, Petitions to the GA, Records of the GA, SCDAH, and Thompson and Lumpkin, *JHR 1783–1784*, 176–77. See Norton, *Liberty's Daughters*, 46; Marylynn Salmon, "Life, Liberty, and Dower: The Legal Status of Women after the American Revolution," in *Women, War and Revolution*, ed. Carol R. Berkin and Clara M. Lovett, (New York: Holmes & Meier, 1980), 91, 102; Salmon, *Women and the Law of Property in Early America* (Chapel Hill: University of North Carolina Press, 1986), 16, 141, 156; and Kerber, *Women of the Republic*, 124–26.

contended that because John Mitchel's heirs supported the American cause and that one had volunteered his services to the state, hers was a just cause:

> Let a few words suffice to plead the cause of the fatherless and Widow against the cultivation of that wretched doctrine of punishing the iniquities of the father in the persons of the innocent children. This is the cause of the widow & Orphan. It is the cause of Justice and mercy, and as such your petitioner is encouraged by a sure and confident hope, that this honorable house will need no other excitement to grant it protection.[18]

Nor did they need any. The 1784 Assembly totally lifted confiscation of the Mitchel estate.[19]

On January 22, 1783, the House heard the petition of Mary Philp, widow of loyalist Robert Philp. She told the legislators that as the daughter of the late James Hartley she was entitled to a significant amount of property; however, "for the want of Some legal formalities, that property was Sold by virtue of the Confiscation Act." Her husband, Robert Philp, "the object of the Said Act" was dead. She implored the legislators to grant her relief, but to little avail. The Assembly responded by lifting confiscation, but then affixing an amercement.[20]

While Mary Philp and most other women who petitioned for dower rights avoided political statements in their claims, Florence Cooke took the opportunity to demonstrate her patriotism. Cooke, the wife of loyalist James Cooke, a Charleston carpenter, utilized her petition to claim her dower rights, establish her daughter's "claim on the inheritance of her father," and to prove herself a patriot. Speaking of herself in the third person, she wrote to the Assembly:

> This law she humbly thinks the more severe as her Child received early & strong impressions of real Attachment to the liberty of her Native Country; with a Confirmed aversion to our Enemies; principally inculcated by yr Petitr who if providence had blessed her with a number of Sons, would have thought herself happily en-

18. Elizabeth Mitchel, February 3, 1783, Petitions to the GA, Records of the GA, SCDAH.

19. Cooper and McCord, *Statutes* 6:635.

20. Thompson and Lumpkin, *JHR 1783–1784*, 15, 613; Adams and Lumpkin, *JHR 1785–1786*, 206; and Cooper and McCord, *Statutes* 6:631, 635.

gaged in employing all the influence & Care of a Mother, to render them fit for the defence and Support of their Country. Conscious of this, she the more regrets that her self and Child should be put out of the protection of the former Laws of this State, with respect to her own Dower, and her Daughters right of future succession to her fathers inheritance.

She claimed that the property under confiscation had been earned as much by her "*own Domestic toil, frugality and attention*" as by her husband's efforts. Furthermore, she said, she was not guilty of any crime. Indeed, she had "a sincere affection for the independence and freedom of her Country, avowed and testified in the worst of times." As far as her husband was concerned, she had "but little to say." He was

> a laborious hardworking man in a Mechanic employment, and not versed in the knowledge of publick troubles, it is not likely he could do any political good or harm. The change that happened in Charles Town was too powerful for his Situation and Circumstances to withstand; he might have said an Idle thing, but your petitioner believes he had neither inclination nor influence to execute any mischievous one.

Florence Cooke explained that the absent James Cooke had left her a house and lot on the Bay, half of a house and lot in St. Michaels Alley, and three Negroes. She was living on the rent of one of the houses but had many debts to pay and a child and female relative to support which had "reduced [her] to very great distress." If that property were sold she would be "utterly undone." She then appealed to the

> members of the legislature as her Country men & fellow Citizens, Humbly entreating, to allow her husband & the father of her Child, to return and have a hearing, if he has Committed any Crime. If he be acquited as she trusts he will, she Pledge herself that she will Exert all the ascendency of a Wife & friend to make him a Good man and useful Citizen.

Cooke added a warning as to the fate that might befall her daughter if the legislature chose not to heed her appeal:

> And lastly she humbly implores of this honorable house, that she may not be deprived of the only resource for herself and the maintenance & education of her Daughter, who must otherwise be turned into the world, without friend or protector, exposed to that

Misfortune and affliction, which Seldom fail to pursue an unhappy female fallen from affluence to poverty.[21]

Florence Cooke represented herself as a patriot, a politically minded
citizen, a confident and assertive woman, one who believed her labors
in building the Cooke estate equaled her husband's. She was a woman
who not only demanded her legal rights but who also recognized and
welcomed her responsibility to raise patriotic children and serve as
helpmeet to her husband. Cooke was, in Linda Kerber's words, a
"Republican Mother." The 1784 Assembly decided to lift the confiscation of James Cooke's property, but then affixed an amercement.[22]

There were other widows who sought and received relief from
confiscation. Among them were Margaret Cunningham, wife of
Andrew Cunningham, Mary Anderson, wife of Culbert Anderson,
Elizabeth Oats, wife of merchant Edward Oats, and Sarah Guest,
wife of William Guest, farmer, surveyor, and justice of the peace. The
South Carolina legislature's Act Number 1265 of 1785 vested in each
widow, her children, and heirs property from her husband's estate,
namely 200 acres to Cunningham, 441 acres to Elizabeth Anderson,
two tenements and 11 acres to Oats, and 500 acres to Sarah Guest.[23]

In 1785 Mary Miller, a widow, filed a suit in the Court of Chancery
claiming dower rights to a house and lot on Church Street, part of the
confiscated estate of loyalist merchant Brian Cape, her son-in-law.
Miller claimed the property had formerly belonged to her husband,
Stephen Miller, and through her dower rights now belonged to her.
But in the meantime, the confiscated house and lot had been bought
by Samuel Beekman whom the court had ordered to pay Mary Miller
£220 with interest from November 23, 1783. Beekman, who said he

21. For this and the preceding quotations, see Cooke, January 21, 1783,
Petitions to the GA, Records of the GA, SCDAH, and Kerber, *Women of the
Republic*, 127–29.

22. Cooper and McCord, *Statutes* 6:635.

23. See the following petitions in Petitions to the GA, Records of the GA,
SCDAH: Margaret Cunningham, January 20, 1785; Mary Anderson, Janu-
ary 8, 1785; and Elizabeth Oats, February 19, 1785. Wallace Brown, *The
King's Friends, the Composition and Motives of the American Loyalist Claimants*
(Providence: Brown University Press, 1965), 222; Lorenzo Sabine, *Bio-
graphical Sketches of Loyalists of the American Revolution with an Historical
Essay*, 2 vols. (1864; reprint, Baltimore: Genealogical Publishing Company,
1966), 1:503; and Cooper and McCord, *Statutes* 6:629–35, 666–67.

could not afford such heavy charges, was seeking compensation from the legislature for his £220 plus interest. The House and Senate finally agreed with Beekman, and Mary Miller's suit was lost.[24]

Margaret Mongin also took her claim to court, with somewhat better results. In 1785 Mongin, the widow of loyalist planter Richard Pendarvis of St. Helena Parish, claimed her dower rights in his estate, but purchasers of the confiscated estate contested her claim because the Confiscation Act did not mention dower. In 1789 Attorney General Alexander Moultrie rebuked Mongin's claim to dower in the estate, saying, "The common law goes upon the idea, that husbands are oftentimes influenced and governed by the sentiment and conduct of their wives. If, therefore, they do not exert this influence, by example and dissuasion, they are considered in the law, as having incurred such a degree of guilt, as to forfeit every right or claim under their husbands." Moultrie reasoned that Mongin had lost her dower right when Pendarvis forfeited his property. The attorney general further argued that if the state had wanted to reserve dower rights it would have stated that fact in the confiscation legislation. Recognizing dower rights, Moultrie contended, "would be productive of endless demands against the state."

Fortunately for Margaret Mongin, the court heard her demand. Her attorney, Henry William DeSaussure, argued that according to English law a wife's dower was only forfeited in the event her husband was tried and found guilty of treason. The Confiscation Act had only banished Mongin's former husband; it said nothing about treason. Judge Elihu Hall Bay at last decided in Mongin's favor: "The court is not bound to give, nor will they ever give such a harsh construction to the act, as to deprive a widow of a common law right, when the act itself is silent upon the subject."[25]

24. Beekman, February 12, 1785, Petitions to the GA, Records of the GA, SCDAH; Adams and Lumpkin, *JHR 1785–1786*, 83–84, 145, 164, 203; and Committee Report on the Petition of Samuel Beekman, 1785, Committee Reports, Records of the GA, SCDAH. The Senate committee report said the court ordered Beekman to pay Miller £420 sterling with interest on the whole sum since November 23, 1783.

25. Mongin, February 12, 1785, Petitions to the GA, Records of the GA, SCDAH, and Cooper and McCord, *Statutes* 6:632. On dower rights see Salmon, "Life, Liberty, and Dower," 91–93, and Kerber, *Women of the Republic*, 129–30.

Loyalist planter Gideon Dupont's daughter, Mary Collett, was not so successful. On January 29, 1784, her petition requesting relief from the confiscation of her father's estate was "referred to the Committee, appointed to Report what further relief shall be made for the Wives and Families of those persons whose Estates have been confiscated." In March her attorney, William Hornby, laid before the House an account against the Commissioners of Forfeited Estates for the maintenance of Mary Collett. It was referred to a committee. Evidently no further action was taken on either petition. Hornby tried again the following year on February 28, 1785, when he petitioned the legislature requesting payment from the Dupont estate to support Mary Collett. His petition was referred to the Committee on Public Accounts. On March 22, the House considered the committee's negative report and denied Hornby's petition.[26]

In February 1787 Collett's husband, John, a loyalist himself, took the matter to the London Loyalist Commission. He told the commission that when he married her in August 1780, she had no money, no marriage settlement, and no hope of any fortune. When her father died in May 1785 he left no will. Collett claimed that his wife had a right to some of the Dupont property in South Carolina, but the only compensation she had received was an annual sum of £20 from the treasury. Dupont's brother, Cornelius, had received £50. Since Cornelius had died, Collett asked the commission to award his wife that sum in addition to her own annuity.[27]

In 1788 Mary Collett appealed to the French Ambassador in London. In her memorial to the ambassador, Mary Collett told him that she was now in England "and in very great distress. That on Account of the late troubles in America her Father was Banished [from] that place and Died in London May 1785 and her Brother in October 1786 leaving . . . [her] the only one alive of that branch of the Family." She explained that her father had owned extensive property in South Carolina "which was sold for the use of the American States and that when the troubles began . . . [she] was but a Child and could not act offensive either way." Her mother had brought into the marriage with her father a large amount of property, which had been confiscated later and sold without any provision for Collett

26. Thompson and Lumpkin, *JHR 1783–1784*, 389, 612, and Adams and Lumpkin, *JHR 1785–1786*, 157, 269, 276–77.

27. Loyalist Transcripts for Great Britain, Loyalist Commission, 58 vols., South Carolina Claims, SCDAH, 54:285–86.

and her children, "tho Children in Similar Circumstances . . . [have] been provided for." She hoped for the ambassador's "Friendly Interference."

John Adams, then minister to Great Britain, forwarded Collett's memorial to the governor of South Carolina along with a letter of February 2, 1788, stating that he did not know the persons involved. On October 9, 1788, Adams's letter to the governor and Collett's memorial were referred to a House committee, and on the following day the committee reported that a portion of the Dupont estate had been sold. Dupont's estate, including proceeds from the sale of the confiscated property, had not been sufficient to pay his debts. The committee concluded that the state no longer owned any of Dupont's property, hence, no award could be made by the state to Collett. The full House and Senate agreed.[28] In this case the state favored the rights of Dupont's creditors over the inheritance rights of Dupont's daughter.

Gideon Dupont's sister, Jane Villepontoux, fared better. In 1786 she petitioned the legislature concerning a sum of money that her brother, by then deceased, had held in trust. A trusteeship placed a married woman's property not in her husband's hands but rather in those of another male adult. This prevented payment of a husband's debts from his wife's property. On March 22, the Assembly honored the trusteeship and ratified an act awarding Villepontoux £462.17.7 sterling.[29]

In 1791 Mary Wells, widow of Charleston printer Robert Wells, took her dower claim to court. She made no apology for her husband's politics nor did she offer any motives for his loyalism. She merely stated that fifteen months before America declared its independence, Wells had traveled to Great Britain and was prevented by the onset of the war from returning home. While Wells was abroad, his attorney, acting in his behalf, bought some land in Charleston. This land was the extent of Wells's real property; his personal property consisted of books, types, and other items associated with his printing business. His entire estate was later confiscated and sold

28. Committee Reports, October 10, 1788, Records of the GA, SCDAH, and Michael Stevens and Christine Allen, eds., *Journals of the House of Representatives 1787–1788* (Columbia: University of South Carolina Press, 1981), 546, 548–49, 558.

29. Adams and Lumpkin, *JHR 1785–1786*, 433, 461–62, 470, 478, 484–85, 511, 525, 528, 595, and Kerber, *Women of the Republic*, 142.

for £13,646. The confiscation, plus losses suffered through a fire in 1770, had claimed all his property. His family had been "reduced to a scanty subsistance." Mary Wells called "on the known humanity & bounty of the Legislature" to restore her husband's property as they had in the cases "of many who were objects of resentment in the Time of War and Confusion." She was "more emboldened in this hope, as the tenth clause of the Confiscation Act holds out a final Provision for the families of those whose Estates were sold." Mary Wells ended her petition with a request for some "allowance" in "consideration of her situation & that of her Children."

The committee considering her petition recommended that an appraisal be made of the Charleston property and that during her lifetime Mary Wells be awarded annually the interest on that sum. After her death, her children were to receive the money. But, without any explanation, the House failed to approve the committee's report. A year later Mary Wells's brother, Robert Rowand, petitioned the legislature on her behalf. Rowand enclosed with his petition a copy of Wells's petition along with the House committee's report, believing that once the legislature reconsidered her case it would rule in her favor. But as 1792 came to a close, Mary Wells had received no assistance from the Assembly.[30]

Finally, as in Margaret Mongin's case, Mary Wells's case ended in a favorable court decision. The cases were oddly similar: the purchasers of the Pendarvis estate and the Wells estate were the same, the presiding judge was the same, and the attorney was the same. Henry William DeSaussure again argued the case, but on the other side: this time he represented the creditors' claims against Wells's dower rights. But Judge Bay found for Wells, ruling that a widow's dower right was one of the law's priorities "and one which the courts of justice have ever held sacred."

Catherine Carne, widow of merchant-doctor Samuel Carne, began her struggle on March 1, 1787, "to have part of her late husband's estate under confiscation restored to her." Two years later on January 28, 1789, she asked the legislature to compensate her for the sale of a house and two lots in Charleston. She petitioned again on

30. See Stevens and Allen, *Journals of the House of Representatives, 1791* (Columbia: University of South Carolina Press, 1985), 115–17, 361, and the following petitions in Petitions to the GA, Records of the GA, SCDAH: Mary Wells, February 1, 1791, and Robert Rowand, November 28, 1792.

January 27, 1791, but this time referred not to her late husband's property, but to her own property and dower rights. In this petition Carne stated that her father, Jacob Bond, left her with £3,000 sterling in money and slaves which she brought to her marriage. Her husband had gone bankrupt, leaving her with nothing. Carne claimed her dower rights in his estate. On February 7, 1791, the House committee recommended an award of £200 sterling "in lieu of Dower in said Estate." Eleven days later on February 18, the House considered a Senate resolution awarding Carne the value of the sold house and two lots. The House agreed.[31]

The legislature's action for Catherine Carne was in accordance with "an Act for the more easy and expeditious obtaining the admeasurement of dower to widows of the lands of their deceased husbands" passed in 1777. In an effort to foster support for widows, the act allowed widows a cash payment equaling one-third the value of the husband's estate in place of dower in the real property. A cash settlement may have been preferred to relying upon proceeds from tracts of land. Marylynn Salmon claims that undoubtedly the state's legislative action was prompted by its concern in protecting the rights and interests of creditors injured by the "encumbrance of a widow's life estate." Salmon argues that as South Carolina focused on its economic recovery and growth after the Revolution, the state's support of widows' rights in land disputes waned in favor of creditors. Indeed, Salmon contends that by 1791 "widows were effectively denied traditional dower rights in all cases involving creditors." After 1791, in the event an estate was bankrupt and creditors made claims on the estate, a widow in South Carolina was not allowed to retain undivided tracts of the family's property. Only when the estate was free of debts and the heirs agreed could a widow be granted such property. If not, the widow would receive a third share from each part of the estate or a cash settlement in lieu of dower.[32]

31. Carne, March 1, 1787, and in Petitions to the GA, Records of the GA, SCDAH; Cooper and McCord, *Statutes* 6:631; and Thomas Waring, *History of Medicine in South Carolina, 1670–1825*, 3 vols. (Columbia: South Carolina Medical Association, 1964), 1:185. See also Michael Stevens and Christine Allen, *Journals of the House of Representatives, 1789–1790* (Columbia: University of South Carolina Press, 1984), 78, and Stevens and Allen, *JHR 1791*, 214, 287.

32. Salmon, "Life, Liberty, and Dower," 92–94. See also Salmon, *Women and the Law of Property*, 169–70.

In the 1795 case of *John Scott's Creditors v. Sarah Scott* the new dower policy is evident.[33] In accordance with her dower rights, the widowed Sarah Scott had been awarded a lot on Broad Street in Charleston with its house, a store, and another lot on East Bay Street, along with a house and outbuildings in Greenwich village, and a pew in St. Philip's Church. Her late husband's creditors protested, arguing that she had received his most valuable property, thereby reducing the value of the remaining estate along with their property rights. In this case the court ruled in favor of the creditors and awarded Sarah Scott a cash settlement instead of her dower share in the real property. Since she no longer held a life interest in the estate, it could then be sold as necessary to meet the demands of her late husband's creditors. But under certain conditions a widow and her heirs could retain ownership forever instead of only during the widow's lifetime.

Coverture was yet another issue in the confiscation of loyalists' estates. Coverture, an aspect of British common law, referred to the husband's control of his wife's property during their marriage. According to this concept, a "woman's identity became submerged, or covered, by that of her husband when she married. A married couple became a legal fiction: like a corporation, the pair was a single person with a single will." The husband absorbed his wife's property; he could do anything with it without her permission. A married woman lost independent control of her property. According to republican theory, political rights derived from owning property. Hence, without property a married woman had no political rights. (The unmarried woman fared little better, since frequently she was denied the political rights that supposedly accompanied her property rights.) "The married woman, 'covered' by her husband's political identity, became politically invisible."[34]

33. Scott was a Charleston merchant. He was included on the fourth confiscation list and was granted a full pardon. Cooper and McCord, *Statutes* 6:631, 645.

34. Kerber, *Women of the Republic*, 120–21. It can be argued that "country ideology" accounts for much of the American resistance to the British. Carolina country ideology was based on a number of related concepts. South Carolinians considered their liberty to be an inheritance, a birthright from their English and Carolina forefathers. Individual freedom was tied to personal independence and that meant owning property. But, women were apparently excluded from that aspect of country ideology. See Robert Weir, *"A Most Important Epocha": The Coming of the Revolution in South Carolina,*

Coverture certainly was a factor in the case of Fenwicke Bull, the public register in Charleston, and Christiana Hoff, the woman who lived with him. In 1785 Martin Miller, Jacob Willeman, and Charles Gruber claimed that the Confiscation Act had denied their children an inheritance from Christiana Hoff.[35] Bull had died in 1778, four years before passage of the Confiscation Act. In his will dated March 9, 1776, Bull had bequeathed to Christiana Hoff,

> now living and dwelling in my house, for and in Consideration of her very great Fidelity to me, in my Business; her great care and Attention to me, and my odd Humours at all Times, as well in Sickness, as in Health; independent of, and free from the Control of her Husband in every Matter which whatever, notwithstanding her Coverture, (she and her said Husband having been separated by mutual Consent, before that she the said Christiana, came to my Aid),[36]

a house and two lots in Charleston, five slaves, household furniture, and £500 sterling. Bull specifically stated the property was given to her "independent[ly]" and for "her sole Use, and without any Controul whatsoever for ever." He added: "Before I now take my Leave of her, I hope she will so far value herself, and remember me, as evermore to be her own Mistress. And to remove every Possibility of a Doubt, I once more repeat, that her Husband, notwithstanding her Coverture shall not have the smallest Controul, Share or Noiety of any or all the foregoing, no, not even one Shilling Currency." In the event of Christiana Hoff's death, Bull had instructed that the property was to be sold and the money dis-

---

Tricentennial Booklet Number 5 (Columbia: University of South Carolina Press, 1970), 5–7.

35. Miller was a Charleston bricklayer, Willeman was a Charleston tanner, and Gruber was a Charleston merchant. They were friends of Bull and executors of his will. See Miller, Willeman, and Gruber, February 16, 1785, Petitions to the GA, Records of the GA, SCDAH; Adams and Lumpkin, *JHR 1785–1786*, 93, 94; Philip Hamer, George C. Rogers, Jr., and David Chesnutt, eds., *The Papers of Henry Laurens* (Columbia: University of South Carolina Press, 1968–), 3:488; and "Correspondence of Arthur Middleton," *SCHGM* 27 (July 1926): 128. The devisees or heirs of Bull were on the first confiscation list; there was no pardon in 1784. Cooper and McCord, *Statutes* 6:629, 634–35.

36. Miller, Willeman, and Gruber, February 16, 1785, with enclosure of Fenwicke Bull's will, Petitions to the GA, Records of the GA, SCDAH.

tributed to the children of his friends, Miller, Willeman, and Gruber. Hoff had since died, and Miller, Willeman, and Gruber, acting as executors of Fenwicke Bull's will, asked the Assembly for an ordinance removing the estate from confiscation and giving it to their children.

The House committee reported on February 23, 1785, that the Bull petition was accurate and that the three petitioners had served their country faithfully and had suffered property losses themselves. The committee recommended that their petition be granted; the House concurred. On March 7, 1785, the Senate returned its resolution and concurrence.[37] Although Fenwicke Bull had been charged with loyalism and punished by the confiscation of his estate, the state upheld Bull's will and his desire not only to bequeath part of his estate to Christiana Hoff, but also to protect it from coverture.

Elizabeth Seabrook Saxby also managed to escape the implications of coverture. On February 17, 1786, John Cogdell, her deceased husband's attorney, informed the legislature that before Elizabeth's marriage to loyalist George Saxby, a merchant, planter, and royal official, she was entitled to a house and a lot in Charleston and a plantation on John's Island. Saxby's marriage to Elizabeth Seabrook had secured his admission to Charleston's social elite, but he became extremely unpopular after his appointment as Inspector of Stamp Duties in 1764. In 1772 he left South Carolina for England and never returned. In 1782 the Jacksonborough Assembly placed him on the first confiscation list; his appeals for relief failed and he died in England in 1786. The Commissioners of Forfeited Estates, Cogdell complained, "Conceived the publick had a Right to the Rent and profitts of the Same during the life of the Said George Saxbey," and they refused to award his client any of the rent or profits, "though her distress for want of a necessary Supply have been great." The commissioners were applying coverture to Elizabeth Saxby's property. Nevertheless, Cogdell asked the legislators to give Elizabeth Saxby all of the rent or at least the amount not already paid to the commissioners. The following month, the Assembly authorized John Cogdell to receive for Elizabeth Saxby the rent

37. Miller, Willeman, and Gruber, February 16, 1785, with enclosure of Fenwicke Bull's will, Petitions to the GA, Records of the GA, SCDAH; and Adams and Lumpkin, *JHR 1785–1786*, 93, 94, 125, 129, 199.

due on the house and lot in Charleston but not yet received by the commissioners, and all subsequent rent.[38]

Along with coverture, trusteeships, and dower rights, marriage settlements further complicated the confiscation of loyalists' estates. A marriage settlement was a prenuptial agreement that allowed a woman or her trustees control over the property she brought into a marriage. It provided, in short, a separate estate to a *feme covert*, a married woman. By the mid-eighteenth century, marriage settlements were becoming common in South Carolina, especially among the wealthy.

Although the 1782 Confiscation Act often disregarded dower rights, it protected marriage settlements. According to Article 12, "all grants, devisees, sales, and conveyances made by the loyalists" between July 4, 1776, and May 12, 1780, and after that date were now "fraudulent." Those made before July 4, 1776, then remained in effect.[39] Several wives of loyalists based their claims on marriage settlements.

One case centering on a marriage settlement concerned the property of Susanna Man Cassels, wife of loyalist planter James Cassels. When she married in 1769, the marriage settlement allowed Cassels to set aside in her will an amount equal to the Negroes she had inherited from her father and was bringing into the marriage. In 1770 she died giving birth to a son, John. She had made no will. When James Cassels's estate was confiscated, he removed all the Negroes he considered his own and left those of his wife's "as the assured inheritance of his Son."

38. Walter B. Edgar and Louise N. Bailey, eds., *Biographical Directory of the South Carolina House of Representatives*, 4 vols. (Columbia: University of South Carolina Press, 1974–1984), 2:598–99; Loyalist Transcripts, 53:553; Weir, *"A Most Important Epocha,"* 17; Cooper and McCord, *Statutes* 6:756, 759; Thompson and Lumpkin, *JHR 1785–1786*, 514, 531, 596; John Cogdell, February 17, 1786, and January 29, 1785, Petitions to the GA, Records of the GA; and Adams and Lumpkin, *JHR 1785–1786*, 421–22.

39. For more on marriage settlements see Norton, *Liberty's Daughters*, 47, 135–37, and Julia Cherry Spruill, *Women's Life and Work in the Southern Colonies* (Chapel Hill: University of North Carolina Press, 1938; reprint, W. W. Norton, 1972), 364–66. See also Marylynn Salmon, "Women and Property in South Carolina: The Evidence from Marriage Settlements, 1730 to 1830," *William and Mary Quarterly* 39 (1982): 655–85, and Cooper and McCord, *Statutes* 6:516–25.

On January 21, 1788, Archibald and Mary Man Taylor and Robert Heriot brought this matter before the Assembly. They contended that the Negroes in question were always "intended" for Susanna Cassels's son. But the Commissioners of Forfeited Estates thought otherwise. The petitioners asked the legislature to "interpose: and not permit the Youth to be stripped of the Patrimony always intended for him by his Ancestors."

The House committee reported on February 5, 1788, that James Cassels had executed a bond based upon the provisions of the marriage settlement. In the event she died before him he was to pay £5,000, the value of the Negroes, in whatever way her will stipulated. Although Susanna Cassels died before making a will, the committee observed that

> James Cassels appears by his conduct to have always considered the negroes secured by the said bond and vested in his son as the representative of his mother; because he never worked them with his other negroes, but suffered them to remain on the plantation belonging to the estate of Dr. Man (Mrs. Cassels' late father) and because he left those [Negroes] in question behind as the property of his son.[40]

The House committee recommended that the Negroes be given to Heriot as trustee for John Cassels. Instead, the Assembly awarded Heriot an undesignated amount of money.[41]

In March 1783, in a case involving the heirs of Charleston lawyer James Michie, a House committee protected the rights of wives to marriage settlement property by ruling that the Confiscation Act was not intended "to affect any property Secured by Marriage Settlements made and Executed bonafide & without fraud or collusion." In 1784 the full Assembly agreed.[42]

As seen in the foregoing, not all women were so fortunate. Of the

40. For this and the preceding quotations see Archibald Taylor and his wife, Mary, and Robert Heriot, January 21, 1788, Petitions to the GA, Records of the GA, SCDAH. See also Stevens and Allen, *JHR 1787–1788*, 335–36. James Cassels was on the fifth confiscation list (Cooper and McCord, *Statutes* 6:631).

41. February 5, 1788, Committee Reports, Records of the GA, SCDAH, and Stevens and Allen, *JHR 1787–1788*, 394–95, 629.

42. Thompson and Lumpkin, *JHR 1783–1784*, 236–37; Cooper and McCord, *Statutes* 6:630, 635; and Edgar and Bailey, *Biographical Directory* 2:452–53.

at least sixty-five loyalist cases in some manner concerning women, the 1784 legislature granted only eight total relief from confiscation. Another seventeen were granted relief from confiscation but had their property amerced. A total then of thirty-one received at least a partial pardon. Another thirty-four were not so lucky. But, of that number, at least fifteen later gained a measure of assuagement, leaving possibly only nineteen not receiving any pardon from the "calamities of war." The state's motives in deciding who would be forgiven and who would not are not always clear. But, in the cases of women, especially those involving a woman's direct appeal to the legislature, courts, or both, the state seemed reluctant to hold a woman responsible for her husband's or other male relative's actions, choosing rather to grant her some form of maintenance, if not restoration of the confiscated property.

In the years after 1776, many South Carolina women found themselves forced to petition the legislature to restore their trusteeships, coverture, dower rights, and marriage settlements, all jeopardized by the loyalism of their husbands or other male relatives. The Assembly's positive response to the majority of these cases provides some insight into gender roles in colonial and post–Revolutionary War South Carolina. A woman's realm was the home and family, not politics, as evidenced in most of the women's petitions. Apolitical women had to be protected. Coverture, dower rights, marriage settlements, and trusteeships all were forms of protection. But there were limits to that protection, as seen in the post–Revolutionary War erosion of traditional dower rights. The state's recovery from the war and business interests sometimes took precedence over a woman's rights. While paying lip service to the protection of women's property rights, the state often acted to protect itself. The 1782 Confiscation Act, for example, acknowledged the state's responsibility to provide only for the *temporary* support of loyalists' families, thus avoiding the possibility that families of loyalists could become a financial drain on the state.

Many Carolina women were thus casualties of confiscation and banishment, even though they generally were not considered loyalists themselves, but rather caught in the "calamities of war" as wives, widows, or relatives of loyalists. In most cases, however, the state moved to relieve them of the harsh consequences of being married or related to loyalists. Like courts in New York and in Massachusetts, which rejected the practice of holding wives of loyalists accountable for their husbands' actions, South Carolina courts evidently had no intention of punishing a woman for the conduct of her husband, father, brother, or other male relative. But sometimes, when the best interest of a woman was at odds with the best interest of the early Carolina republic, the woman lost.[43]

43. At least seven of the sixty-three loyalists were not found on the 1782 confiscation lists but petitioned for relief. Since these involved women, they are included here in the total number. Those seven cases involved the estates of Edward Oats, Robert Rowand, William Creighton, James Keith, John Champneys, Henry Peronneau, and Lachlan McIntosh. See their respective petitions to the General Assembly, Records of the GA, SCDAH. Not included here are the cases of Robert Cooper and Peter Taylor. From the available evidence, no woman or her representative made any appeals to the South Carolina legislature or courts in either case. Instead, in each case a woman appealed only to the London Loyalist Commission. For Cooper, see Loyalist Transcripts, 52:588. For Taylor, see Loyalist Transcripts, 57:494–99. See also Robert M. Calhoon, "The Reintegration of the Loyalists and the Disaffected," in *The American Revolution, Its Character and Limits*, ed. Jack Greene (New York: New York University Press, 1987), 68–69.

✖ Kent Anderson Leslie

Amanda America Dickson
An Elite Mulatto Lady in Nineteenth-Century Georgia

One day in the middle of February 1849, David Dickson rode across his fallow fields. A wealthy Georgia planter, age forty, of medium height and weight, he wore his black hair long and straight, "Indian style." As he rode, Dickson spotted a young slave playing in a field. He knew the slave. She belonged to his mother; in fact, she was a great favorite of his mother's. Deliberately he rode up beside the slave child and reached down and swung her up behind him on his saddle and, as her descendants would say years later, "That was the end of that." The slave's childhood ended, and Amanda America Dickson's life began on that day when her father raped her mother. Amanda Dickson lived her life on the margins of a system of racial categorization that proved both useful and artificial. She struggled to remain outside these racial boundaries through acceptance by her father's elite white family, and she sought to erase the stigma of blackness in the white world with the ties of family and class.

Various sources record this process of family definition from different perspectives. Because of David Dickson's extraordinary wealth, legal records abound in the courthouses of Hancock and Richmond counties, Georgia. These sources present a picture of a father transferring the control of his wealth to the "sound judgment" of his daughter, without the interference of any court or husband.[1] Be-

1. Will of David Dickson, Probate Court of Hancock County, Ga., Index to wills, 246–52, July 21, 1884.

cause David Dickson's will left the bulk of his estate to his mulatto daughter, contemporary newspaper articles are also plentiful.[2] They describe Amanda America Dickson as the wealthiest black woman in Georgia, or the southeast, or the world. An oral history also exists, a story that Amanda America's mother, Julia Frances Lewis Dickson, passed down to her great-granddaughter, Kate Dickson McCoy-Lee. Julia Dickson told this story from the perspective of one who lived in a world where class could override race. Julia remembered that Amanda America defined herself as a "lady" in the ornamental sense, and her family as the family of David Dickson. With nostalgia, the black descendants of Amanda America Dickson looked back to a time when the power of wealth created a safe space for a black "lady" and her family. In this extraordinary case, the gender conventions that governed the lives of upper-class white women would shape the life of this slave woman as well.

Elsa Barkley Brown has stated that elite black families and individuals in the nineteenth-century South had to choose between retreating into a world of "personal privilege" or engaging in the black community's struggle for racial uplift. Amanda America Dickson chose the former. If we compare Amanda's story with other stories about mixed families in the antebellum South, the differences are illuminating. Kathryn L. Morgan's *Children of Strangers*, Pauli Murray's *Proud Shoes*, and Adele Logan Alexander's "Ambiguous Lives" chronicle the racial definition of other mixed families with different experiences.[3]

2. *Sparta Ishmaelite:* obituary of David Dickson lists the beneficiaries of the will (March 4, 1885); editorial explaining that the *Ishmaelite* will not print the contents of David Dickson's will (March 11, 1884); editorial describing the caveators' (Dickson's white relatives who objected to the will) arguments against the will (July 14, 1885); editorial describing the communities' anticipation of the upcoming trial (July 15, 1885); editorial describing the summary arguments during the Dickson will case trial (November 25, 1885); articles describing the Georgia Supreme Court's verdict (June 17, 1887). *Sandersville Mercury,* June 21, 1887; *Milledgeville Union Recorder,* June 21, 1887; *Augusta Chronicle,* June 14, 1887; *Atlanta Constitution,* June 14, 1887; *Cleveland Gazette,* June 25, 1887; *Savannah Tribune,* August 6, 1887.

3. Brown, "Weaving Threads of Community: The Richmond Example" (paper delivered at the Southern Historical Association meeting, Norfolk, Virginia, November 1988); Morgan, *Children of Strangers: The Stories of a Black Family* (Philadelphia: Temple University Press, 1980); Murray, *Proud Shoes: The Story of an American Family* (New York: Harper & Row, 1956); Alexander, "Ambiguous Lives: Free Women of Color in Rural Georgia, 1787–1879" (Master's thesis, Howard University, 1987).

Morgan, for example, remembers the stories of her great-grand-mother, "Caddy," who was born a slave. The stories themselves change and appear in different versions but the message to the family remains the same: "You have to fight every inch of the way to be free." In essence, Caddy's family utterly rejects its white ancestry and defines itself as black-against-white. Pauli Murray's *Proud Shoes* records the story of Murray's aristocratic mulatto grandmother, Cornelia Smith Fitzgerald, her black grandfather, Robert Fitzgerald, and their descendants. As the mulatto daughter of one of *the* Smiths, Cornelia Fitzgerald was raised in her father's household. There she learned that because of her aristocratic white background, "she was inferior to nobody," a notion that, according to Murray, made it impossible for her grandmother to adjust to her later "Negro status." When Murray describes herself as standing "very tall in proud shoes," she is describing herself as standing in the shoes of her grandfather, and choosing to be black and proud.

Adele Logan Alexander's "Ambiguous Lives" describes the stories of women in a mixed family of material privilege, a family in which a white parent acknowledged his paternity and, at least temporarily, protected his children from racial definitions. The Hunt-Logan family used education and decorum to transcend racial definitions altogether. Alexander chronicles the struggles of her grandmother, Adella Hunt Logan, as she tried to live with racial ambiguity as an adult, away from the protection of her white father.

All of these texts describe the varied mechanisms through which mixed families faced the complex issues of racial identification and the need for the protection of an intermediate identity. Amanda America Dickson's story does not reflect the defiance of Caddy's stories or the pride in blackness of Pauli Murray's, but rather the racial ambiguity of Adella Logan's life, the struggle to escape the boundaries of race by finding shelter inside the boundaries of a white family and its class.

Conventional history texts have erased Amanda America Dickson's story. However, because of her father's extraordinary wealth and fame, agricultural historians of Georgia have preserved a record of David Dickson's public life. One of these historians, Ralph Betts Flanders, added a footnote to his description of David Dickson, which reads:

> David Dickson was as unusual in his marital relations as he was successful in the planting industry. According to one of his close

friends, while still a young man he became attached to a mulatto girl, about his age, who was a waiting maid in his father's house. Falling heir to this slave upon the death of his father, Dickson lived with her as man and wife, becoming the father of several mulatto children. So open was Dickson in this respect that he was banned from polite society. Upon his death in 1885, he left his entire estate, some half million dollars to his concubine, who bore his name, Amanda A. Dickson.[4]

Flanders is correct in stating that David Dickson was an innovative and successful planter-farmer. From 1860 until his death in 1885, he remained the wealthiest individual in one of the wealthiest counties in Georgia. But on several other counts the picture painted here is flawed: Amanda America Dickson was David Dickson's daughter, not his concubine. Her mother, Julia Frances Lewis Dickson, belonged to David's mother, not his father. In fact, Julia Dickson's birth took place nine years after David's father, Thomas Dickson, had died. A monolithic "polite society" did not ostracize David Dickson; in fact, his fame and generosity made his plantation a modern Mecca for farmers throughout the Southeast who sought information on the "Dickson method." It would have been a simple task for Flanders to correct this misinformation by examining contemporary newspapers and legal documents.[5] Instead this white male historian either transformed, or recorded another's transformation of, a mulatto daughter into a more acceptable concubine.

Kate Dickson McCoy-Lee (1894–1986), Amanda America's granddaughter, told a different story.[6] She was born the year after Amanda America's death and was the third child of Amanda America's son, Charles Green Dickson, and his wife, Kate Holsey Dickson. Kate's sources of information about her grandmother included Julia Frances Dickson, Amanda America's mother; Kate Holsey Dickson, Amanda's daughter-in-law; and "Aunt Mary" Long, Amanda's lifelong personal servant. By the time McCoy-Lee told her stories for

4. Ralph Betts Flanders, *Plantation Slavery in Georgia* (Chapel Hill: University of North Carolina Press, 1933), 272.

5. *Georgia Supreme Court Reports* 78:413–47; *Augusta Chronicle*, by "L," February 19, 1885, June 14, 1887; *Sparta Ishmaelite*, February 25, and November 25, 1885.

6. The story has been distilled from a series of interviews with Kate McCoy-Lee, which took place from 1981 until 1986. In addition, the author has relied on a taped interview with McCoy-Lee that her granddaughter, Jean Jackson of Annapolis, Maryland, recorded.

the last time in the 1980s, she was a well-educated and well-traveled individual who had lived a long and productive life as an educator, wife, mother, grandmother, and great-grandmother. What McCoy-Lee chose to remember fulfills the needs of the born storyteller and, to a certain extent, the needs of her family, a family that lived in a racist society. What did she want her descendants to believe about Amanda America's life? The slave child Julia Frances never forgave David Dickson for forcing her to have sex with him when she was young. In retaliation, as his concubine, "she ruled David Dickson with an iron hand; had the keys to the plantation and controlled everything."[7]

At the time of Amanda America Dickson's birth on November 21, 1849, her mother was thirteen and her father forty. She was born on the Dickson plantation in the pine barrens of southwestern Hancock County, in the fertile Black Belt of Georgia. The Dickson plantation, located nine miles from the county seat, Sparta, consisted of two thousand acres of land. The Dickson family had come to the country before the turn of the century and staked out a claim to a 170-acre plot of scruffy land. There Thomas and Elizabeth Dickson, David's parents, built a small house and raised ten children. By 1827 they had managed to accumulate enough property for Thomas to leave an estate that included at least twenty-eight slaves, thereby placing the Dicksons' holdings in the top 20 percent in Hancock County. Thomas Dickson's son added to the family fortune and at the time of Amanda America's birth in 1849, David Dickson was a wealthy man in his own right. Owning fifty-three slaves, he belonged to the wealthiest 5 percent of slaveholders in Hancock County.[8]

In 1849, at forty years of age, David Dickson lived on the Dickson homeplace in a household of older, widowed, or unmarried white people: his mother Elizabeth, seventy-two; his brother, Green, thirty-five; and his sister, Rutha, forty-three. Julia Frances Lewis Dickson lived in a slave house "in the yard" of the Dickson homeplace, with her mother, Rose Lewis. According to family tradition,

7. Interview with Kate McCoy-Lee by the author, November 10, 1981.

8. *Tax Digest*, Hancock County, Ga., District 114, 1849. Georgia Department of Archives and History, Atlanta, Ga.; 1800 United States Census of the State of Georgia; will of Thomas Dickson, 1827, Probate Court of Hancock County, Ga., Will Book M, 182–96. See also Forest Shivers, *The Land Between: A History of Hancock County, Georgia, to 1940* (Opelika, Alabama: n.p., 1990), 131.

Julia's father was "Portuguese, not black," and Julia was "a small copper colored person, with soft hair and beautiful teeth," a person who was "very temperamental and high-strung," a person who "claimed to have no black blood in her."[9] The child Julia bore in October of 1849 captivated the Dickson family. Soon after the birth, Amanda America's white relatives took her from her mother's breast, and her white grandmother took the infant to her own room. She slept in a trundle bed that Elizabeth Dickson had made specially for her. For the next fifteen years Amanda America lived in that same room, in the white Dickson household, until Elizabeth Dickson died in 1864.

Unfortunately, Amanda America's naming is left out of the family's story. "America" is a curiously patriotic name for a slave, and it seems unlikely that her mother, Julia, chose it. Why would her father, or perhaps her white grandmother choose it? As a cruel oxymoronic joke? As an expression of their own patriotic view of the sectional conflict that raged over slavery in the territories at the time? Or in the belief that in America this child could be brought into their family in spite of her color, and be rescued from slavery by their individual wills?

The decision to bring a slave infant into the household may have been made by David alone or by David and his mother. During the antebellum period, it was not unusual for slaveholding families to bring a slave into a white plantation household. According to Mary Chesnut, her mother-in-law slept with two slave women in her room in case she needed attention during the night, and with two others in the next room for protection.[10] But, in this case, the slave was an infant who, for a time at least, required care. Perhaps Elizabeth Dickson made the decision to retrieve the child in an effort to make amends for her son's loss of control. Perhaps she simply wanted the company and affection of her grandchild. Perhaps David and Elizabeth made the decision together to create a "family" that excluded the infant's mother, a family they had the power to design.

McCoy-Lee described Amanda America as the "darling of David Dickson's heart." He "adored her and gave her everything she wanted. She was bathed in sweet milk to lighten her skin and allowed to

9. Taped interview of Kate Dickson McCoy-Lee by Jean Jackson.

10. Mary Boykin Chesnut, *Mary Chesnut's Civil War,* ed. C. Vann Woodward (New Haven: Yale University Press, 1981), 202.

claim newborn slaves as her own and name them whatever she liked."[11] As she grew older, David bought Amanda America a house on Green Street in Augusta so that she and her mother could go shopping. Amanda America often traveled to and from Augusta on the train with her pet parrot and monkey. In addition to shopping in Augusta for clothing, she had a seamstress who came down to the plantation to make clothes for her. Everyone on the plantation called her "Miss Amanda," including her father and, one would presume, her mother.

Why would David Dickson and his mother treat a mulatto slave child as a "pampered darling"? And why would that child's granddaughter, Kate McCoy-Lee, the storyteller, choose to remember that treatment this way? To the outside world Amanda America Dickson remained a slave. If this picture of her childhood is correct, then we must assume that David Dickson and his mother raised this child for their own pleasure, as a pet, believing that someone in the family would always be there to protect her. They raised Amanda America in what E. Franklin Frazier would later describe as "a world of make believe" in which class theoretically erases race.[12]

If David and Elizabeth Dickson had wanted to free Amanda America between 1849 and 1864, it would have been virtually impossible for them to do so and keep her with them in the state of Georgia. In 1801 the state outlawed manumission in the state except by petition to the legislature.[13] This process became more and more difficult after the Nat Turner rebellion in 1831. Until 1859 masters and mistresses could free their slaves outside the state during their lifetimes or in their wills; Amanda America could have been freed in another state, but she could not have legally returned to Georgia as a free person of color. In order for David and Elizabeth to keep Amanda with them on the Dickson homeplace, the child had to remain a

11. McCoy-Lee, November 10, 1981.

12. McCoy-Lee, November 10, 1981. The word *pet* is defined in *American Heritage Dictionary* (2d college edition, 1982, 1985) as 1) An animal kept for amusement or companionship. 2) An object of affection. 3) A person especially loved or indulged; a favorite daughter; teacher's pet. Adj. L. Kept as a pet; a pet daughter; a pet aversion. V. petted, petting, pets. *Tr.* to stroke or caress gently; pat-Intr. informal. To make love by fondling and caressing. Orig. unknown. Frazier, *Black Bourgeoisie* (Glencoe, Illinois: Free Press, 1957), 25.

13. See Lucius Q. C. Lamar, ed., *A Compilation of the Laws of the State of Georgia, 1810–1819* (Augusta: n.p., 1821), 811–12.

slave and thus continually at risk, a fact that the white Dicksons—and Amanda's descendants—largely ignored. In McCoy-Lee's memories, Amanda America was never a slave or black; these facts were erased because she was David Dickson's daughter.[14]

The category of Free Persons of Color would not have been unfamiliar to Elizabeth and David Dickson. In 1859 the census taker recorded sixty-two black individuals as free in Hancock County. In 1860 the census recorded thirty-seven names of free people of color, two of whom lived in households with white individuals. This census also revealed that the wealthiest Free People of Color in Hancock County in 1860 were both women: Cresa Ruff, who owned property worth $1,000, and Nancy Wadkins, who owned property worth $2,000 including two slaves who were probably family members.[15]

If we look carefully at the description of Amanda America's childhood from her granddaughter's perspective, then we are left to wonder what these remembrances meant to the later black Dickson family. One message is that David Dickson tried to make Amanda appear as white as possible; another is that as a child she had a kind of exalted status as "Miss Amanda" and that Amanda America's white father loved her unreservedly. The role would be common for the daughter of an elite white planter in preparation for her "ladyhood," but hardly a common role for a mulatto daughter in a family of aging white slaveholders.

Family tradition has it that Amanda America went to school in Paris and professors came to the plantation to teach her, including a Dr. Porter from Atlanta University and a Reverend Ambrose. Amanda Dickson read widely, including *Camille,* Alexander Dumas's 1852 play about a young courtesan in Paris who was doomed to be ostracized by polite society. Amanda also attended Atlanta University briefly from 1876 to 1878. But, according to McCoy-Lee: "David Dickson had a fireplace built for her in the North Hall because she did not like a stove. She left because she didn't like the discipline."[16]

14. McCoy-Lee, November 10, 1981.

15. United States Census for 1850, 1860, 1870, Hancock County, Ga.; *Register of Free Persons of Color,* Hancock County, Ga., 1855–1862, Georgia Department of Archives and History, Atlanta, Ga.

16. McCoy-Lee, November 10, 1981. See Alexander Dumas, fils, *Camille,* in *Camille and Other Plays,* ed. Stephen S. Stranton (New York: Hill and Wang, 1957), 105–64. Amanda America Dickson attended Atlanta Univer-

McCoy-Lee recalled that while Amanda America Dickson grew up in "the Big House," her mother, Julia, became David Dickson's "housekeeper." Julia may have continued to have a sexual liaison with Dickson, but in 1853, at the age of seventeen, she gave birth to another daughter, Julianna, whose father was a slave on the plantation. Julianna was "not related to David Dickson, who was her owner." Julianna eventually married a black man, Raibon Youngblood, and had several children, one of whom, Will, "took care of Granny Julia when she got old."[17]

When Amanda America Dickson reached young adulthood, David Dickson arranged for her marriage to his white cousin, Charles Eubank.[18] Since marriages between black persons and white persons were illegal in Georgia, the couple married in Baltimore. After the marriage Dickson gave them a plantation on the Ooustanala River near Rome, Georgia.[19] In 1866 Amanda America and Charles had a son, Julian Henry, and in 1870 they had a second son, Charles Green. Aunt Mary Long, Amanda America Dickson's lifelong "servant," remembered the couple as traveling across the Ooustanala on a ferry with the two boys and their nurses. Marriage apparently did not alter Amanda America's status in an elite white world.

By 1870, however, both Amanda America's marriage and her opportunity for independence from her father failed. Amanda left Charles Eubank and came home to David Dickson with the explanation, "I want to live with you, Pappie." Eubank arrived in a buggy one day and tried to retrieve his wife, but Amanda "put her hands

---

sity in 1876–1877 and 1877–1878. *Atlanta University Catalogue,* 1876–1877, 1877–1878, Atlanta University, Special Collections.

17. Julianna Dickson Youngblood is listed in the census of 1880 as a twenty-seven-year-old mulatto female, the wife of Raibon Youngblood, a thirty-five-year-old black male. Their children were Willie, age ten; Edgar, age nine; Lula, age six; Bessie, age five; and Emma, age one.

18. Charles Eubank was a white Civil War veteran who served with the Hancock County Confederate Guards, Fifteenth Regiment, Georgia Volunteer Infantry. He enrolled in the Army of Virginia as a private on July 15, 1861, and was discharged at Farmville, Va., in April of 1865 (*Roster of Confederate Soldiers of Georgia 1861–1865,* comp. Lillian Henderson [Hapeville, Georgia: Longino and Porter, 1964], 2:476).

19. From 1750, when slaves were admitted to the colony of Georgia, until 1979, biracial marriages were forbidden by law. Charles Eubank purchased seventeen and seven-tenths acres of land from S. C. Johnson for $600 on February 22, 1866 (*Deeds,* Floyd County Courthouse, Rome, Ga.).

on her hips and stormed at him and he never returned." Despite the separation, her two sons remained close to the Eubank family. They often went to visit their white grandmother. Their grandfather, David Dickson, changed their names to Dickson, took them to New Orleans, and had them declared white. As McCoy-Lee recalled, "He loved the little boys, called them my little men and slept with them. He [David] never wanted them to do anything but ride over the plantation with him and see what was going on. David Dickson indulged them all."

Again, the black Dickson family remembered these events in a revealing way. The failed marriage was perceived as Amanda's act of defiance against a white husband. However, she willingly returned to her role as a dependent daughter. Her omnipotent father then transformed his grandchildren into Dicksons and had them declared white. Nevertheless, they all lived in Hancock County, Georgia, where people understood their background, if only through rumor. The only way that David Dickson's grandchildren could have escaped the stigma of race would have been for them to have abandoned their place. But in Hancock County David Dickson had the power to eliminate the problem of racial categories and then "indulge them all." In retrospect, the idea of indulging a mulatto daughter and mulatto grandchildren in Reconstruction Georgia seems unwise, even if one assumes that these individuals could one day play the roles of gentlemen and ladies on their own. Indulgence also created a precarious balance between affection and dependence. According to McCoy-Lee, David Dickson did not take into account his own mortality. Amanda America and her children lived in a world in which they were loved as if there were no other world, no public sphere with racial barriers that they would have to confront. They assumed that David Dickson would always be in charge.

McCoy-Lee remembered, for example, how David Dickson dealt with visitors. "David Dickson lived in an unorthodox way. When guests came, Julia served them. People came from all over the country to see him. His favorite expression was 'By God.' White visitors would look at Amanda and the boys and say, 'Have I got to eat with them?' David would say, 'By God, yes, if you eat here.' " Years later, Rebecca Latimer Felton, a Georgia suffragist, remembered the position of guests in the Dickson household: "I remember well a noted home in middle Georgia where a rich man lived in open alliance with a colored woman and where Governors and Congressmen were often invited to dine and where they were glad to go. The visitors understood conditions in the Dickson home. They knew there were children born of a slave mother and the law of Georgia forbade such miscegenation."[20] David Dickson, the patriarch, eliminated the boundary of race and destroyed a social taboo.

How was David Dickson able to maintain this protected place for Amanda America and her children? From the time of Amanda America's birth in 1849 until David Dickson's death thirty-six years later, the Dickson estate increased steadily. By 1860 David owned 150 slaves, which made him the wealthiest planter in Hancock County. Measuring his estate in dollars after the Civil War, Dickson remained the wealthiest farmer in Hancock County from 1867 until 1885. At the end of his career he controlled three times as much property as the person closest to him in wealth.[21]

In addition to being wealthy, David Dickson demonstrated other characteristics that were useful to the citizens of Hancock County: generosity, hospitality, and fame. Before the Civil War, Dickson and his good friend, James Thomas, operated the only banking business in the county, a network of personal loans. At the time of his death 140 individuals owed Dickson money, including black and white farmers, merchants, lawyers, judges, and ordinary folks.[22] Beginning in 1859, Dickson published articles and letters in the widely circulated agricultural journal, the *Southern Cultivator*, encouraging farmers to increase their yields by using deep plowing, shallow cultivation, crop rotation, and commercial fertilizers. He explained that these techniques had made him wealthy and that farmers who were interested in seeing his experiments with the "Dickson method" should come to Hancock County and see for themselves. By 1870 the *Southern Cultivator* described David Dickson as the "Prince of Southern Farmers," a man who was "constantly" interrupted by visitors and letters from farmers seeking advice.[23]

While David Dickson invited strangers to come to his farm and

20. Sylvia Hoffert, "One Great Evil," *American History Illustrated* 12, no. 2 (May 1977): 3–41.

21. *Tax Digest for Hancock County, Georgia, 1849–1885*, Georgia Department of Archives and History, Atlanta, Ga.

22. Elizabeth Wiley Smith, *The History of Hancock County, Georgia* (Washington, Ga.: Wilkes Publishing Co., 1975), 122. Inventory of the Estate of David Dickson, Probate Court, Hancock County Courthouse, Sparta, Ga.

23. Willard Range, "The Prince of Southern Farmers," *Georgia Review* 2 (Spring 1948): 92–97; David Dickson, *A Practical Treatise on Agriculture* (Atlanta: Burke and Co., 1873).

observe his methods for themselves, he also continued to lavish care on his "outside" family: as McCoy-Lee recalled, Amanda America's children were educated in a schoolhouse that David Dickson had built on the plantation. One of her sons, Charles, went to Amherst College but stayed only one year. Amanda took him there and bought a house in the area. The family does not remember that either son prepared for an occupation, but they hardly needed to do so with their wealthy grandfather as a patron.

On February 11, 1885, the inevitable occurred: David Dickson died. According to McCoy-Lee, Amanda America clung to her father's body, repeating over and over again, "Now I am an orphan." But in fact, Amanda Dickson's mother remained alive. Here the family remembers that Amanda America had one parent who was white, but she chose to be alone rather than identify with her mother, to be kinless rather than acknowledge blackness. It is curious that Amanda America's descendants, who identify themselves as black, remember the story this way, as if Amanda America thought she could be made white by denying her black mother.

David Dickson's will bequeathed several small amounts of property to certain of his friends and relatives. He left his brother, Henry Dickson, one thousand acres of land in Rusk County, Texas, and to various other relatives a sum of twenty thousand dollars in cash. But the bulk of the estate, which included seventeen thousand acres of land and approximately three hundred thousand dollars in cash, stocks, and bonds, went to Amanda America Dickson and, upon her death, to her sons, Julian Henry Dickson and Charles Green Dickson. The will declared that the estate was left to Amanda America Dickson "free and clear and exempt from the marital rights, powers, control or custody of any husband which she might have with full power in her without the interposition of any court."[24] The will then charged Amanda America to educate and support her children "in an ample but not extravagant manner," all of which the deceased left to the "sound judgement and discretion of the said Amanda America Dickson without interference from any quarter."

David Dickson had "paid all the lawyers in the county $10,000 not to contest the will." Nevertheless, some of them did file objections for David Dickson's white relatives in the Macon, Georgia, Superior

24. Will of David Dickson, Probate Court of Hancock County, Ga., Index to wills, 246–52, July 21, 1884.

Court. After the court settled the case in favor of the will, however, Amanda America "handled everything herself" with legal advice from her lawyers. "They had so much money that they didn't know what to do with it." David Dickson also bequeathed a plantation to each of Amanda's sons who were also the children of David's nephew, Charles Eubank.[25]

David Dickson's will presents a picture of the relationship between father and daughter as one of extraordinary trust and respect. Dickson could have left a trustee in charge of his estate. Instead he expressly directed his executors to turn the management of the estate over to his thirty-six-year-old mulatto daughter, leaving everything to her "sound judgement." But Amanda America's granddaughter, Kate McCoy-Lee, did not describe her as a person with sound judgment; instead the black Dickson oral history presents a picture of a "lady" in the attractively helpless sense.[26] That was obviously not the case.

According to Kate McCoy-Lee, when Amanda Dickson's sons wanted to marry black women, they had to ask permission. Would these young men have had to ask permission to marry white women? McCoy-Lee seemed curiously apologetic that both sons married into elite mulatto families. Amanda America's sons had to ask permission to marry outside a boundary—the family boundary that their mother had drawn around herself and her white father. That boundary did not make Amanda America white, but it made her, for a limited time, not black—at last in the realm of her father's power and influence.

The oldest son, Julian Henry Dickson, married a young mulatto woman, Eva Walton of Augusta, in 1884. According to family tradition, Eva was the granddaughter of the George Walton who signed the Declaration of Independence for Georgia. Some while after their marriage, Julian and Eva left Hancock County. They moved to Beaufort, South Carolina, and set up a compound called Dickson Village. Julian Dickson became an alderman there. "A relative found some of the family in recent years. They were rich. Julian's children scat-

25. McCoy-Lee, November 10, 1981.

26. Kent Anderson Leslie, "A Myth of the Southern Lady: Antebellum Pro-Slavery Rhetoric and the Proper Place of Woman," *Spectrum* 6 (1986): 31–39.

tered."[27] In spite of his grandfather's wealth and prestige and his mother's inherited wealth, Julian Dickson left Hancock County and moved to Beaufort where black people were in the majority. There he and his family identified themselves as black and Julian became a civic leader.

In October of 1887 Amanda's other son, Charles Green Dickson, married Kate Holsey of Augusta, the daughter of Bishop Lucius Henry Holsey of the African Methodist Episcopal Church. Bishop Holsey's father was the son of a Scotsman, William Holsey. The couple's daughter, Kate McCoy-Lee, remembered her grandfather: "There are books about Bishop Holsey, *The Incomparable Holsey,* and a book of poems which the Bishop wrote himself, *Little Gems.* The Bishop had blue-gray eyes and red hair and skin like an Egyptian from staying out in the sun."[28]

Kate Holsey Dickson later divorced Charles because he spent his fortune on fast horses, white friends, and women. The family stayed out on a plantation called the Lockhart Place until Kate built a "rather large" house in town and moved there, "taking her servants with her." After Charles Green Dickson left Kate and her children, he moved to Stockton, California, where he died in his early forties of Bright's disease. "He lost one fortune in Georgia only to make another one in California." Charles escaped his racial definition as black by passing into the white world in California. He lost his inherited fortune, his name, and his racial identity, but he regained his class.

McCoy-Lee recalled that in 1899, when she was five years old, her mother moved from Sparta, Georgia, to Bishop Holsey's home on Auburn Avenue in Atlanta. "Bishop Holsey was a fabulous gardener. He [had] had tuberculosis when he was seventeen and was told to work outside as a cure." The Holseys had a large garden where young Kate McCoy-Lee once sat and ate strawberries. Years later, in 1981, she recalled that "Dr. Martin Luther King, Jr., is buried in the same spot."

McCoy-Lee remembered visiting her great-grandmother, Julia Dickson, at Sparta, where the family was allowed to use the Dickson silver.

27. McCoy-Lee, November 10, 1981. The children were Julia Frances, born in 1887; David, born in 1889; and William, born in 1899.

28. John Brother Cade, *The Incomparable Holsey* (New York: Pageant Press, 1969); Lucius Henry Holsey, *Little Gems* (Atlanta: Franklin, 1905).

> Granny Julia said that when Sherman came through Georgia, they hid the silver in bags under a locust tree and she was not sure that they ever dug it all up. David Dickson had a silver pitcher with an English patent mark 1829. He also had a big safe brought out to the plantation from Augusta and a big hole was dug to put it in. The safe had "D.Dickson" on the dial. People said that he had barrels of gold in the safe.

Julia Dickson, who had the keys to everything on the Dickson plantation, apparently did not have access to the safe "with barrels of gold in it." "Granny Julia" controlled the domestic sphere, not David Dickson's wealth, which he bequeathed to his daughter after his death.

On June 10, 1893, Amanda America Dickson died. She was forty-four and died at her home at 452 Telfair Street in Augusta, Georgia, of neurasthenia or nervous exhaustion. Her mother, "Granny Julia," later moved to Sparta and bought a house on Elm Street. Subsequently, she moved "Mr. Dickson's" body to town and had a monument erected. As her great-granddaughter McCoy-Lee remembered, "Granny Julia's house was full of beautiful things. The furniture was covered with mohair." Julia Dickson died in 1914. After her death said McCoy-Lee, "Everybody in town came to her house and took everything they wanted. There was nobody to stay them. I am all that is left now." Kate Dickson McCoy-Lee's story ends with the death of Julia Dickson, the slave girl raped by David Dickson in 1849.

Between 1885, when David Dickson died, and 1893, when Amanda America Dickson died, a battle raged in the public sphere over the issue of race. Black people in Georgia and across the South struggled to vote, to get an education, to earn a living, and to avoid violence against themselves and their families. In 1883 the United States Supreme Court declared the Civil Rights Act of 1875 unconstitutional, leaving black citizens no protection for their right to equal access in public accommodations including railroad cars, steamboats, hotels, theaters, places of entertainment, cemeteries, and public schools. During this era Georgia maintained a poorly funded, dual public school system, which spent less for black students and teachers than it did for whites. Moreover, the state legislature constantly threatened to reduce its meager contribution to education for black citizens.[29] In 1887 the Georgia legislature with-

29. Dorothy Orr, *A History of Education in Georgia* (Chapel Hill: University of North Carolina Press, 1950), 374.

drew eight thousand dollars in public funds from Atlanta University and created Georgia State Industrial College where "Negroes might receive a more appropriate education." In 1890 the United States Congress defeated the Lodge Bill, which would have provided federal protection for black men's voting rights. After 1890 white Georgians forced black artisans out of the skilled trades.[30] In addition to these problems black Georgians struggled to protect themselves from violence. In 1892 more people were lynched in the United States than in any year before or since.

Between 1885 and 1893 black citizens also struggled to maintain their dignity in the public sphere. During the 1880s black people complained of being excluded from public accommodations and the theater. By 1891 the Georgia legislature passed a statute segregating railroad cars, excluding Pullman cars. In that same year, several city councils tried to pass statutes that would segregate streetcars. Black citizens thwarted these efforts with boycotts until 1898, the same year that Pullman cars were finally segregated.[31] White Georgians abandoned personal arrangements that tolerated exceptions and turned the color line over to the law, which allowed no public distinction between black individuals regardless of class or family connections.

If Amanda America Dickson had ventured into the outside world after her father's death, she would have encountered a reality that demanded a racial definition. But without a racial identity, the mulatto daughter of a white planter who lived and died in Hancock County remained unaware of her real choices. In essence, the Amanda America Dickson of this oral history sacrificed a chance for autonomy as a black woman, choosing instead to live a life of privilege in a make-believe world.

---

30. John Michael Matthews, "Studies in Race Relations in Georgia" (Ph.D. diss., Duke University, 1970), 50–54.

31. Ibid., 126, 127–32.

ॐ Cheryl Thurber

The Development of the Mammy Image and Mythology

Mammy waits by the door for the white children she has cared for all their lives. She is old and remains a reminder of their past, her past, and the legacy of an Old South that is also past. Ever since the movie *Gone with the Wind* the image has been that of Hattie McDaniel, a large and imposing figure who controls her charges with her presence. But in the early part of the twentieth century, the image was that of a frail woman who reminded people of the "ol' time befo' de war darkies" on the old plantation. Mammy did not exist to the extent that the mythology would lead people to believe. She was a character probably created by nostalgic southern whites to ease their troubled racial consciences. Significantly, the mammy, one of the central figures in the plantation legend of the Old South, reached her greatest popularity in the era of the New South and Progressivism.

The word *mammy* evokes strong and ambiguous feelings, especially in its racial overtones and implications and the confusing message of female sexuality and motherhood. The mammy, in contrast to the stereotype of the "loose" young black woman, was repre-

The author would like to thank Phoebe Evans, Elizabeth Fox-Genovese, Jan Hawks, and Charles Wilson for extensive comments and editorial assistance; Ann Abadie, Roberta Church, Jim Cobb, Chloe Evans, Bill Ferris, Robert Ginn, Kenneth Goings, Jacquelyn Dowd Hall, James R. Humphreys, Tera Hunter, Winthrop Jordan, Charles Joyner, Mary Montanus, Sheila Moore, June Patton, Bobby Rogers, Stephanie Shaw, Carrol Treese, and the staff of the Mississippi Valley Collection at Memphis State University for additional suggestions; also William Thomas of the *Memphis Commercial Appeal* for an interview in that paper on October 11, 1988.

sented as a sexually nonthreatening older black woman in intimate contact with white children and part of white families. Yet the mammy's mothering qualities also convey ambiguous messages for both black and white ideals of motherhood, since to have been a perfect mammy a black woman would have had to neglect her own family. Her success in mothering white children, moreover, implies neglect on the part of the white mother who used a black mammy to care for her children. Susan Tucker states the black perspective in regard to the mammy's being more instinctive with children: "They did not wish to be cast as mammies, and they did not perceive their child-rearing as romantically as whites did, but they did see themselves as warmer and more balanced in their approach to children. They felt that white women 'didn't know how to love children' or that 'white women didn't stay around to know how.'" The love that the white children felt for mammy could be seen as a replacement, or supplement, for their love for their own natural mother.[1]

Scholars have not been immune to the legacy of southern mythology. The mammy of myth has been credited with a variety of often contradictory characteristics. Historians have accepted elements of the mythology of the mammy and have then tried to prove or disprove her existence on the basis of antebellum experience; they have tended to concentrate on only one aspect of her character and roles, which they have then been able to discredit. Several recent studies on slavery, notably those by Catherine Clinton, Deborah Gray White, Joan Cashin, Herbert Gutman, and Jacqueline Jones, have found little evidence for real mammies in the antebellum period and have even questioned the historical evidence for the existence of mammies in the period immediately after Emancipation.[2]

1. Tucker, *Telling Memories among Southern Women: Domestic Workers and Their Employers in the Segregated South* (Baton Rouge: Louisiana State University Press, 1988), 43. There is a contrast between mammy the "instinctual" caretaker and nanny the trained efficient childcare worker. In recent years there has been an emphasis on the importance of the training programs of the black institutes such as Tuskegee and Hampton; while they trained domestic workers, and they may have taught young women how to be child nurses, it does not appear that they trained mammies.

2. Clinton, *The Plantation Mistress: Woman's World in the Old South* (New York: Pantheon, 1982), 201–2; White, *Ar'n't I a Woman?: Female Slaves in the Plantation South* (New York: W. W. Norton, 1985), 46–61; Cashin, "Women's Work and Culture in the Old Southwest" (paper presented at the meeting of the Southern Association for Women Historians, Fall 1987); Gutman, *The Black Family in Slavery and Freedom 1750–1925* (1976; reprint, Vintage Books,

Clinton, in particular, discusses the lack of antebellum evidence for the stereotype. She finds "this familiar denizen of the Big House is not merely a stereotype, but in fact a figment of the combined romantic imaginations of the contemporary southern ideologue and the modern southern historian." Clinton discovered only a handful of examples who fit even portions of the image "of female slaves who served as the 'right hand' of plantation mistresses." Clinton concludes: "The Mammy was created by white Southerners to redeem the relationship between black women and white men within slave society in response to the antislavery attack from the North during the ante-bellum era, and to embellish it with nostalgia in the post-bellum period. In the primary records from before the Civil War, hard evidence for her existence simply does not appear."[3]

White's interpretation is consistent with Clinton's recognition that most of the evidence for real mammies came from memoirs written after the war. White and Clinton also agree in seeing the mammy as a contrast to the Jezebel, or promiscuous young black woman. Mammy was an asexual figure who invited an ambiguous resolution of sexual tensions. Elizabeth Fox-Genovese has also presented the idea of mammy as a resolution of sexual tensions: "Mammy signaled the wish for organic harmony and projected a woman who suckled and reared white masters. The image displaced sexuality into nurture and transformed potential hostility into sustenance and love. It claimed for the white family the ultimate devotion of black women, who reared the children of others as if they were their own." The ambiguous word *nurse* adds to the confusion surrounding mammy; to nurse can mean both to suckle and to care for. Nurse was the most commonly used word to describe the role of the person who took care of young children, but, as Fox-Genovese also points out, nursemaids were not automatically transformed into mammies. The use of black women to suckle white infants is in many ways a separate issue. Mammies were not necessarily wet nurses, nor did wet nurses automatically become mammies.[4]

1977), 443–45, 630–35; and Jones, *Labor of Love, Labor of Sorrow* (New York: Basic Books, 1985), 24–25, 127–32.

3. Clinton, *Plantation Mistress*, 201–2.

4. Fox-Genovese, *Within the Plantation Household: Black and White Women of the Old South* (Chapel Hill: University of North Carolina Press, 1988), 292, also 136–37, 147–48, 151–52, 158, 161–62, 279, 291–92. White, *Ar'n't I a Woman?*, 46–61. Jezebel is a familiar Judeo-Christian symbol of female depravity. In the Bible she is wicked and scheming rather than promiscuous. Suckling

Similarly, Herbert Gutman concluded that there was little hard evidence for the existence of mammies. He found that even in the 1880s there were few older black women who served in the role of mammies taking care of white children. Most black domestic workers in white households were young single women and thus did not fit the stereotypical image of a mature woman who loved her white children more than her own. Most married black women were washerwomen working out of their own homes rather than in white households. Gutman found that black house servants on the whole were very young single women, many under the age of twenty. "This evidence contradicts yet another erroneous but popular belief about ex-slave women: the assertion that the typical house servant was an aged 'mammy' who remained in her antebellum place out of loyalty to a white family or because whites had a special concern for such women. Elderly black women worked as domestics for these and other reasons, but visitors to white households much more regularly found there a young woman or child servant rather than a loyal and aged 'mammy.' "[5]

Among recent studies, Eugene Genovese's *Roll, Jordan, Roll* is exceptional in presenting a significant role for the mammy in slavery times. However, he concentrates his attention on the mammy as a powerful figure in the middle, who could mediate between the Big House and the slaves who worked in the fields. Focusing on mammy as mediator, moreover, Genovese gives less attention to her role as the primary caretaker of white children. A careful examination of his sources reveals that again much of the evidence for mammy is based on memoirs that were written after the war had disrupted the slave system.[6]

---

white infants is not a common part of the mythology of mammy in the turn-of-the-century material. The use of wet nurses was not prevalent in the South, although because of summer heat and disease southern white women had many problems with pregnancy; the high death rate for these women was associated with childbirth. For a discussion of wet nurses see Sally McMillen, "Mother's Sacred Duty: Breast-feeding Patterns among Middle- and Upper-class Women in the Antebellum South," *Journal of Southern History* 51, no. 3 (August 1985): 333–56. In *Along This Way: The Autobiography of James Weldon Johnson* (New York: Viking, 1933), 9–10, the author, executive director of the NAACP, notes that he was nursed by a white neighbor as an infant.

5. Gutman, *Black Family*, 632, also 443–45, 630–35.

6. Genovese, *Roll, Jordan, Roll: The World the Slaves Made* (1972; reprint, Vintage Books, 1976), 353–65, 494–501.

Edward A. Pollard's *Black Diamonds Gathered in the Darkey Homes of the South*, a series of semi-fictionalized letters published as a book in 1859, is a carefully worked defense of slavery and one of the few antebellum sources that discusses mammy and provides evidence for the existence of the stereotype.

> I am not ashamed, my dear C., to confess to be attached by affection to some of the faithful slaves of our family, to have sent them remembrances in absence, and, in my younger days, to have made little monuments over the grave of my poor "mammy." Do you think I could ever have borne to see her consigned to the demon abolitionist, man or woman, and her lean starved corpse rudely laid in a pauper's grave? No! At this moment my eyes are tenderly filled with tears when I look back through the mists of long years upon the image of that dear old slave, and recollect how she loved me in her simple manner; how when chided even by my mother, she would protect and humor me; and how, in the long days of summer, I have wept out my boyish passion on her grave.[7]

The Federal Writers' Project of the Works Progress Administration's interviews with former slaves reflect the variety of the slave experience but give very little indication of the widespread existence of mammies. Very few former slaves mentioned any older relatives who had the role of mammy in antebellum times. In fact, they more commonly mentioned former slaves as having been raised by the white mistress as opposed to the adult black women who took care of the white children.[8]

The few references to mammy by former slaves usually include a

7. Pollard, *Black Diamonds Gathered in the Darkey Homes of the South* (1859; reprint, New York: Negro Universities Press, 1968) 38–39, also 23, 33, 95.

8. The Federal Writers' Project of the Works Progress Administration narrative interviews with former slaves are reprinted in George P. Rawick, ed., *The American Slave: A Composite Autobiography,* 22 vols. (Westport, Conn.: Greenwood Publishing Co., 1972, 1977, 1979). See Benjamin A. Botkin, ed., *Lay My Burden Down: A Folk History of Slavery* (Chicago: University of Chicago Press, 1945); Works Progress Administration, Savannah Unit Georgia Writers Project, *Drums and Shadows: Survival Studies among Georgia Coastal Negroes* (Athens: University of Georgia Press, 1940); and Norman R. Yetman, ed., *Life under the "Peculiair Institution": Selections from the Slave Narrative Collection* (New York: Holt, Rinehart, and Winston, 1970). Numerous studies have used the narratives as a major source including this author's "'Belongin' to the White Folks': Slavery in Marshall and DeSoto Counties, Mississippi" (paper presented at the American Historical Association, Cincinnati, December 1988).

story about the special protection the role provided, or the continued concern shown by the white folks toward their former mammy. One example tells of a mammy who was whipped by the overseer, and when the mistress discovered what had happened she exploded to the overseer, "What you mean by whupping Mammy? You know I don't allow you to touch my house servants. . . . I'd rather see them marks on my own shoulders than to see 'em on Mammy's." When the overseer was sent off the former slave commented, "He wasn't nothing but white trash nohow."

This story is consistent with the general picture of the relationship between mammy and the families she was associated with. There are numerous instances where the devotion of the white children to their black mammy was mentioned, including their care for her as she grew older and after slavery times. But the continued support was inconsistent at best. While anything was welcome, especially in her old age and during the 1930s when the interviews were conducted, the support was usually minimal and irregular. Many former slaves mentioned that they were devoted to the white children that they had been raised with or to their former mistresses, but former slaves did not mention mammy's devotion to her white children.[9]

Many former slave women had had the experience of assisting in the care of the white children of their masters while they were children or teenagers themselves. This pattern of older children babysitting younger children is a universal cultural phenomenon that continues today and probably was practiced in antebellum households. While many women mentioned having worked as cooks or maids as adults, very few said that they, or their female relatives, had been mammies.[10]

It is likely, however, that mammies did exist in the antebellum period, but in much smaller numbers than the mythology would indicate. The mythology had in fact developed prior to the Civil War but drastically increased during a much later period. One difficulty

9. Botkin, *Lay My Burden Down*, 173.

10. A number of former slaves related stories about dropping a baby or being careless while watching children. This in fact is a universal tale type, and it can be found in Stith Thompson, ed., *Motif Index of Folk Literature*, 6 vols. (Bloomington: Indiana University Press, 1955–1958). These stories usually serve as moral lessons about being more careful and about the consequences of getting caught.

is that most of the antebellum evidence for mammies comes from fictional sources, not from actual cases. Mammy fit into the plantation legend, although most discussions of the plantation legend mention her only briefly with much less attention to her than to any of the other characters—the Plantation Lord, the Plantation Mistress, the young Lord, the Belle, the Happy Darkies who worked in the fields, the loyal House Servants, and the storytelling old Uncle. Francis Pendleton Gaines, in a book on the image of the southern plantation, devoted less than a page to his discussion of mammy. Similarly, William R. Taylor, in *Cavalier and Yankee*, barely refers to mammy and tends to lump mammy with the other contented slaves.[11]

Jessie W. Parkhurst's 1938 article offers the most extensive previous examination of the role of mammies, including a lengthy discussion of the various traditional characteristics that are ascribed to the mammy. From Parkhurst's research it can again be deduced that most of what we know about mammy comes from romanticization found in later memoirs. Parkhurst offered an especially thorough litany of the characteristics that the mythology ascribed to mammy, although she insisted that "the qualities and characteristics attributed to the 'Black Mammy' indicate a first hand and personal knowledge of her, which became standardized and institutionalized by sentiment." In Parkhurst's view mammy was ascribed virtues that "were generally denied to slave women as a group," and their number increased over time. By the 1930s when Parkhurst wrote, she could say that, unlike her sisters, mammy

> was considered self-respecting, independent, loyal, forward, gentle, captious, affectionate, true, strong, just, warm-hearted, compassionate-hearted, fearless, popular, brave, good, pious, quick-witted, capable, thrifty, proud, regal, courageous, superior, skillful, tender, queenly, dignified, neat, quick, tender, competent, possessed with a temper, trustworthy, faithful, truthful, neither apish nor servile.[12]

11. Gaines, *The Southern Plantation: A Study in the Development and the Accuracy of a Tradition* (1924; reprint, Gloucester, Mass.: Peter Smith, 1962), and Taylor, *Cavalier and Yankee: The Old South and American National Character* (1961; reprint, New York: Harper & Row, 1969).

12. Parkhurst, "The Role of the Black Mammy in the Plantation Household," *Journal of Negro History* 23, no. 3 (July 1938): 349–69, esp. 352–53. Trudier Harris, *From Mammies to Militants: Domestics in Black American Literature* (Philadelphia: Temple University Press, 1982), bases most of her brief discussion of the mammy on Parkhurst's article.

Significantly, Parkhurst's work was written when Margaret Mitchell's *Gone with the Wind* (1936) was yet more powerfully shaping the popular image of mammy. In 1939 Hattie McDaniel's rendition of Mammy in the film further reinforced the image and, in effect, represented the archetype. Thus, although the existence of historic mammies may be questioned, the mythological mammy has gained wide recognition.[13] With Mitchell's creation of Mammy in *Gone with the Wind* the mythology had coalesced, the epitome of the character had been created, both in the book and in McDaniel's portrayal, and required no further development. This was particularly true since the real existence of mammies was in a process of decline to near extinction and no additions to the mythology were needed. Just as Scarlett O'Hara and *Gone with the Wind* served the needs of the new southern woman who was emerging in the 1920s and 1930s, even earlier the mammy had served as a necessary character in the southern pantheon, which then formed the backdrop for the new vision that emerges from Mitchell's work.[14]

Never widespread in the antebellum period nor even immedi-

13. Mitchell, *Gone with the Wind* (New York: Macmillan, 1936); Jamaica Kincaid, "If Mammies Ruled the World," *Village Voice Anthology, 1965–1980* (New York, 1982), provides an interesting perspective on *Gone with the Wind* and also the decline of the mammy: "What I imagine black people are really objecting to when they disapprove of Mammies . . . is the system that produced those things. . . . Scarlet and Rhett and Melanie and Ashley were not civilized people and that's why they didn't deserve a Mammy. But the worst part of it is, they have successfully ruined for us any ideas about having Mammies" (55). When the film version of *Gone with the Wind* premiered in Atlanta none of the black performers, including Hattie McDaniel, was permitted to attend the opening. Her performance won an Academy Award, the first for any black performer.

14. For the relationship between *Gone with the Wind* and the New Woman, see Elizabeth Fox-Genovese, "Scarlet O'Hara: The Southern Lady as New Woman," *American Quarterly* 33 (Fall 1981): 391–411. *Gone with the Wind* has been extensively examined for its place in American culture, but surprisingly the mammy character has received little attention. Some of the other perceptive studies of the book and film's cultural impact include: Edward D. C. Campbell, Jr., *The Celluloid South: Hollywood and the Southern Myth* (Knoxville: University of Tennessee Press, 1981), 118–40; Richard Harwell, ed., *Gone with the Wind: As Book and Film* (Columbia: University of South Carolina Press, 1983); Willie Lee Rose, "Race and Region in American Historical Fiction: Four Episodes in Popular Culture," in J. Morgan Kousser and James M. McPherson, eds., *Region, Race, and Reconstruction: Essays in Honor of C. Vann Woodward* (New York: Oxford University Press, 1982), 113–39.

ately after the war and Emancipation, the mythology of the mammy actually emerged and expanded many years later to serve the needs of a generation of nostalgic southern whites searching for their past and perhaps seeking to justify existing race relations. References to mammy in the *Confederate Veteran* magazine, American popular songs, memoirs, and fiction confirm that more was written about mammy at the turn of the century than during the antebellum period, the Civil War, or Reconstruction. The real expansion of the mammy mythology coincided with Progressivism, the New South movement, and the later phases of the Confederate Lost Cause movement.[15]

In *Ghosts of the Confederacy,* Gaines M. Foster argues that the Confederate Lost Cause movement fell into three distinct phases. The first·was characterized by local associations and unsuccessful efforts to organize on the part of the Virginia leadership. The second phase saw the rise of the organizational structure to celebrate the Confederate tradition and included the founding of the United Confederate Veterans, the Sons of the Confederacy, and the United Daughters of the Confederacy, in addition to the *Confederate Veteran* magazine, which became the organ for all of these organizations. These broad-based organizations cut across class divisions but remained dominated by the middle class.[16]

The third phase, following 1907, witnessed a steady decline. The organizations' members constricted and increasingly represented an elite segment of the middle class. As the Confederate veterans declined in numbers, the Daughters replaced the Sons as guardians of the tradition. Unfortunately, Foster's excellent book did not carry the story forward fully to include the period of the UDC dominance.

15. Research on three other topics, "'Dixie': The Cultural History of a Song and Place," "'Are You From Dixie?': The South in Popular Song from the 1890s to 1920," and "'Belongin' to the White Folks': Slavery in Marshall and DeSoto Counties, Mississippi," led this author to the wealth of references to mammy c. 1900 and the discovery that other researchers such as Clinton, *The Plantation Mistress*, and White, *"Ar'n't I a Woman?"*, had made brief comments about how little evidence there was for the existence of mammy in the antebellum period.

16. Foster, *Ghosts of the Confederacy: Defeat, the Lost Cause, and the Emergence of the New South* (New York: Oxford University Press, 1987). For other relevant works on the Lost Cause, see Thomas L. Connelly, *The Marble Man: Robert E. Lee and His Image in American Society* (New York: Alfred A. Knopf, 1977); Paul M. Gaston, *The New South Creed: A Study in Southern Mythmaking* (New York: Alfred A. Knopf, 1970); and William W. White, *The Confederate Veteran* (Tuscaloosa: Confederate Publishing Co., 1962).

In a discussion of southern memoir writing, John Blassingame found that women played a key role in writing memoirs and in encouraging men to write them, especially around the turn of the century. It is significant that most of the references to mammy in the *Confederate Veteran* magazine appeared in pieces written by women.[17]

Although memoirs that mentioned the mammy appeared throughout the period from the 1890s to the end of the 1920s, the number of references to mammy increased from about 1906 to 1912, which was the peak time for the glorification of mammy. From 1912 to 1918 a gradual pattern of decline emerged and that decline increased so that by the late 1920s there was very little mention of mammy. There were qualitative differences in the ways mammy was discussed. Most of the remembrances before about 1906 include references to a particular mammy, usually called by names such as Aunt Chloe, Aunt Amanda, or Aunt Mary, rather than Mammy. The articles described specific incidents in the life of a specific individual. A number of novels also had mammy characters. After about 1906 the specific references continued, but general comments about the mammy also began to appear, as did poems to mammy and general odes to her virtues. All of these later discussions tended to glorify mammy in the abstract, as the idea rather than as a person.[18]

17. John Blassingame, Ford Foundation Lecture in Southern Culture, University of Mississippi, Fall 1987. *Confederate Veteran* magazine served as the organ for all of the organizations and quickly became a general popular magazine for the South. By about 1910 the women of the United Daughters of the Confederacy were setting the nostalgia agenda, as has been noted by Foster and others, but the role these women played needs more attention. The women who wrote for *CV* seem to have been largely the daughters of veterans. By this time the common soldier had become glorified, so the women were just as proud to be daughters of privates as they were of officers. In the early and middle periods of the organizations, the membership cut across class lines and represented all segments of white society. Gradually, the upper and lower classes dropped out of active involvement. A few blacks were also involved in the organizations and ceremonies. Papers of the *CV* at Duke University give the impression that many of the articles were voluntary contributions sent by the readers.

18. For examples of the earlier types of *Confederate Veteran* articles see: "Burial of 'Aunt' Mary Marlow," 14 (March 1906): 101; A. J. Emerson, "Stonewall Jackson: a Homily," 20 (February 1912): 58–59; Cornelius B. Hite, "Bravery of Southern Women," 34 (June 1926): 220; Sally B. Hamner, "Mammy Susan's Story," 1 (September 1893): 270–71; Julia B. Reed, "Bluecoats at Liberty Hall," 7 (July 1899): 303–4; and Rev. G. L. Tucker, "Faithful

In conjunction with both the Confederate Lost Cause tradition and the New South ideology, the heightened glorification of mammy from 1906 to the mid-1920s corresponded to significant trends in American culture, notably in race relations and conditions for women in general. The ideal of the southern belle also flourished, for example in popular songs, between 1905 and 1918. Paradoxically, the ideal of the traditional, sweet, innocent, and beautiful southern girl emerged with special force during the greatest push for woman suffrage.[19]

The New South movement frequently used the mythology of the Old South to promote its cause because it helped to present the picture of the South as a utopian community of harmonious relations. The beginning of the twentieth century thus witnessed a lull in the criticism of the South that had occurred earlier and would recur later. During this period a southern president was elected for the first time since before the Civil War, the South resumed a major

---

to the 'Old Mammy,' " 20 (December 1912): 582. Fiction included examples such as Mrs. Bernie Babcock, *Mammy: A Drama* (New York: Neale Publishing Co., 1915), and Albert Morris Bagby, *Mammy Rosie* (1904; reprint, Freeport, N.Y.: Books for Libraries Press, 1972). A transitional article by Mary Brabson Littleton, "Howard Weeden, Poetess and Artist," *CV* 14 (April 1906), 162, discussed a young white woman who wrote poetry and painted, both with mammy as the subject. The later *Confederate Veteran* articles may have been ostensibly about a specific individual, but they include generalized comments about mammy: William Preston Cabell, "How a Woman Helped to Save Richmond," 31 (May 1923): 177–78; Captain James Dinkins, "My Old Black Mammy," 34 (January 1926): 20–22; Margaret Heard Dohme, "Alexander Hamilton Stephens," 40 (March 1932): 91–94; "In Memory of a Faithful Servant," 24 (October 1916): 476; Laura Herbert MacAlpine, "War Memories of a Virginia Woman," 21 (December 1913): 579–81; Mrs. C. D. Malone, "The Franklin County Monument," 22 (December 1914): 537; "Mammy—and Memory," 28 (February 1920): 55; Chapman J. Milling, "Illium in Flames," 36 (May 1928): 179–83; "The Old Black Mammy," 26 (January 1918): 6; Estelle T. Oltrogge, "My Old Black Mammy," 25 (January 1917): 45; Mrs. Samuel Posey, "The Crimson Battle Flag," 31 (March 1923): 98–100; "Preserving Amiability of Black Mammy," 17 (August 1909): 427; Howard Weeden, "Me and Mammy" 34 (November 1926): 415; Julia Porcher Wickham, "My Children's Mammy—An Appreciation," 34 (November 1926): 413–15.

19. Gaines, *Southern Plantation*; Anne Firor Scott, *The Southern Lady: From Pedestal to Politics 1830–1930* (Chicago: University of Chicago Press, 1970); and Cheryl Thurber, " 'Are You From Dixie?' " (work in progress).

position in national politics, and the Old South came to be viewed as an idyllic society.[20]

With the growth of black migration northward, the North was having its own difficulties with race relations and was ready to believe that the South had solved its racial problems. Certainly the ideal of a loving and faithful mammy contributed to the illusion of peace. With the expression of pious devotion and support for mammy, proper southerners could convince themselves and others of their own goodness. In a sense they were attempting to redeem themselves for the other wrongs they had done to blacks because, of course, "I loved my old mammy." Using the specific relationship between individuals to explain and justify race relations in general has been a frequently repeated pattern in southern culture. The implication is that if all blacks could be like mammy then race relations would be harmonious.[21]

A few people saw through the myth. In 1918 Mrs. W. L. Hammond writing in the *Confederate Veteran* magazine in 1918 of the efforts made by southern white women through personal effort and club work to improve the condition of the Negroes in their communities, said: "One of the first steps necessary is to bury the old black mammy. . . . Her removal will clear the atmosphere and enable us to see the old soul's granddaughters, to whom we must in justice pay something of the debt we so freely acknowledge to her."[22]

About the same time, a mild controversy ensued in newspapers, with an article in the New York *Sun* to which the "Hon. Bridges Smith" responded in the *Macon Telegraph*. Smith's statement is typical of the response the discussion of mammy elicited. "Bless your ignorant souls, honey, the old black mammy has been dead and buried these many moons. And if flowers were laid upon her grave

20. See Paul H. Buck, *The Road to Reunion 1865–1900* (Boston: Little, Brown, 1937). Numerous articles in the *Confederate Veteran* from the late 1890s to the early 1900s conveyed the message of reunion.

21. Patting themselves on the back may have also been a way for adult children to triumph over the "mother" figure. *CV* reprinted articles from northern newspapers and magazines that praised the South's handling of race relations. For black migration to the North, see Allan H. Spear, *Black Chicago: The Making of a Negro Ghetto, 1890–1920* (Chicago: University of Chicago Press, 1967). For racial attitudes see George M. Fredrickson, *The Black Image in the White Mind: The Debate on Afro-American Character and Destiny, 1817–1914* (New York: Harper & Row, 1971).

22. Hammond, "The Old Black Mammy," 6.

and tears were dropped on the mound, it was right and proper. She deserved every flower and was due every tear. We shall never look upon her like again." Smith, like many other writers, asserted that there were no longer any living mammies who fulfilled the ideal found in people's memories. "She is dead and long since buried, and she should rest in peace." He also recognized that reviving mammy was not appropriate to efforts to improve conditions for her descendants who did not imitate her ways.

It is only the imitations, the caricatures, of the devoted, the loyal, the ever-faithful old black mammy that the present generation knows. And this is why the *Sun,* in its ignorance of the original, says she is trotted out on so many occasions that she has become a racial type, a political institution, and a good deal of a bore. That the imitation should be got out of the way, and the sooner the better, may be all well and good; but as for the old black mammy as we knew and loved her, she is dead beyond resurrection.

As Smith's last statement made clear, by 1918 mammy was beginning to be seen as part of the past, not the present.[23]

From about 1910 on, suggestions for memorials to the mammy made their appearance culminating in 1923 with a United Daughters of the Confederacy proposal to erect a monument to her memory in the nation's capital. After extensive and bitter controversy, the bill was finally killed in the House of Representatives. Many black opponents of the bill felt that it would be better to improve conditions for blacks by working to end lynching, inequality in education, discrimination, separation on public conveyances, and denial of suffrage rights.[24]

In celebrating the mammy, the increasingly middle- and upper-class United Daughters of the Confederacy were reclaiming and reinterpreting the past in conformity with their own middle-class, progressive values and shifting the focus away from the veterans and the war. Having a mammy became a badge of having been "raised right" as a proper southerner. In the mythology, the white folks were firmly left in control of the subservient and dependent mammy who knew her place, and because of that mammy could be

23. Ibid.
24. On the efforts to erect a monument see Genovese, *Roll, Jordan, Roll,* 353; and Parkhurst, "Role of the Black Mammy," 349–50.

seen as having power within the household. The literature also used mammy as the symbol of a world that was rapidly disappearing.

Popular mythology portrayed mammy as loyal to her white family even to the point of loving "her white children more than her own." In memoirs about mammies, there were several passing comments that mammy had done a better job of raising her white children than she had done with her own, who frequently disappointed her.[25] Consistent with this viewpoint is the suggestion that, after the abolition of slavery, she chose to remain with her former master's family. Loyalty and affection were tied together. The historical record for the continued loyalty of house servants, however, leaves a very mixed impression. At the end of the Civil War innumerable former masters were devastated when the slaves with whom they had the greatest personal contact left. James L. Roark in *Masters without Slaves* cited numerous examples of shock in the face of such departures: One woman lamented, "Those we loved best, and who loved us best—as we thought—were the first to leave us." Another woman wrote, "As to the idea of a *faithful servant, it is all a fiction.* I have seen the favorite & most petted negroes the first to leave in every instance."[26]

After the Civil War, domestic service changed dramatically. During the latter part of the nineteenth century, American middle-class households began to expect to have domestic service. In the early 1900s in the South, with a good supply of black labor, middle-class, and even some working-class, households expected to employ black women. As David Katzman pointed out in *Seven Days a Week*, some of the tensions between mistress and servant were different in the South than in the North. Katzman maintained that in the North the mistress looked upon the servant as an adopted child to be controlled; while in the South black domestics were viewed from a perspective that did not include any sense of kinship, much less equality. Katzman suggested that in the North the tensions were in the interpersonal relationship, while in the South tensions between mistress and servant were cultural and racial. On the other hand, as Tucker's *Telling Memories* demonstrates, while interpersonal rela-

25. For disappointment with her own children see Tucker, *Telling Memories*, 132–33, 138.

26. Roark, *Masters without Slaves: Southern Planters in the Civil War and Reconstruction* (New York: W. W. Norton, 1977), 89, 82.

tions in the South were not without strains, there were also many examples of long-term domestic worker and employer relationships.[27]

Servant status was intimately linked with race relations. As one former black nursemaid recalled in a 1912 article in the magazine *Independent:* "Sometimes I have gone on the street cars or the railroad trains with the white children, and, so long as I was in charge of the children, I could sit anywhere I desired, front or in back. If a white man happened to ask some other white man, 'what is that nigger doing in here?' and was told, 'Oh she's the nurse of those white children in front of her!' immediately there was the hush of peace."[28] In a peculiar way, being a mammy gave a woman a position that she was otherwise denied, although she viewed it less as a privilege than as a prescribed role. Tucker presented several examples of such situations, including one in which the young nursemaid was dressed in a bathing suit to accompany her young charges on the beach. The people she worked for wanted her to play with their children, but other families at the resort objected. The resort then began to include in its advertisements that servants must be in uniform; thereafter older women, who were more accustomed to wearing uniforms, accompanied children to the beach. As a young child another woman remembered begging her family's maid to take her to the Memphis zoo on a Tuesday, the one day when blacks were permitted admittance on their own. "Tuesday was colored day at the zoo. I used to wonder how 'colored' people could take their children to the zoo, when the ones I knew worked on Tuesdays."[29]

27. Katzman, *Seven Days a Week: Women and Domestic Service in Industrializing America* (1978; reprint, Urbana: University of Illinois Press, 1981); Tucker, *Telling Memories.* See also Jones, *Labor of Love,* and Susan Strasser, *Never Done: A History of American Housework* (New York: Pantheon Books, 1982). There were several articles in popular magazines that discussed the servant-mistress relationship but tended to be published anonymously. Southern examples include: A Georgia Negro Peon, "The New Slavery in the South—An Autobiography," *Independent* 56 (1904): 409–14; M. E. M., "Parlor and Kitchen," *Lippincotts* 4 (August 1869): 207–10; A Negro Nurse, "More Slavery at the South," *Independent* 72 (January 1912): 197–200; A Southern White Woman, "Experiences of the Race Problem," *Independent* 56 (1904): 590–94.

28. A Negro Nurse, "More Slavery at the South," 198.

29. Tucker, *Telling Memories,* 236. Frances Randle, "Free Admission Can Pay Off," *Commercial Appeal,* July 5, 1989, A9.

In the antebellum period the mythological mammy had power within the household, which she purportedly ran. She held the keys, an important symbol of status, and answered only to the plantation mistress and master. Because of her power, mammy could not be crossed by either the white or black members of the household. Before the war, wealthy slaveholding women had had many house servants; after it they usually had only one to fill the combined role of nurse, cook, maid, and housekeeper. In reality servants often complained about being expected to watch the children and do other tasks as well. Although servants were usually called lazy, careless, and incompetent, the mythical mammy was praised for just the opposite traits. The glorification of mammy was a way of praising some blacks while criticizing all the others who did not live up to the ideal. The praise was not for a specific individual but for the abstract idea of mammy. Specific women generally received praise for their work as mammies after they were no longer actively working, or after they had died. The praise was for the memory of the past, not an assessment of the present quality of their work.

In a society where racial tensions were all too common, the mammy's role within white families was frequently as a neutral figure functioning as a mediator and sympathetic ear. As one woman told Tucker, "Psychologically these maids balanced the white family. They helped many a white child to grow up in an easier way." They also were believed to provide white girls with a role model of stoical acceptance and resourcefulness.[30]

According to the myth, the mammy exercised immense influence over her white charges. She told them stories with moral examples and taught them manners. A child who was "mammy raised" was taught right. A poem entitled "Me and Mammy," by Miss Howard Weeden, expressed some of the sentiment about being raised right by mammy.

> Me and Mammy know a child
> About my age and size

30. Tucker, *Telling Memories*, 132, 138. Domestic workers also function as confidantes by listening to marital, family, and personal problems of the white women who employ them. For many women their maid is the one person to whom they have revealed the most personal and intimate details of their lives and is probably one reason why there have been so many long-term employer-employee relationships.

Who, Mammy says, won't go to heaven
　'Cause she's so grown and wise.

She answers "Yes" and "No" just so
　When folks speak to her,
And laughs at Mammy and at me
　When I say "Ma'am" and "Sir."

And Mammy says the reason why
　This child's in such a plight
Is 'cause she's had no Mammy dear
　To raise her sweet and right;

To stand between her and the world,
　With all its old sad noise,
And give her baby heart a chance
　To keep its baby joys.

Then Mammy draws me close to her
　And says: "The Lord be praised,
Here's what I calls a decent chile,
　'Cause hit's been Mammy-raised."[31]

The poem is in a nostalgic childhood style reminiscent of Eugene Field. In addition to writing poetry, Weeden also painted a number of idealized portraits of former slaves called "Old Voices." In a 1906 *Confederate Veteran* article about Weeden, Mary Brabson Littleton described one of her paintings *Me and Mammy:* "The typical nurse, is positively lovable in the spirit of kindly sympathy and natural goodness that oozes from her rough features. The world of childhood might be intrusted to her care without fear of any greater harm to them than overkindness and indulgence in their whims and fancies. The face wears a smile that belongs to the whole race— indescribably warm and young and sweet."[32]

The mythological mammy was also very class conscious. Several memoirs and stories describe her as concerned about the status of the people who associated with her white children. In a 1926 "Appreciation," Julia Porcher Wickham of Virginia described that side of mammy. "They were extremely aristocratic in their ideas, and it was difficult for 'skim milk' to masquerade as 'cream' with them. 'Who dat young gentleman what come here las' night?' one of them would

31. Weeden, "Me and Mammy," 415. This poem was apparently written and published in the first decade of this century.
32. Littleton, "Howard Weeden, Poetess and Author," 162–63.

ask. 'He ain't none of our white folks.' She had seen the difference at once, and didn't want any 'po' white trash,' as she would have expressed it, coming around her young mistress." Tucker cited a similar example at a wedding reception where two maids discussed their respective members of the couple with pride: "And the maid said to Lucretia, 'I hope you know that your Edward is marrying the cream of Mobile.' 'Well,' Lucretia said, 'Mr. Edward, he ain't no skim milk himself.'" These class statements not only present mammy as upholding the white class structure, but also her association with only the "best" whites.[33]

The glorification of the mammy was intimately connected with nostalgia and the longing to return to childhood days and a simpler, peaceful life. In the early twentieth century the South was seen as embodying traditional American values. There were several hundred popular songs about the South from this period. Mammy songs, which had their greatest popularity from about 1910 to 1920, expressed nostalgic desires—to return from the city to my old country home where mammy would be waiting for me by her old cabin door ready to welcome me to her arms as in childhood days of old. The flowers—magnolias or dogwoods usually—would be in bloom to add to the joyousness of the occasion. Typically, the sheet music covers would have cotton bolls and pickers in the background.[34]

Mammy represented the black world to her white folks. Because they knew her, whites could say they understood blacks. The concrete example was used as justification for knowledge of the abstract. Domestic workers in general have frequently been cited as exceptional examples of "good" blacks. Tucker suggested that a reverse reasoning was used to explain the exception: "These white women felt they did know blacks or knew enough about blacks to proclaim them a generally lazy, childlike, inferior, and sometimes

33. Wickham, "My Children's Mammy—An Appreciation," 413; Tucker, *Telling Memories*, 226.

34. Very little has been published on images conveyed in popular music; of some relevance here is Sam Dennison, *Scandalize My Name: Black Imagery in American Popular Music* (New York: Garland Publishing, 1982). These points about popular music are expanded in Thurber, "'Are You From Dixie?'" Most of these popular songs were Tin Pan Alley and northern compositions.

violent people. And they were surprised that the ones known to them as domestics were 'not like other blacks.' "[35]

Mammy belonged to her white family. In her old age she was supposed to be taken care of by the white children she had cared for in their youth. Numerous examples suggest that this frequent part of the mythology had at least some basis in reality, or at any rate it was something to be noted and praised when it did occur, even if it was insufficient. At a mammy's death scene she was surrounded by the white family, who then organized her funeral. It is surprising how many times mammy's coffin was carried by white pallbearers and her funeral conducted by white ministers, usually Presbyterian or Episcopal. She belonged to the white world; the perfect mammy presumably had no time for a black family or black world. The few blacks who had obituaries published in white newspapers and magazines were usually loyal servants. In many cases a mammy had both a white and a black funeral in her two different worlds.[36]

William Faulkner's Mammy Callie came to his family in 1907 at the height of the mammy glorification, although she was in fact fairly old. Faulkner modeled many of his fictional mammies after Mammy Callie. He continued to care for her over the years; and, when she died in 1940, Faulkner conducted the funeral for her at his home at Rowan Oak. He dedicated his book *Go Down, Moses* to her, with the words: "To Mammy Caroline Barr Mississippi [1840–1940] Who was born in slavery and who gave to my family a fidelity without stint or calculation of recompense and to my childhood an immeasurable devotion and love." The tombstone he erected for her said, "Mammy / Her white children bless her."[37]

Although Faulkner's mammy was an older woman, most women who worked as child nurses were actually young. The popular con-

35. Tucker, *Telling Memories*, 227, also 191–94.

36. See for example, "Burial of 'Aunt' Mary Marlow," and Rev. G. L. Tucker, "Faithful to the 'Old Mammy,' " 582.

37. Faulkner, *Go Down, Moses* (1940; reprint, Vintage Books, 1973); John Faulkner, *My Brother Bill: An Affectionate Reminiscence* (1963; reprint, Oxford, Miss.: Yoknapatawpha Press, 1975), 47–52; Joseph L. Blotner, *Faulkner: A Biography* (New York: Random House, 1974), 1034–36. Mammy Callie also had a funeral at a black church that Faulkner and his family attended. Faulkner's characters Dilsey Gilson and Mollie Beauchamp are both said to be based on Mammy Callie.

ception of the mammy as an older woman constituted a legacy from a bygone era. William Alexander Percy in *Lanterns on the Levee* pointed out that his mammy did not meet the stereotype. "Southerners like to make clear, especially to Northerners, that every respectable white baby had a black mammy, who, one is to infer, was fat and elderly and bandannaed. I was a respectable and a white baby, but Nain was sixteen, divinely cafe-au-lait, and she would have gone into cascades of giggles at the suggestion of a bandanna on her head. I loved her devotedly and never had any other nurse." Percy appreciated her for childlike qualities: "I shall continue to believe I loved her for her merry goodness, her child's heart that understood mine, and her laughter that was like a celesta playing triplets." Percy then described, with ambiguous sexual feelings, being held close to her bosom and listening to her sing to him. His conclusion reflects the abstract idea of mammy, even though he referred to a specific individual: "Nain possibly comes back to me more as an emanation or aura than as person." Several years after the height of the mammy glorification, Lillian Smith, in her provocative study of southern society, *Killers of the Dream* (1949), also recognized the mixed emotions and sexual feelings that young boys and men had about their mammies.[38]

Mammy was generally referred to as "Old Black Mammy" rather than just as "Mammy." Although Percy recognized the stereotype, his experience reflected the reality that it was young women who most often worked in white households. It is easy to view the mammy as old from a child's perspective no matter what her age. But the adjective *old* was increasingly used as a reference to the old-time "befo' de wa'" slaves, the holdovers from another era. To talk about mammy can sound like the glorification of an old-time subservient person. The same articles frequently refer to mammy's granddaughters as being very different from her. Black mammy was used to distinguish the caretaker from the mother, but it also gave a sense of distinction. Mammy was black not white, and she belonged to the general class of blacks and therefore was not equal to or the same as the white child.

The physical image of mammy has been heavily influenced by

38. Percy, *Lanterns on the Levee: Recollections of a Planter's Son* (New York: Alfred A. Knopf, 1941), 26–27. Smith, *Killers of the Dream* (New York: W. W. Norton, 1949), 123–31.

popular culture, especially toys and advertising. Doris Y. Wilkinson, in two articles about black representation in dolls and toys, has pointed out that black dolls and toys seem to have peaked about 1912, which coincides with the period of the glorification of mammy, although most of the examples Wilkinson uses are male toys. Mammy is supposed to be a large woman, wearing a colorful bandanna on her head and a white apron. The Aunt Jemima products still promote that image. Aunt Jemima dolls began to be manufactured in the late 1890s, but their production expanded from about 1908 to 1925. In actual fact, the Aunt Jemima image represented a cook, not a mammy.[39]

Surprisingly, the Aunt Jemima description does not seem to be a common part of the early image of the mammy, even though today the two separate characters of cook and mammy have merged. Most descriptions from the first two decades of this century and earlier often describe mammy as small, and hunched over; she is always very black, and the glow is just beginning to be part of her facial description. She is usually described in a modified nurse uniform with a white apron and white bandanna. Today we tend to envision the mammy as Hattie McDaniel in *Gone with the Wind*, perhaps the supreme example of the popular image.

Has mammy disappeared? Increasing use of child-care centers has lessened the demand for her, and those black women who do care for white children are no longer called mammy. Today, as women try to juggle careers and motherhood, mammy might represent the model of an instinctive caretaker who provides love and support for the children; yet rather than resurrecting mammy, many white

39. Wilkinson, "Play Objects as Tools of Propaganda: Characterizations of the African American Male," *The Journal of Black Psychology* 7, no. 1 (August 1980): 1–16; "The Doll Exhibit: A Psycho-Cultural Analysis of Black Female Role Stereotypes," *Journal of Popular Culture* 21, no. 2 (1987): 19–29; Kenneth Goings, "Memorabilia That Have Perpetuated Stereotypes about African Americans," *Chronicle of Higher Education* 36 (February 14, 1990): B76; and Kenneth Goings, "Black Collectibles as Gender-Based Advertising: 1880s–1950s" (paper presented at The Second Southern Conference on Women's History, June 7, 1991). For black male images, see Joseph Boskin, *Sambo: The Rise and Demise of an American Jester* (New York: Oxford University Press, 1986). Dawn Reno, *Collecting Black Americana* (New York: Crown, 1986), shows a number of examples of mammy and Aunt Jemima collectibles, but she does not differentiate the item as a cook (Aunt Jemima) or a mammy.

middle-class Americans have tended to adopt the English nanny as the ideal of efficient child care. As a result of the civil rights movement, many of the gross distortions of blacks in caricatures and stereotypes are no longer an acceptable part of popular culture or advertising. Younger generations are frequently unaware of the mammy stereotype, though mammy is still an item to be sold to tourists: mammy dolls, cookie jars, salt and pepper sets, toaster covers, magnets, and other souvenirs continue to be found in New Orleans and at roadside stops. In recent years, country craft shops that cater to middle-class suburbanites frequently feature mammy and pickaninny dolls. Mammy has now become a commercialized expression of quaintness for craft kits.[40]

Mammy is best understood as the product of the New South ideology and Progressivism rather than antebellum reality. Most of the previous discussions of the mammy have examined the antebellum record through the lens of the later mythology, but the concept of the mammy is more appropriate to the period of her glorification, from about 1906 to the mid-1920s. While mammy is now an ambiguous legacy of the past, the myth of mammy offered a way of praising the past and dealing with a younger generation of blacks that was viewed as "uppity." The mammy mythology followed the typical southern pattern of using a specific example to tell a story in order to illustrate general principles. A specific type of person—in this instance, the mammy—was glorified in the abstract and became a stereotype in order to demonstrate that the South was capable of harmonious and loving race relations. The plantation legend enshrined a picture of a peaceful and idyllic society with mammy waiting there among the memories of childhood. The ideal mammy was presented as someone who loved unconditionally with forgiveness for the past, who was worthy of admiration and adoration, and who at the same time offered strength and shelter from the realities of the adult and modern world.

40. Rheta Grimsley Johnson, "Oprah Puts Mammy Doll in the Shade," *Commercial Appeal,* March 19, 1989, B1, discusses the quandary of what to do with a recent handmade mammy doll.

❧ Mary Martha Thomas

The Ideology of the Alabama Woman Suffrage Movement, 1890-1920

The suffrage movement in the South, and Alabama in particular, developed a generation later than it did in the rest of the nation.[1] While the American Woman Suffrage Association was founded in Boston and the National Woman Suffrage Association in New York in 1869, it was not until the 1890s that southern women began to organize. It was not the gender conventions of the "southern lady," however, but the politics of race that caused the delay. Woman suffrage was held back in the South at least partly because women's rights had long been associated with the emancipation of slaves. Not until that link was broken would southern women join in the campaign for woman suffrage. White southerners did not seriously consider enfranchising women until the demand for the vote was separated from the abolition movement.

Pre–Civil War leaders believed in universal suffrage on the theory that women and blacks had the same inalienable right to consent to the laws they obeyed as did white males. However, after the Civil

1. A. Elizabeth Taylor has written extensively on the suffrage drive in several southern states. See *The Woman Suffrage Movement in Tennessee* (New York: Bookman Associates, 1957); "The Woman Suffrage Movement in Texas," *Journal of Southern History* 17 (May 1951): 194–215; "The Woman Suffrage Movement in Arkansas," *Arkansas Historical Quarterly* 15 (Spring 1956): 17–52; "The Woman Suffrage Movement in Florida," *Florida Historical Quarterly* 36 (July 1957): 42–60; "The Woman Suffrage Movement in Mississippi, 1890-1920," *Journal of Mississippi History* 30 (February 1968): 1–34; "The Woman Suffrage Movement in North Carolina, Part I," *The North Carolina Historical Review* 38 (January 1961): 45–62; "The Last Phase of the Woman Suffrage Movement in Georgia," *Georgia Historical Quarterly* 43 (March 1959): 11–28.

War, the historic connection between racial and sexual equality gradually faded until suffragists could argue that the two issues were really not related. By the 1890s racism had become so nearly universal in the nation that southern attitudes toward blacks were not unlike those of northerners. The National American Woman Suffrage Association (NAWSA) began to separate the two issues during the 1890s, but the seeds had been sown earlier.[2]

The early woman suffrage leaders had been concerned with both their rights and those of the blacks. But after the war, women discovered that they had to choose between the two causes. This dilemma was especially evident in the discussions leading to the adoption of the Fourteenth Amendment. The Stanton-Anthony wing of the suffrage movement insisted that the cause of human freedom would be set back by an amendment that inserted the word "male" into the Constitution for the first time. They believed that singling out black men made it harder for women to get the ballot. The Lucy Stone wing, on the other hand, argued that women ought to acquiesce in the enfranchisement of blacks and be happy that one group at least had won its rights.[3]

Some former abolitionists actively collaborated with southern suffragists in developing a new rationale for suffrage, the most prominent of whom was Henry B. Blackwell, Massachusetts abolitionist and husband of Lucy Stone. In 1867 he published an essay, *What the South Can Do*, containing statistics that showed that there were more white women in the South than there were black men and women combined. Hence, the enfranchisement of women would greatly increase the white majority in the electorate and thus ensure white supremacy. The aim of this strategy was to prove that the enfranchisement of white women would further, rather than impede, the power of a white ruling class that was fearful of black domination. In a society laden with class strife, imperialist venture, and colonization, the equality of all people was no longer taken for granted.[4]

2. Aileen S. Kraditor, *The Ideas of the Woman Suffrage Movement, 1890–1920* (New York: Columbia University Press, 1965), 163–218.

3. Ibid.

4. Kraditor, *Ideas of the Woman Suffrage*, 168–69; Elizabeth Cady Stanton et al., eds., *The History of Woman Suffrage*, 6 vols. (1881–1922; reprint, New York: Arno and the *New York Times*, 1969), 4:246; Paula Giddings, *Where and When I Enter: The Impact of Black Women on Race and Sex in America* (New York: William Morrow, 1984), 123–24.

White suffrage leaders accordingly dispensed with the theory of natural rights. Desire for an educated electorate and the preservation of Anglo-Saxon power overwhelmingly influenced NAWSA's call for enfranchisement. This in time became the single most important argument used in the South. National suffragists were in the process of making the shift from an argument based on justice to one aimed at expediency. Instead of emphasizing the inalienable rights of women as individuals, this newer argument was designed to achieve woman suffrage in a manner that seemed politically possible in a racist society. Old-timers like Susan B. Anthony could not go so far as to advocate withdrawal of political power from the blacks, but the time had passed when she believed that black suffrage and woman suffrage were interdependent. By the turn of the century, Anthony and other suffrage veterans were making way for a new generation of activists in NAWSA. Included were southern white women and others who had not been weaned in the abolitionist or natural-rights tradition.[5]

Other events taking place in the 1890s made possible the growth of a southern suffrage movement. Alabama and other southern states were seeking ways to disfranchise blacks and ensure white supremacy. To limit black voting, state after state passed a poll tax, a literacy test, or property qualifications. As state legislatures considered these measures, several also considered giving women the ballot in order to counteract the black vote. Suddenly suffrage leaders saw an opportunity that they had not even known existed. In 1890 the Mississippi Constitutional Convention considered granting suffrage to women who owned $300 worth of property. This proposal was not adopted, but it had been given serious consideration with no organized support from women. As a result of these events, Laura Clay of Kentucky persuaded NAWSA to create a southern committee to organize the South, and all states of the Old Confederacy established suffrage associations in the 1890s. Suffrage

5. Kraditor, *The Ideas of the Woman Suffrage Movement*, 96–122. See also Eleanor Flexner, *Century of Struggle: The Woman's Rights Movement in the United States* (1959; reprint, New York: Atheneum, 1968); Anne F. Scott and Andrew M. Scott, *One Half the People: The Fight for Woman Suffrage* (New York: J. B. Lippincott, 1975); William H. Chafe, *The American Woman: Her Changing Social, Economic, and Political Roles, 1920–1970* (New York: Oxford University Press, 1972).

leaders hoped that the South's "Negro problem" might be the key to female enfranchisement. Black women who favored suffrage soon discovered that white suffrage leaders, who should have been their natural allies, became their most formidable adversaries. Many white suffrage leaders either acquiesced in, or took advantage of, the anti-black sentiment of the period.[6]

The first suffrage organizations in Alabama, formed in Decatur, Huntsville, Verbena, Gadsden, and Calera, joined together in 1892 to create the Alabama Woman Suffrage Association. Ellen Stephens Hildreth, a kindergarten teacher who moved from St. Louis to Decatur, was the first president of the state organization, but this group did little except mail suffrage literature. Interest in suffrage increased in 1897 after Alberta C. Taylor of Huntsville visited Colorado where women were allowed to vote. Taylor revived the organization in Huntsville, which elected one of Alabama's most distinguished women, Virginia Clay Clopton, president. Clopton had married Clement C. Clay, United States senator from Alabama, in 1834; after his death she married David Clopton, chief justice of the Alabama Supreme Court. She was the author of *A Belle of the Fifties* (1904), a reminiscence of Washington society in the decade before the Civil War. The activity of this early organization was limited because of the strong anti-suffrage sentiment that existed in the state.[7]

Frances Griffin of Verbena became the state president in 1901, and under her leadership the organization became slightly more active. Griffin was educated at Judson College and taught school in Montgomery. She left her career as a school teacher in 1885 to work

6. C. Vann Woodward, *Origins of the New South 1877–1913* (Baton Rouge: Louisiana State University Press, 1951), 321; Paul E. Fuller, *Laura Clay and the Woman's Rights Movement* (Lexington: University Press of Kentucky, 1975), 56–60; Marjorie Spruill Wheeler, "Southern Suffragists and the 'Negro Problem'" (paper presented at the First Southern Conference on Women's History, Converse College, June 1988); Giddings, *When and Where I Enter,* 123–24.

7. Stanton et al., eds., *History of Woman Suffrage* 3:830, 4:465; Lee Norcross Allen, "The Woman Suffrage Movement in Alabama" (Master's thesis, Alabama Polytechnic Institute, 1949), 1–16; John Irvin Lumpkin, "The Equal Suffrage Movement in Alabama, 1912–1919" (Master's thesis, University of Alabama, 1949), 4–6; Gillian Goodrich, "Romance and Reality: The Birmingham Suffragists, 1892–1920," *The Journal of the Birmingham Historical Society* 5 (January 1978): 6–8.

for the Woman's Christian Temperance Union. By the 1890s she added suffrage to her interests and was soon in great demand as a speaker and organizer. In 1896 she helped Arkansas women organize; the following year she made a six-week tour of Tennessee; and in 1898 she was invited to New Orleans where the Louisiana constitutional convention was considering enfranchising women.[8]

In 1901 Griffin had an opportunity to address the Alabama constitutional convention, which was called for the purpose of disfranchising blacks. In her half-hour speech, she based her argument on the abstract principle of justice, namely that governments derive their just powers from the consent of the governed. She reminded the delegates that this principle "is the guaranty of liberty of the American Republic—it is the watch-word of every people striving for political freedom. Now comes the declaration that women as well as men belong to the 'governed,' and upon that belief, I ground my demand to the application of the principle to citizens regardless of sex." The condition of woman had changed, she said, from being that of a ward of the state to being "an agent of intelligence where she touches the Government all the way along her life, and the Government touches her." Griffin believed that women should have a voice in the adoption of laws and the appropriation of taxes. In short, she argued that men and women should be equal in the eyes of the law.[9]

Griffin also argued that men and women were different. She said that women were asking for the ballot not because they thought men were unjust or unfair or that men were unwilling to speak for women. But women needed the vote because they should be able to speak for themselves. "Men," she said, "by their very nature never can speak for women. It would be as impossible for all men to understand the needs of women and to care for their interests as it would be for all women to understand the needs of men and care for the interests of them."[10]

In addition, she refuted the common arguments against woman suffrage. To objections that politics was too corrupt for women, her

8. Stanton et al., eds., *History of Woman Suffrage* 4:475, 583, 680–81, 926.
9. *Official Proceedings of the Constitutional Convention, of the State of Alabama, May 21st, 1901, to September 3rd, 1901*, 4 vols. (Wetumpka, Ala.: Wetumpka Printing Company, 1940), 1:464–65.
10. Ibid., 1:471.

answer was that women would purify politics. To claims that women were not able to vote intelligently, she pointed out that a higher percentage of women than men had a grade school education, and that women were as capable of voting as recently naturalized citizens. She also added that women "neither steep themselves in tobacco nor besot themselves with liquor, so that whatever brains they have are kept intact." To arguments that women should not vote because they did not bear arms, her answer was that many men did not do so either, yet they could vote. Some men advanced the argument that voting would place an added burden on women. On the contrary, Griffin said, the "immense work in which women are engaged, in charities and reforms in the constant repairing of the damages of society, would be infinitely less, if they had some power to prevent the evil." Others suggested that only a handful of women wanted the vote. Her answer was "rights are not measured by the number who want them. So long as there is one women who wants the right to vote, she is, according to the spirit of the Constitution and the Declaration of Independence, entitled to that right."[11]

Griffin closed by pointing out that women needed to be able to protect themselves. They resented being classed with traitors, idiots, criminals, and children. She said that women want full justice before the law; they want equal pay for equal work. She stressed that there were some women who have no men to represent them. "I live in a household of women, educated women. My sisters are widows and I am an old maid; we have no representation at the polls. There is not a man on the face of the earth interested particularly in how the affairs of our household go. . . . I should like to remind you gentlemen that so long as laws affect both men and women, men and women together should make those laws." Nowhere in her speech did Griffin make a racial appeal; she did not argue that the vote of white women could be used to uphold white supremacy.[12]

At the conclusion of the speech, Griffin was warmly applauded by the delegates as well as the audience in the gallery. The press, however, refused to take her efforts seriously. One paper commented, "No matter how modest a constitutional convention is

11. Ibid., 1:466–67, 469.
12. Ibid., 1:471.

nowadays some female suffragist will find it out and insist on making a speech."[13]

After Griffin's speech, several ordinances were placed before the convention granting the franchise to women. The strongest support came from those who saw it as a check on black suffrage. One delegate declared, "It would double the available white vote of the states and would not increase the Negro vote five per cent." However, there were several delegates who advocated woman suffrage on its own merits as Griffin did. They argued that women who have no one to represent them and who own property should be allowed to vote on tax and bond issues as had been done in Louisiana and other states of the union. This approach would provide "equal justice, common and even-handed, to the women of the land." Other supporters maintained that any woman who owned property had as much right to vote upon tax and bond issues as a man who owned property. Granting women the vote was a "question of right, fairness and justice" not a question of poetry and sentiment. After a spirited discussion, the convention considered a proposal that allowed women taxpayers to vote. It eventually passed a resolution that would have permitted unmarried women over the age of twenty-one who paid taxes on $500 of property to vote on municipal tax issues. However, the next day the delegates had second thoughts and rescinded even this minor concession.[14]

The delegates to the convention had traditional ideas about women and women's role. The theory of southern culture was that a woman was the "Queen of the Household" and the domestic circle. If women departed from this role, the result might be the complete destruction of cherished convictions regarding woman's sphere. Voting would degrade women; it would involve them in the dirt of politics. It would be in opposition to the highest southern civilization where women are the loveliest creatures on the face of the earth. Opponents argued that the finest southern woman was too pure, too refined to lower herself by going to the polls where she would undoubtedly be put into contact with poor white women and black

13. *Huntsville Republican*, June 15, 1901.

14. *Official Proceedings of the Constitutional Convention, 1901* 1:323, 606; Malcolm Cook McMillan, *Constitutional Development in Alabama, 1798–1901: A Study in Politics, the Negro, and Sectionalism* (Spartanburg, S.C.: Reprint Co., 1978), 278; *Official Proceedings of the Constitutional Convention, 1901* 3:3817–18, 3823, 3873–74.

women. Rather than expose herself to such disagreeable contact, the southern lady should stay at home and leave voting to those of low station and morality. As far as the delegates were concerned, women should remain in the private sphere of the hearth and home and only men should operate in the public sphere of politics and the workplace. Rejection of women's suffrage by the Alabama legislature and other southern legislatures shortly brought an end to the "southern strategy" of the suffragists. [15]

After 1904 all organized activity virtually came to an end, and the Woman Suffrage Association ceased to function. It was not until 1910–1911 that Alabama women were once again interested in the right to vote. This new concern was largely the result of the Progressive movement, which supported a wide range of civic and community projects. The Alabama Federation of Women's Clubs, which had been organized in 1895, originally consisted of literary clubs, but by the turn of the century the women had become interested in various reform movements in the state. They sought to improve the educational system by making school attendance compulsory, by placing women on school boards, by attacking illiteracy, and by introducing kindergartens, manual training, and domestic science into the school system. They worked to secure a women's dormitory at the University of Alabama and to provide scholarships for women. They were instrumental in establishing industrial reform schools for both boys and girls. Leading the drive to abolish child labor, they helped to secure the passage of one of the early child labor laws. [16]

Black women of the state established their clubs at the same time as white women. The first of these was created in Montgomery in 1890, and others followed until by 1904 there were a total of twenty-six clubs in Birmingham, Selma, Mobile, and several smaller towns. These clubs established the Alabama Federation of Colored Women's Clubs in 1899. The most active of these was the Tuskegee Woman's Club established in 1894 by Margaret Murray Washington, the wife of Booker T. Washington. The major project of this organization was the establishment of a reform school for boys at Mt. Meigs, which was later taken over and administered by the state. These women

15. *Official Proceedings of the Constitutional Convention, 1901* 3:3858, 3869–71.
16. Lura Harris Craighead, *History of the Alabama Federation of Women's Clubs, 1895–1918* (Montgomery: The Paragon Press, 1936), 350.

also visited the local jail, providing fruit, clean clothes, and religious services for the prisoners. They established a settlement school and cottage where mothers and children could take cooking and sewing classes. They held Mothers' Meetings to create an interest in self-improvement and the development of children. As these projects suggest, black women were concerned with education, self-improvement, and community projects. In addition there was always a strong emphasis on race pride, on the defense of the black community and home, and on race advancement. The motto of these associations was "Lifting as We Climb."[17]

After the hiatus of nearly a decade, Alabama's white women created new suffrage organizations as the result of a National Child Labor Conference held in Birmingham in 1911. At that meeting Jean Gordon of Louisiana and Belle Bennett of Kentucky argued that child labor would never be abolished until women had the vote. Alabama's Nellie K. Murdock, who had long worked for abolition of child labor, came to believe that suffrage was necessary to carry out other reforms. Murdock held a series of meetings in her home that eventually led to the establishment of the Equal Suffrage Association of Birmingham. Pattie Ruffner Jacobs was elected president. Associations in other towns quickly followed, and in 1912 these groups combined to form the Alabama Equal Suffrage Association which affiliated with NAWSA. Jacobs became president of the state organization and provided the Alabama suffrage movement with strong leadership.[18]

Pattie Jacobs was a remarkably perceptive, free-spirited southern woman who kept a youthful diary in which she showed a restless

17. Minutes of the Ninth Annual Session of the Alabama Federation of Colored Women's Clubs, July 3–6, 1907, Washington Collection, Tuskegee University, Tuskegee, Ala.; Mrs. Booker T. Washington, "Synopsis of the Lecture by Mrs. Booker T. Washington on the Organizing of Women's Clubs, June 2, 1910," and "Report of the Tuskegee Woman's Clubs, October 1909–May 1910," Booker T. Washington Papers 1909–1910, Box 982, Manuscript Division, Library of Congress, Washington, D.C.; Mrs. Booker T. Washington, "The Tuskegee Woman's Club," *The Southern Workman* (August 1920): 365–69.

18. Minutes of the Alabama Equal Suffrage Association, 1912–1918, Alabama Department of Archives and History, Montgomery, Ala.; Allen, "Woman Suffrage Movement," 18–20; Goodrich, "Romance and Reality," 5–21; *Birmingham News*, March 9 and 13, 1911; *Birmingham Age-Herald*, November 12 and 26, 1911.

and independent soul. The institution of marriage troubled her, but she eventually married Solon Jacobs who gave her unswerving support throughout the suffrage fight. Jacobs was destined to become a prominent suffrage leader, not only in the state, but at the national level as well. At the meeting of NAWSA in 1913, she was much heralded as a representative of the "New South" and southern womanhood. When she was not serving as president of the Alabama Equal Suffrage Association, she headed the critically important Legislative Committee. She also served the National Association as auditor. Jacobs, a shrewd and sophisticated strategist, led the association through the campaign of 1915 and the 1919 state battle over ratification.[19]

Black women also supported the demand for the vote, but black and white women never worked together. Instead of creating separate suffrage associations, black women worked for suffrage through their various women's clubs. Indeed, black women had a more consistent attitude toward the vote than did white women; by the 1890s blacks tended to support a political philosophy of universal suffrage, while white women advocated a limited, educated suffrage. Like white suffrage leaders, black women saw the franchise as a cure for many of their ills, with sexual exploitation heading the list. These black women felt they needed the ballot to uphold their virtue and to foster sentiment in favor of their own protection. They also felt that woman suffrage would be a boon to education by providing them a voter's influence with legislators and school boards. Being able to vote would allow women to work for improved schools and compulsory education. Black women were also interested in the vote because, unlike white women, the vast majority of them had to work for a living. They believed as voters they would be better able to protect themselves in the workplace.[20]

Their most immediate concern, however, was the loss of the vote by black men and the charge that the men had "sold" their votes to white supremacist politicians. Disfranchised, racially conscious black women were highly critical of black men who had the ballot but who did not know its value. Underlying these attitudes was the

19. J. Wayne Flynt and Marlene Hunt Rikard, "Pattie Ruffner Jacobs: Alabama Suffragist" (paper presented at the First Southern Conference on Women's History, Converse College, June 1988).

20. Giddings, *When and Where I Enter,* 119–21. See also Rosalyn M. Terborg-Penn, "Afro-Americans in the Struggle for Woman Suffrage" (Ph.D. diss., Howard University, 1977).

conviction that unlike the masses of black men, women would never betray the race if they had the power of the vote. Their exalted sense of themselves as a group extended to their feelings about the suffrage issue. W. E. B. Du Bois applauded the greater tenacity of black women as a group. "You can bribe some pauperized Negro laborers with a few dollars at election time," he said, "but you cannot bribe a Negro woman." Evidently this thought also occurred to white supremacists in the South, especially in the states with large black populations, which gave them further reason for opposing woman suffrage.[21]

The leading black suffragist was Adella Hunt Logan of the Tuskegee Woman's Club, who supported woman's suffrage as early as the turn of the century. Born in Sparta, Georgia, in 1863, she graduated from Atlanta University in 1881 and began teaching school in south Georgia. She joined the Tuskegee faculty in 1883 and within a few years became the "Lady Principal." But she retired as a teacher in 1888 when she married Warren Logan, Tuskegee's treasurer. Tuskegee did not allow more than one member of a family to draw a salary from the Institute's limited financial resources. Logan soon became interested in the suffrage drive and worked for women's right to vote for nearly two decades. Indeed, she was a life member of the National American Woman's Suffrage Association as early as 1901. As a charter member and officer of the Tuskegee's Woman's Club, she participated in many of their activities, but her major work was on behalf of suffrage. She led spirited monthly discussions at club meetings and established a large personal library on the subject which she opened to all who were interested. Working regionally and nationally within the National Association of Colored Women, she helped to educate her associates about suffrage by establishing a department of suffrage within the organization and headed it for several years. She died tragically in 1915 when she committed suicide by jumping from the second story of a building on the campus of Tuskegee Institute.[22]

21. Miss N. H. Burroughs, "Black Women and Reform," *The Crisis* 10 (August 1915): 187; Giddings, *Where and When I Enter,* 121–23.

22. Adele Logan Alexander, "How I Discovered My Grandmother," *MS.* (November 1983): 29–33; Giddings, *When and Where I Enter,* 121; Louis R. Harlan, ed., *Booker T. Washington Papers,* 13 vols. (Urbana: University of Illinois Press, 1972), 2:30. Alexander suggests that her grandmother's life was plagued with problems, including the strain of leading a "double life" in a racially hostile environment, that eventually overwhelmed her.

The declarations of white women in the Alabama Equal Suffrage Association echoed the voices of the Progressive movement in their aims to promote "equal and exact justice," to improve the "civic, social, economic, educational and sanitary conditions in Alabama," and to mitigate "the cruelties of industrialism." Women were ready and able to help men with this heavy burden. The suffragists, however, were concerned primarily with protecting the home. They maintained that women should be concerned with the "food supply of every community, water, milk and meat inspection, all housekeeping conditions and school affairs, highways, lighting, drainage and sewerage systems," and they were convinced that the enfranchisement of women was now at last stirring in the southern states. "It is coming like sunrise over Alabama—a great light, sound and sweet and wholesome, born of the desire of women for a chance to help in the world's work."[23]

Instead of emphasizing the inalienable rights of women as individuals, as Frances Griffin and others had done earlier, Pattie Jacobs and her Progressive-era colleagues tended to emphasize the necessity of the ballot as an agent for reforming society. Instead of basing their appeal on the similarity of men and women as human beings, they stressed the differences that distinguished the sexes and gave each a unique role to play in politics. Now the suffragists argued that women needed the vote in order to be better wives and mothers. The nation, they said, was simply a macrocosm of the home and women should be able to make decisions about pure food, fresh milk, clean water, and adequate drainage. Women were still primarily wives and mothers, but the world had changed and they needed the ballot to protect the home and family. With the advent of Progressivism, women were able to identify their own cause with the larger reform effort to extend democracy and eliminate social injustice. Suffrage and social welfare were linked together.[24]

Jacobs expressed these views in a letter to the editor of the *Birmingham Age-Herald.*

23. "Call to Organize the Alabama Equal Suffrage Association," unidentified newspaper article in volume 1 of Pattie Ruffner Jacobs's scrapbook 1911–1914, Birmingham Public Library, Birmingham, Ala.

24. "Woman Suffrage After All Tends to the Making of the Home, Says Mrs. Jacobs," *Montgomery Advertiser,* November 20, 1914.

> Nobody of women is more staunchly upholding the home than the woman suffragists, but we do not understand the home to mean the four walls in which we live.
>
> One after another the duties that formerly belonged exclusively to the individual household have become the common duties of the community. . . . The modern city is now a big, co-operative house-keeping business and what was the family's duty has been transferred to the municipality. . . . The ballot is the quickest, most effective, most dignified weapon which women may use to defend the home. So that when the assertion is made that "woman's place is in the home," we suffragists say, "Amen."[25]

Adella Logan's thinking regarding the ideology of suffrage also evolved over the period she was active as a suffrage leader. In a 1905 article she argued for suffrage on the basis of abstract justice as other suffrage leaders of the day were doing. She quoted Jefferson's famous statement in the Declaration of Independence about governments deriving their just powers from the consent of the governed. She pointed out that women must obey the laws made by men, must pay taxes levied by men, but had no voice in writing these laws. She cited some of the benefits that accrued when women voted—better schools, less crime, better laws for women and children. She refuted some of the common objections to women voting: that women do not want the vote, that they are not interested in politics, that the home would be neglected, and that women are represented by their husbands. She concluded: "If white American women, with all their natural advantages, need the ballot . . . how much more do black Americans, male and female, need the strong defense of a vote to help secure their right to life, liberty and the pursuit of happiness?"[26]

By 1912 Logan believed that more black women were becoming interested in studying public issues and in voting. Under the influence of Progressivism, black women along with white women were beginning to realize that in order to be good housekeepers, they must be able to vote on such issues as pure food, sanitary and safe buildings, adequate school facilities, reform schools, and juvenile courts. "Colored women feel keenly that they may help in civic betterment, and that their broadened interests in matters of good government may arouse the colored brother, who for various rea-

25. *Birmingham Age-Herald,* June 27, 1913.
26. Logan, "Woman Suffrage," *The Colored American Magazine* (September 9, 1905): 487–89.

sons had become too indifferent to his duties of citizenship." Logan felt that black women had the motivation and skills to contribute to the improvement of conditions in the black community.[27]

The Alabama Federation of Colored Women's Clubs officially endorsed suffrage in 1910, but it was the 1913 convention that took decisive action under the leadership of Logan who headed the Committee on Resolutions. The convention approved a strongly worded resolution that favored unrestricted suffrage and looked forward to the day when "our broad country woman shall share with man the responsibility of deciding questions—social, economic, and civic—which have to do not only with her welfare, but with the deepest interests of those dearer to her even than herself." The leaders believed that when women were enfranchised, the black women would be equal to the situation because they would be educated well enough to cast their ballots wisely.[28]

Aileen Kraditor, in her influential book *The Ideas of the Woman Suffrage Movement*, was the first to identify this shift in an argument from "justice" to an argument from "expediency." Instead of emphasizing the inalienable rights of women as individuals, the suffragists—black as well as white—tended to emphasize the necessity of the ballot as an agent for reforming men and society. And rather than base their appeal on the similarity of men and women as human beings, they underlined the immutable differences that distinguished the sexes and gave each a unique role to play in politics. Thus, women had begun by talking about justice among human beings and ended by talking about what women could contribute to politics *as* women. By the early twentieth century, women had accommodated themselves to political realities and based their arguments on the doctrine of the two spheres. By invoking accepted gender conventions, they ceased to challenge the established order. By reassuring men that women would continue to operate in the female sphere, the suffragists hoped to gain male support.[29]

27. Logan, "Colored Women as Voters," *The Crisis* 4 (September 1912): 242–43.

28. "Mrs. Warren Logan Writes of the Doings among Club Women around Tuskegee," *The Colored Alabamian,* April 10, 1915; Minutes of the Alabama Federation of Colored Women's Clubs, July 1913, July 1919. The white Alabama Federation of Women's Clubs did not endorse suffrage until 1918.

29. Kraditor, *Ideas of the Woman Suffrage,* 96–122.

It is easy to understand why the suffragists made this shift from challenging women's sphere to emphasizing women's special role; they realized they would not win votes by attacking the accepted social order. By avoiding issues that might alienate potential supporters while emphasizing traditional concepts of women's proper role, the suffragists acquired growing respectability. More and more, they occupied the moderate center of the political spectrum and mirrored the views of the society around them. Both Kraditor and William H. Chafe saw this shift as a turning point in the suffrage drive that contemporary observers did not perceive. Chafe, in his pathbreaking work *The American Woman: Her Changing Social, Economic, and Political Roles, 1920–1970*, described this shift as a "narrowing of vision." He believed women had to abandon their goals of gender equality in order to win votes. Both he and Kraditor saw this shift as a significant break with the past.[30]

Other historians have viewed the suffrage strategies differently. Nancy F. Cott, in *The Grounding of Modern Feminism*, believed that the women of the Progressive period did not see a dichotomy. She felt that suffragists could talk about being treated as equals with men and in the same breath speak of the differences between the sexes and women's special contribution. They could view men and women as alike in their common humanity, yet categorically different from each other. Progressive women firmly believed in their stereotypical domesticity while at the same time aiming toward goals of equality between the sexes. They simply recognized that the paradox existed. Women wanted a sexual equality that included sexual differences and apparently saw no contradiction in this position. Kraditor built her expediency argument in part by focusing on southern suffrage, and Cott challenged it by looking only at the North.[31]

In Alabama, suffrage leaders recognized the existence of the two arguments but continued to argue both ways at the same time. Frances Griffin based most of her arguments in 1901 on justice, but she clearly felt women had a special role. Pattie Ruffner Jacobs and Adella Hunt Logan made gender equality part of their arguments a decade later. But simultaneously they described the world as a mac-

30. Chafe, *American Woman*, 3–22.

31. Nancy F. Cott, *The Grounding of Modern Feminism* (New Haven: Yale University Press, 1987), 3–10.

rocosm of the home and believed that women should vote in order to preserve the health of their children and the cleanliness of their homes. The experience of Alabama women supports Cott's analysis of the interweaving of the justice and expedience arguments.

The Alabama Equal Suffrage Association also was interested in goals other than the franchise. At the second annual convention, which was held in Huntsville on February 4 and 5, 1914, the association showed an awareness of wider women's issues. Their goals included demanding a compulsory education law, favoring equal pay for women who do equal work with men, raising the age of consent from twelve to twenty-one for females, abolishing child labor, supporting an eight-hour day and minimum wage for women, and encouraging a law to make mothers as well as fathers coguardians of their children.[32] The association also studied the legal status of women and was concerned with state laws regarding women's property rights, marriage and divorce, and laws affecting working women.

Nonetheless, the immediate goal of the association was to present a petition to the state legislature requesting a woman suffrage amendment be added to the state constitution. The Alabama legislature met only every four years, and the next scheduled meeting was in 1915. The suffragists believed that Alabamians, because of strong states' rights traditions, would be more receptive to enfranchising women by state action than by federal action. Widespread fear of federal authority over voting rights was common in the southern states, and for this reason, most southern legislators opposed a federal amendment. Alabama women were quick to explain that they saw a federal amendment only as a last resort and urged that the state give them suffrage. The Suffrage Association waged a hard and emotional campaign, but the legislature rejected the proposal in August 1915.[33]

Even though the legislative campaign was unsuccessful, the issue of woman suffrage had been raised and widely debated. It became a major item on the Progressive agenda. New members flocked to the

32. Minutes of the Alabama Equal Suffrage Association, February 4–5, 1914; *Huntsville Mercury-Banner,* February 5, 1914.

33. *Journal of the House of Representatives of the State of Alabama, 1915,* 2 vols. (Montgomery: Brown Printing Co., 1915), 2:2963; Bossie O'Brien Hundley's scrapbook, Birmingham Public Library, Birmingham, Ala.; Allen, "Woman Suffrage Movement," 81–82; Goodrich, "Romance and Reality," 15.

suffrage associations, which experienced substantial growth and activity for about a year and a half, until the United States entered World War I. The number of associations in the state increased more then three times, the state was organized into congressional districts according to the direction of NAWSA, and NAWSA even sent a paid organizer into the state. However, the entrance of the United States into World War I in April 1917 brought almost all of the suffrage activity to a halt. The women shifted from their suffrage work to a variety of war work, which occupied them until the war was over in November 1918. This hiatus proved to be disastrous to the suffrage organization.

The state organization that had carefully been built up seemed to disappear almost overnight. One local organization after another disbanded, board members received no answers to their letters, and no leaders existed for many districts. When Congress passed the Nineteenth Amendment in 1919, the women had difficulty waging a campaign for ratification. Organizing for the ratification campaign, NAWSA divided the states into three categories: hopeful states, fighting states, and hopeless states. The executive council of NAWSA placed Alabama in the "hopeless" class. Despite this pessimistic outlook, the state suffrage association appointed a ratification committee to wage a campaign to ratify the Nineteenth Amendment.[34]

Opposition does not develop until an issue has considerable support or is on the verge of success, and by this time opposition to woman suffrage had organized. The Alabama Association Opposed to Woman Suffrage was established in 1916 but did not become active until 1919. Its motto was "Home Rule, States' Rights, and White Supremacy." The president was Nell V. Baker, and the opposition shortly claimed a membership of 1,000. Members protested against having the issue of "Votes for Women" thrust upon them and affirmed their belief that the men of Alabama would always love, honor, and protect their women as long as they remained within the sphere to which nature and God had assigned them. Despite such rhetoric, this group seems to have engaged in little activity.[35]

A more active group was the Woman's Anti-Ratification League of

34. Stanton et al., eds., *History of Woman Suffrage* 6:4–5. This account was written by Jacobs.

35. *The Woman's Protest*, National Association Opposed to Woman Suffrage, March 1916, Manuscript Division, Library of Congress, Washington, D.C.; *Selma Times*, February 12, 1916.

Alabama, which was created in Montgomery in June 1919. Mrs.
James S. Pinckard was selected president, and Marie Bankhead
Owen, the daughter of Senator John H. Bankhead and a bitter foe of
suffrage, headed the legislative committee. The group selected as its
motto "Alabama for Alabamians." The debate this time centered
entirely on the questions of states' rights and white supremacy, two
issues that southerners had supported since the Civil War and Reconstruction and that continued to shape southern politics until
well after World War II.[36]

The Anti-Ratification League believed that the suffrage amendment had been conceived by Susan B. Anthony fifty years earlier for
the very purpose of destroying white supremacy. The league maintained that the amendment was a "wolf gnawing at the vitals of both
state and national government. It is the seed from which may spring
untold misery in the future. The fifteenth amendment is not dead.
It only sleepeth. Why arouse it from its slumber?" Moreover, contained in advancing the states' rights argument was the underlying
fear that Congress would have the power to enforce the amendment, and black women would be voting along with white women.
Opponents feared the ballot would be opened to all women regardless of color. In this light, the amendment was seen as a threat to
"the established civilization of the South."[37]

The issue of race was not a major debating point in the 1915 campaign, although it was always just below the surface, as it was in all
southern states. However, the 1919 ratification contest turned on
the race issue. Once the race issue was raised, the suffrage cause
was doomed. The suffrage leaders attempted to respond to the
charges. Pattie Jacobs pointed out that women must have the same
qualifications as men in order to vote and that the poll tax and the
literacy test would still apply to black women as well as to black
men. These arguments had little effect, and the Alabama legislature
defeated the amendment in July 1919.[38]

36. Alabama Woman's Anti-Ratification League Scrapbook, 1919–1920,
Department of Archives and History, Montgomery, Ala.; *The Woman's Protest*, March 1916.

37. "Legislators Urged to Defeat Susan B. Anthony Amendment," un-
identified newspaper article, June 22, 1919, Alabama Anti-Ratification
League Scrapbook; "The Anti-Ratification League," *Montgomery Advertiser*,
June 9, 1919.

38. *Journal of the Senate of the State of Alabama, 1919*, 8 vols. (Montgomery:

It is difficult to believe that the Nineteenth Amendment posed any real danger to white supremacy. The Alabama Constitution of 1901 had been successful in disfranchising black voters. In 1900 approximately 181,315 eligible black voters were registered, but that number declined to 3,742 in 1908 and continued to decrease. The poll tax and the literacy test also prohibited poor white men from voting. By 1919 the electorate was only half of what it had been in 1901, and the Democratic regime had long since gained control of politics.[39] Yet, whites seemingly felt they must pursue every avenue to maintain white supremacy.

Some of the proponents of suffrage saw white supremacy as a bogus issue. One editorial writer said that there was no danger to the South except in the imagination of the opponents of suffrage. Reactionary elements, who did not want women voting under any circumstances or conditions, capitalized on the fear of blacks voting. Another editorial said the opponents of woman suffrage, by appealing to the ignorant masses' racial hatred and prejudice, were trying to create an issue that was in itself dangerous to the public welfare.[40] The Alabama suffrage leaders themselves did not use the race issue; they did not attack black women, yet they could easily have done so. It was the antisuffragists who raised the race issue and resorted to race baiting.

Despite the talk of the fear of the black vote, it would appear that the real objection to woman suffrage in Alabama, as in other states, was a perceived threat to gender roles. Suffrage was a radical proposal because it challenged the separation of the male sphere of the public world and the female sphere of the private world. Suffrage called into question all the traditional activities of women. It not only gave women the opportunity to act in politics but also recognized them as individuals within the family. In the traditional or patriarchal family, a woman was expected to subordinate her individual interests to those of her family; thus a husband could quite properly represent his wife at the polls because a woman's interests

Brown Printing Co., 1920), 1:838–39; Alabama Woman's Anti-Ratification League Scrapbook; Allen, "Woman Suffrage Movement," 122–38; Minutes of Alabama Equal Suffrage Association, 1918.

39. McMillan, *Constitutional Development in Alabama*, 352–55.

40. "Why the Suffrage Amendment Will Be Ratified," *Montgomery Journal*, June 10, 1919; "Anti-Suffragists Try to Evade the Issue," *Birmingham Age-Herald*, June 6, 1919.

were no different from those of her husband. But as citizens and
voters, women would participate directly in society as individuals,
not indirectly through their subordinate position as wives and mothers.[41] In 1919 Alabamians, it would seem, were not yet ready to
recognize women as individuals with independent identities separate from the family.

41. Ellen DuBois, "The Radicalism of the Woman Suffrage Movement:
Notes toward the Reconstruction of Nineteenth-Century Feminism," *Feminist Studies* 3 (Fall 1975): 63–71; Carl N. Degler, *At Odds: Women and the Family in America from the Revolution to the Present* (New York: Oxford University
Press, 1980), 342–43, 355.

Elizabeth Hayes Turner

"White-Gloved Ladies" and "New Women" in the Texas Woman Suffrage Movement

The existing articles and books on the woman suffrage movement in the South stand as beacons to those who are trying to make sense of women's experiences below the Mason-Dixon line. At present these works are primarily studies of state organizations or of individuals who gave their wholehearted energies to the cause.[1] Although the subject is far from exhausted, we now have a better picture of the politics involved at the state, regional, and national levels. Perhaps it is not too soon to begin asking questions about the rise as well as the role and function of *local* suffrage societies in the South—to try to discover if, in fact, the grass had any roots, and if so, how healthy they were, and whether they advanced or held back

1. For a survey of the literature, see Jacquelyn Dowd Hall and Anne Firor Scott, "Women in the South," in John B. Boles and Evelyn Thomas Nolen, eds., *Interpreting Southern History: Historiographical Essays in Honor of Sanford W. Higginbotham* (Baton Rouge: Louisiana State University Press, 1987), 461, 496–99. For a history of the leaders of the woman suffrage movement in the South see Marjorie Spruill Wheeler, "New Women of the New South: The Leaders of the Woman Suffrage Movement in the Southern States" (Ph.D. diss., University of Virginia, 1990). Two helpful publications on the Texas woman suffrage movement are Ruthe Winegarten and Judith N. McArthur, eds., *Citizens at Last: The Woman Suffrage Movement in Texas* (Austin: Ellen C. Temple, 1987), and Janet G. Humphrey, ed., *A Texas Suffragist: Diaries and Writings of Jane Y. McCallum* (Austin: Ellen C. Temple, 1988). See also Patricia B. Nieuwenhuizen, "Minnie Fisher Cunningham and Jane Y. McCallum: Leaders of Texas Women for Suffrage and Beyond" (Senior thesis, University of Texas at Austin, 1982); and Anastatia Sims, "The Woman Suffrage Movement in Texas" (Senior thesis, University of Texas at Austin, 1974).

the greening of the general suffrage movement. And, remembering that there were many more foot soldiers than commanders mobilizing for suffrage, we need to ask what kind of southern woman was willing to organize, campaign, march, and hold meetings in townships across her state for the ideal of equal voting rights. How were clubwomen, the so-called "white-gloved ladies" of the South, able to transcend their domestic culture in order to emerge as "New Women" campaigners for suffrage? What forces brought them publicly to espouse such goals? Was it religion, professional training, club work, youthful idealism, or some combination of several influences? And, finally, how did local societies sustain suffrage in their immediate communities while fostering state-level associations and leaders?

The answers are beginning to emerge, at least for one middle-sized prosperous community, Galveston. Texas is a good place to begin to seek answers, for it was the first state of the Old Confederacy and the ninth state in the nation to ratify the Nineteenth Amendment. It is no doubt axiomatic to point out that strong popular suffrage sentiment in the South was most likely to be found in cities. The urbanization of the South in the postwar years provided an essential foundation for the development of women's civic reform and suffrage associations.

In Galveston the roots for a suffrage movement had been developing since at least the 1880s with the growth and spectacular rise of the city as the state's leading cotton export center. Prosperity promoted an ever more sophisticated citizenry, and as the community of 22,000 in 1880 almost doubled to 40,000 by 1900, so too did the diversity of economic prospects in the form of merchant houses, cotton factoring, shipping, railroading, banking, and insurance. Industries such as cotton mills, presses, seed and oil companies, bagging and cordage manufactories, flour mills, foundries, and cracker and barrel factories provided employment for thousands of working men and women.[2] Local entrepreneurs in 1891 billed Gal-

2. For a discussion of Galveston's economic and business history, see David G. McComb, *Galveston: A History* (Austin: University of Texas Press, 1986), 112; *Galveston Daily News*, April 11, 1942; for banking: June 16 and July 4, 1926; March 9, 1930; October 1, 1932; September 23, 1931; September 8, 9, 1958; for cotton: November 7, 1915; September 5, 1920; October 1, 1927; September 1, 1929; March 21, 1930; April 11, September 11, 1942; for the Port of Galveston: June 11, 1906; April 11, 1917; for merchants: July

veston as "the wealthiest city in the world of its size."[3]

Accompanying the impressive aggregation of wealth was an equally imposing growth of clubs, societies, and private associations. By 1910 the city directory listed no fewer than sixty-eight church and synagogue societies (of which forty-four were women's), eight benevolent institutions (six managed by women), thirty clubs (eight for women), forty-six fraternal associations (six for women), and fourteen immigrant relief societies (three managed by women). All this points to the fact that membership in societies, clubs, leagues, unions, and associations was an important element of town life at the turn of the century for both men and women and added a sense of integration for individuals into community life. Discrete groups provided the necessary preconditioned environment for the formation of women's reform associations. But the fact that Galveston in 1910 was swimming with little clusters of self-defined groups did not alone set the stage for the formation of a suffrage society.[4]

More essential to the process was the *type* of groups that women created both before and after the turn of the century. Between 1880 and 1895 four permanent benevolent institutions—two orphanages, a home for elderly women, and a free kindergarten—were conceived and managed by white women to provide leadership and training for elite, civic-minded women. In 1891 women interested in furthering their education and broadening their intellectual horizons founded the city's first exclusive literary club, the Wednesday Club. It was followed by several more women's literary and patriotic clubs. Then, six months after the disastrous hurricane of 1900, which almost destroyed Galveston, women survivors united to form the

22, 1922 and 1923; July 4, 1926; September 1, 1927; April 26, 1932; September 9, 1958; February 21, 1971; and *Galveston Tribune,* September 14, 1932; for railroads: *Galveston Daily News,* December 16, 1928; December 31, 1933.

3. "Galveston and Deep Water," pamphlet, p. 11 in Subject Files, Rosenberg Library, Galveston.

4. *Directory of the City of Galveston, 1909–1910* (Galveston: Morrison and Fourmy Directory Co., 1909). For a discussion of the specialization represented in clubs and societies see Robert H. Wiebe, *The Search for Order, 1877–1920* (New York: Hill and Wang, 1967), 123, and Don H. Doyle, *New Men, New Cities, New South: Atlanta, Nashville, Charleston, Mobile, 1860–1910* (Chapel Hill: University of North Carolina Press, 1989), 208–59. For a women's history perspective, see Suzanne Lebsock, "Women and American Politics: 1880–1920," in Louise A. Tilly and Patricia Gurin, eds., *Women, Politics, and Change* (New York: Russell Sage Foundation, 1990), 35–62.

Women's Health Protective Association (WHPA), the first citywide progressive reform association open to all white women.[5]

At precisely the same time that the city's first women's reform group emerged, male civic-commercial elites were planning the nation's first commission form of municipal government. This urban structural reform held great portent for women activists who believed that the city's needs would best be met with a "progressive" form of government. Both the city commissioners and the members of the WHPA sought the welfare of the city and its people as they attempted to refashion, reform, and rebuild their community in the post-storm era.

The city commission plan, founded on the principle of efficiency, consolidated power in a five-member board. It tackled the work of reconstructing the storm-devastated city by building a four-mile-long, seventeen-foot-high protective seawall, and it raised the elevation of the island several feet by dredging the bay and pumping millions of cubic yards of sand onto the island. City commissioners secured money through complicated bond and tax maneuvers involving the county, state, and federal treasuries for these expensive improvements and reestablished the city's advantageous business position. The commission system, however, eliminated city ward representation, thereby breaking up bloc voting patterns among working-class and immigrant neighborhoods. As it turned out, city government was becoming more exclusive just as female civic associations were becoming more democratic.[6]

The Women's Health Protective Association grew from sixty-six concerned veterans of the pre-storm benevolent institutions, literary clubs, and church societies in 1901 to a powerful five-hundred-member, investigative, inspection, and city-lobbying group in 1915.

5. The four benevolent institutions were the Galveston Orphans' Home (1880), the Letitia Rosenberg Woman's Home (1888), the Lasker Home for Homeless Children (1894), and the Johanna Runge Free Kindergarten (1893). Elizabeth Hayes Turner, "Women, Religion, and Reform in Galveston, 1880–1920," in Char Miller and Heywood T. Sanders, eds., *Urban Texas: Politics and Development* (College Station: Texas A&M University Press, 1990), 75–95; and Turner, "Women's Culture and Community: Religion and Reform in Galveston, 1880–1920 (Ph.D. diss., Rice University, 1990).

6. Bradley Robert Rice, *Progressive Cities: The Commission Government Movement in America, 1901–1920* (Austin: University of Texas Press, 1977), 15.

Between 1901 and 1920 the WHPA replanted the island with trees and shrubs killed by the grade raising (elevating the island) and inspected streets, alleys, markets, bakeries, restaurants, dairies, and housing. Members demanded enforcement of the pure milk and pure food and drug ordinances. They helped establish regular medical examinations for schoolchildren, public playgrounds, hot lunch programs, and well-baby and tuberculosis clinics. The WHPA was a typical Progressive Era women's reform group. It stayed within the realm of municipal housekeeping and employed efficient but ladylike tactics to meet its goals. Still, in politicizing women's domestic goals for the city, the WHPA brought women actively into the political process and thus became the most important predecessor to a Galveston suffrage society.[7]

Also critical to the issue of suffrage was the fact that constituent members elected WHPA officers. For the first time, white women from all classes, denominations, and economic stations were able to cast votes for their organizational officers. Previously, elite groups of women confined their voting to officer elections in clubs or in church societies, neither of which had the advantage of size or openness. In a sense, the WHPA officers paralleled male elected officials; they were the city's highest elected women officials, and their constituency was the female members of the WHPA. Male voters elected their representatives to the city commission, and women elected theirs to the WHPA and thus initiated, for the women who favored civic improvement, the habit of voting.

True, the WHPA was an extralegal body and was only able to influence urban policy through petition, demonstration, and activity. But its influence had force. The WHPA constituency had actually elected officers who were much like their male counterparts in the city commission—the same class, same circle of friends, even the same goal of promoting a more healthful and therefore more prosperous community. City-elected officials and WHPA officers

7. For WHPA activities see the Morgan Family Papers, WHPA File, Rosenberg Library, Galveston, and the *Galveston Daily News,* December 11, 1921. Examples of progressive women's municipal reform associations are found in Marlene Stein Wortman, "Domesticating the Nineteenth-Century American City," *Prospects: An Annual of American Cultural Studies,* 3 (1977): 531–72; Mary Ritter Beard, *Woman's Work in Municipalities* (1915; reprint, New York: Arno Press, 1972).

were social equals, and parlor politics played no small role in winning support for the women's vision of a more beautiful urban environment.

Because they were often family friends, city commissioners were more accessible to and more compatible with WHPA officers than aldermen had been in the pre-storm decades. A harmonious period of cooperation between male and female elected officials lasted for ten years until 1911 when, the grade raising completed, the WHPA turned its attention to sanitation in the markets, restaurants, bakeries, and dairies. Then the thornier issue of imposing middle-class and elite values of cleanliness on middling shopkeepers and dairymen in conjunction with the state's Pure Food and Drug Act brought business-oriented city commissioners and the idealistic WHPA into conflict. Commissioners, afraid to interfere with free enterprise, were unwilling to enforce the pure food codes or create new ones. Progressive women reformers, on the other hand, understood the critical need for unadulterated milk in the raising of healthy infants, which for the most part was a woman's job. Thus male and female political cohesiveness broke down over gender issues. By employing experts to testify that the milk was watered down, bacteria laden, and possibly dangerous, by taking dairymen to court, and by forming coalitions with commercial and labor organizations (voters), the women were eventually able to extract cooperation again from the city commission. But power would never be theirs, the women reasoned, until *they* had the vote.[8]

Having learned to vote within a woman's association, and for the first time having cooperated closely and then struggled against city hall over issues peculiar to women, WHPA members thus set the stage for the advent of a suffrage society. It was a great leap, and not every woman was willing to travel the distance from civic-mindedness and arguing a woman's agenda before the city commission to joining a suffrage society. Nevertheless, in February 1912 seventy-four women and seven men became charter members of the Galveston Equal Suffrage Association (GESA). The *Galveston Daily News* reported sardonically, "If the men of Galveston doubt that the

8. *Galveston Daily News*, February 22, 23, 1913; January 7, 9, November 4, 1914; July 6, 1915; November 3, and December 1, and 7, 1916; *Galveston Daily Herald*, March 5, 1913; *Galveston Tribune*, December 1, 1914; May 4, 1915. Clipping, January 1915, WHPA File, Morgan Family Papers, Rosenberg Library, Galveston.

cause of woman's suffrage is knocking loudly at their doors clamoring for admission they need but have peeped into the ballroom of the Hotel Galvez Thursday . . . where . . . [150] Galveston women . . . were in session to discuss the question."[9]

Several women gave their reasons for wanting the vote. Mrs. Sally Trueheart Williams, daughter of a prominent realtor and a staunch Presbyterian, went right to the heart of the conflict with city government. "Housekeeping," she reasoned,

> used to begin at home and end there. But time has changed all this. It begins now . . . in the public laundry, the grocery, the dairy, the meat market, or the candy store; it only ends in the home. . . . The woman who keeps house must in a measure also keep the laundry, the grocery, the market, the dairy, . . . and in asking for the right to vote they are following their housekeeping in the place where it is now being done, the polls.[10]

Rebecca Brown, one of the wealthiest women in the city, argued that "every property holder should have the vote." Julia Runge, a kindergarten teacher, wanted "equal salary for men and women who do equal work."[11] This being a southern town no one brought up the issue of votes for black women, nor did any woman address the more radical view that as women they were all—black and white— entitled to equal citizenship based on natural rights. Privately Galveston suffragists wrote what they could not express in public. "I feel humiliated over the position of woman," wrote Cordia Sweeny, "and the way she has been looked on in the past, as a slave or a plaything. I want to be neither, and want woman equal with man before my daughter grows up."[12]

9. *Galveston Daily News*, February 16, 1912. For a discussion of feminism and woman suffrage see Gerda Lerner, *The Creation of Patriarchy* (New York: Oxford University Press, 1988), 236; Ellen Carol DuBois, *Feminism and Suffrage: The Emergence of an Independent Women's Movement in America, 1848– 1869* (Ithaca: Cornell University Press, 1978), 18; Nancy F. Cott, *The Grounding of Modern Feminism* (New Haven: Yale University Press, 1987).

10. *Galveston Daily News*, February 16, 1912.

11. Ibid.

12. Mrs. John S. Sweeny to Annette Finnigan, February 25, 1915, Jane Y. McCallum Papers, Austin Public Library, Austin. Some Galveston men used the natural rights argument for women's right to vote. See *Galveston Daily News*, February 16, 1912; and Edmund R. Cheesborough to Minnie Fisher Cunningham, November 18, 1916, McCallum Papers.

Although Galvestonians were relatively late in organizing for suffrage compared with more western states, in Texas they were actually riding a wave of organizational fervor as women formed local societies in San Antonio, Dallas, Waco, Tyler, San Marcos, and Houston. (Austin had organized in 1908.) Suffragists from New York and Dr. Anna Howard Shaw, president of the National American Woman Suffrage Association (NAWSA), stumped the state in 1912, thus aiding Texans in their struggle to mobilize for suffrage. By 1913 seven local societies carried the banner, by 1915 twenty-one, by 1916 eighty, and in June 1918, one year before ratification, ninety-eight societies and leagues across Texas supported votes for women.[13]

The founding of local suffrage societies was critically important to the movement as a whole. No viable, permanent state-level association in Texas existed before the forming of strong local societies. Sentiment for suffrage in the cities, supported by women active in local affairs, ensured the establishment and maintenance of a state organization. And support for the franchise, as demonstrated in the case of Galveston, depended upon a sufficient level of women's club activity that addressed community problems.[14]

In 1913 Texas suffragists formed a state association that eventually positioned itself to work in three major directions: first, at the national level, to support and remain under the guidance of the NAWSA; second, at the state level, to lobby the Texas legislature for passage of a state suffrage amendment; and third, at the local level,

13. A. Elizabeth Taylor, "The Woman Suffrage Movement in Texas," reprinted from the *Journal of Southern History* 27 (May 1951), in Winegarten and McArthur, eds., *Citizens at Last*, 26, 30 (hereafter cited with reprinted page numbers). See also "Austin Woman Suffrage Association Minutes," March 1, 1912, in *Citizens at Last*, 124; Jacquelyn Dowd Hall, *Revolt against Chivalry: Jessie Daniel Ames and the Women's Campaign against Lynching* (New York: Columbia University Press, 1979), 21–26; and Elizabeth Cady Stanton et al., eds., *History of Woman Suffrage*, 6 vols. (1881–1922; reprint, New York: Arno & *The New York Times*, 1969), 6:631–32.

14. Prior to 1913 women in Texas had formed two state organizations. In 1893 the Texas Equal Rights Association was formed and remained active until 1896. Another Texas Woman Suffrage Association was formed in 1903, but by 1908 it had become dormant. That same year, however, Austin formed a permanent local society when Dr. Anna Howard Shaw stumped the state for suffrage. It remained the only suffrage society in Texas until 1912. Taylor, "The Woman Suffrage Movement in Texas," 16–26.

to aid and guide the activities of the local suffrage societies, particularly in organizing new suffrage leagues within their same counties. This put tremendous pressure on the state officers, especially the president and the state field-workers, to give of their time exclusively to suffrage work. The state association needed dedicated, energetic women who were willing to make enormous personal sacrifices for the sake of the cause and who would be able to reside in Austin when the legislature met. Texas women who were "called up" to lead the state suffrage association more closely resembled "career" suffragists, whether salaried or not. Their past lives as southern ladies quickly blurred under the demands for suffragist leadership.

Local suffrage societies differed from the state organization in their responsibilities to the movement. Their duties fell into five basic categories: to educate and agitate their own members as well as nonmembers and male voters; to increase membership in their own city and aid the field-workers in establishing new associations within their county; to petition the legislature with as many local signatures as possible; to help raise money for their own work and for the campaign at the state level; and occasionally to send delegates to state and national meetings and to lobby the state legislature.

Local suffragists differed from state suffrage workers also in style and level of commitment. It is here that we find some white-gloved ladies and New Women acting together, although not always in concert, for the goal of enfranchisement. White-gloved ladies should be understood as a synonym for clubwomen, who represented respectability without controversy, who took part in the round of women's teas and fund-raisers for worthy causes, or who studied Shakespeare and Milton in discussion groups. Many clubwomen were content with the status quo and were unwilling to campaign for suffrage or risk their positions as community leaders even after 1912, a period when suffrage was considered safe. A few white-gloved ladies made the important decision to campaign for women's votes openly and joined the Galveston Equal Suffrage Association. But they quickly learned that the commitment to suffrage needed not only a decision to struggle for rights for women, which they made, but also a change in the way they approached the struggle. No mere conventional club tactics of endorsing national issues at the local level and then adjourning for refreshments would suffice in the campaign for political equality. Nothing less than aggressive and determined action, much like the efforts of the civic-reforming Women's Health Protective Association, would win the fight.

In short, suffrage demanded that New Women in both mind and deed stir the southern conscience. New Women saw themselves as movers and motivators of others, not as protectors of status, convention, and the social order. All suffragists were ideologically New Women in endorsing voting rights, but those with conservative tendencies fostered by years of club work remained motivated by old patterns wherein they made few challenges to the existing order. They offered the movement respectability without innovation. State-level officers observed this when they evaluated the fire and determinism of individual local suffrage societies. They clearly saw the difference between aggressive New Women and those with the habits of white-gloved ladies.

Because so many suffragists had been involved in club work and were familiar with the traditional methods of women's organizations, they often preferred to carry these organizing techniques—teas, entertainments, endorsements, polite requests for funds—to the campaign for equal rights. Many favored the traditional white-gloved ways, while others sought more aggressive approaches to gaining enfranchisement—marches, outdoor rallies, and lobbying efforts at the statehouse. Yet for the sake of the movement in the South, southern women needed to tread cautiously; too much militancy could turn voting and supporting men against the cause. A fine tension presented itself between the usefulness of aggressive tactics and genteel confrontations of the sort southern women dispatched with grace.[15]

15. Anne Firor Scott offers the best description to date of the meaning of the term *New Woman* for southerners: "Like the lady, the new woman represented only a small minority of all women in the South. Unlike the lady she did not become the universal ideal. At her best, she maintained the graciousness and charm which had been the sound part of the chivalric ideal and, without losing her femininity or abandoning her responsibility for the propagation of the species, became an important force in public as well as in private life" (Scott, *Making the Invisible Woman Visible* [Urbana: University of Illinois Press, 1984], 220). See also Scott, *The Southern Lady: From Pedestal to Politics, 1830–1930* (Chicago: University of Chicago Press, 1970). Marjorie Spruill Wheeler offers a thorough examination of the southern woman suffrage leader at the state level in "New Women of the New South." For a picture of clubwomen nationwide and in Texas see Karen J. Blair, *The Club-woman as Feminist: True Womanhood Redefined, 1868–1914* (New York: Holmes

In cities like Galveston, women supporters contended with these conflicting ideals and processes. Many, though committed in principle to votes for women, were unable or unwilling to rearrange their lives to make the movement their sole activity or to adopt measures that would brand them as controversial. This did not mean that their efforts were nonessential or immaterial. A. Elizabeth Taylor is correct when she states that "local societies played an important part in the votes-for-women movement, for on them rested the chief responsibility for promoting favorable sentiment in their communities."[16]

In order to gain "favorable sentiment," an image of white-gloved respectability with involvement in many other community and club activities needed to accompany their commitment to equal suffrage (white gloves symbolized both purity and activism; gloves were worn for public occasions). Local suffragists were not entirely free to abandon their club and church work, for these interests proved to male opponents that Texas suffragists were not wild-eyed harpies but civic leaders whose dedication to home, family, and community entitled them to a deferential hearing. Local suffragists also differed from their state-level sisters in their inability to remove themselves for long periods from the community or from civic work. But by honoring their pledge to the city as well as to suffrage, local suffragists protected the movement from the taint of radicalism.

Most Galveston suffragists continued their involvement in the circle of women's associations. During the Progressive Era there were multiple distractions: the WHPA sanitation fight with city hall waged for six years until 1917; then the war effort commenced with Liberty Loan drives, anti-vice committees, and soldier comfort stations. All claimed the attention of activist island women. During this same period women formed branches of the YWCA, the Red

and Meier Publishers, 1980), 119, and Megan Seaholm, "Earnest Women: The White Woman's Club Movement in Progressive Era Texas, 1880–1920" (Ph.D. diss., Rice University, 1988). For a study of clubwomen in a southern city that views their organizations as "cultural phenomena" rather than "political bodies," see Darlene Rebecca Roth, "Matronage: Patterns in Women's Organizations, Atlanta, Georgia, 1890–1940" (Ph.D. diss., George Washington University, 1978).

16. Taylor, "Woman Suffrage Movement in Texas," 30. For a study that discusses the consciousness of women relevant to their public activism, see Nancy F. Cott, "What's in a Name? The Limits of 'Social Feminism': or, Expanding the Vocabulary of Women's History," *Journal of American History* 76 (December 1989): 809–29, esp. 827.

Cross, and the Anti-Tuberculosis Association, which required teams of women to canvass for both members and money. In a general sense the suffragists' involvement in these varied activities supported the argument that equal dedication to community and nation earned equal voting rights. But involvement meant time away from suffrage campaigns, limiting the wholehearted advancement of the movement. This proved extremely frustrating to the women at state suffragist headquarters who wanted maximum commitment to the cause. They understood the need for credibility and respectability but also saw opportunities for suffrage slipping away.

This was understandably discouraging for the locals as well. As white-gloved ladies they wanted to maintain their involvement in the community because their work directly and tangibly affected themselves and their families. But as New Women they often felt shackled by the very commitments that gave them access to public life. In order better to understand the problem these women faced, we need to discover who these white-gloved New Women were.

The suffrage association rolls make it very clear that in an open (to white) membership association there were two types of members: those who supported the association nominally and those who committed themselves to work as officers. Nominal members, who comprised by far the largest percentage, were willing to be listed as suffrage supporters in print and were often tapped more heavily for financial support. By 1913 the GESA had grown to 175 members and by 1915 to 300. This compares favorably with other Progressive Era women's associations in Galveston. The Woman's Christian Temperance Union (WCTU) climbed to 100 members and the WHPA reached a maximum of 500 members in 1915; the YWCA opened with 2,000 members in 1914, a level it maintained until 1920. Of the 300 members of the GESA 36 were men, about two-thirds of the women were active in at least one other women's group (many of the members were from other towns), and 29 were active as officers in the years 1912 to 1919.[17]

It is the officers' biographical and organizational profiles that provide the clearest picture of who southern grass-roots suffragists were (information is available for twenty-four of the twenty-nine). At least twelve Galveston suffragists were native Texans, nine were born in Galveston, seven were from other states, and five were of unknown origin. With respect to age, eight or 32 percent were in

17. *Galveston Tribune,* Special Edition between March 17 and 18, 1915.

their thirties in 1915, six or 24 percent were between forty and fifty, while five or 20 percent were in their fifties; only one was older, but four were in their twenties. The southern women who marched for votes were not necessarily young and idealistic; most were mature women in the prime of life.[18]

With respect to religious ties one might expect to see a high percentage of Methodist women, as historians have often linked Methodism in the South with a lively reform tradition including the establishment of settlement (Wesley) houses and, of course, the endorsement of prohibition. But a search through the suffrage officer rolls turned up only two Methodists and one Baptist. The majority of suffrage officers were Episcopalian (ten) and Presbyterian (four). A significant number of suffrage officers came from Episcopal and Presbyterian backgrounds because in these churches status and wealth interfaced with a strong tradition of community service.[19]

18. Biographical entries for these twenty-four suffragists were acquired by combing the two daily newspapers, the *Galveston Daily News* and the *Galveston Tribune* between 1900 and 1920, the Galveston Equal Suffrage Records, Wednesday Club Records, Morgan Family Papers (for WHPA officers), Galveston YWCA Records, the four benevolent institution records, Galveston Red Cross Records, blue books, city directories, the 1880, 1900, and 1910 manuscript census returns for Galveston County, obituaries, and community histories and biographies, all in the Rosenberg Library, Galveston. A similar project using the *Woman's Who's Who of America, 1914–1915* can be found in Barbara Campbell, *The "Liberated" Woman of 1914: Prominent Women in the Progressive Era* (Ann Arbor: UMI Research Press, 1979).

19. In order to discover the suffragists' religious affiliation, church and synagogue records and directories have been thoroughly searched along with any existing women's church and synagogue society records. Three remain unidentified (or unchurched); the other suffragists were Lutheran (1), Jewish (1), Catholic (1), and Swedenborgian (1). For a discussion of the activist roles of Episcopal women in community affairs, see Elizabeth Hayes Turner, "Episcopal Women as Community Leaders: Galveston, 1900–1989," in Catherine Prelinger, ed., *Episcopal Women: Gender, Spirituality, and Commitment in a Mainline Denomination* (New York: Oxford University Press, forthcoming). For a history of Methodist women and their reform activities in the South, see Hall and Scott, "Women in the South," 489, and John Patrick McDowell, *The Social Gospel in the South: The Woman's Home Mission Movement in the Methodist Episcopal Church, South, 1886–1939* (Baton Rouge: Louisiana State University Press, 1982). Education, even for upper-class women, was more difficult to determine. No information for fifteen of the twenty-four could be found. The remaining nine received professional training appropriate to their careers.

Particularly striking was the fact that sixteen of the officers (66 percent) were married. Two of the married women, Dr. Ethel Lyon Heard and Mrs. Jens Moller, combined marriage with careers as a physician and a real estate agent respectively. Mrs. Moller served as president of both the WHPA and the GESA. The fact that Mrs. Moller and Dr. Heard were childless may, in part, explain their ability to spend time with the movement outside of their professional lives. But the majority of the other Galveston suffrage officers were also childless; of those who could be identified as mothers in 1915, only four had children under the age of ten at home. Perhaps the most unifying characteristic of these married suffragists was the fact that their husbands belonged to the white-collar and professional classes: three lawyers, two physicians, two shipping agency owners, two prosperous merchants, one newspaper publisher, four transportation agents, one court clerk, and one bookkeeper. A comfortable middle- to upper-class lifestyle and the relative absence of maternal responsibilities provided the leisure time necessary to organize for club and suffrage work.[20]

Eight of the active suffragists in 1915 were single (two widows); here wealth clearly marked the difference in their status. Three were independently wealthy with sizable inheritances, three were teachers, one was a librarian, and one was a medical student. Discrepancies in wealth did not appear to prejudice one worker from another, but every active suffragist was considered "socially acceptable." No Galveston suffrage officer came from the working class

20. The 1910 manuscript census for Galveston shows that Mrs. Jens Moller had no live-in servants, but her parents lived with her. Only three suffragists employed live-in servants, but of these, two also kept boarders. Of the twenty-four officers, seven bore children. (It was impossible to verify if four others had children or not). If anyone should wonder about birth control among southern women, one need only look at the drop in the number of children per childbearing suffragist between 1890 and 1915. Mary Fowler Bornefeld, first president of the GESA, born in 1860, and married in 1882, bore her first child in 1883 and continued to have a baby every two years thereafter until 1893 when her sixth and last child was born. By contrast, younger suffragists who married after 1900 limited their families to a maximum of three. Although the sample is too small to make generalizations about the efficacy of the birth control movement in the South, the fact that so few suffragists had children at all is a significant factor in considering who joined the movement at the local level.

where, for working women, finding leisure even for union activities was a problem. Suffragists and labor spokeswomen lamented the absence of working women in the suffrage ranks but found few solutions to the problem.

State suffrage president Annette Finnigan wrote to Eva Goldsmith, a member of the Legislative Committee of the State Federation of Labor, about the situation. "Galveston women of their own accord brought up the subject of reaching the working woman and said that they felt that they were not reaching the people." Finnigan asked Goldsmith if she would travel to Galveston and help the suffragists "in reaching the working women and the labor element." Goldsmith complied but recommended that the young state field-worker, Pearl Penfield, "go down and speak for them. . . . I think Miss Penfield can do some good work at this time by visiting the different shops and making the girls talks, for suffrage is being talked of more and more all the time and some outsider could do more good than my continued talk every day." But she cautioned that not every suffragist could do the job: "Now I am going to be frank with you, do not send Mrs. [Edward] Harris to Mr. Young [president of the Galveston Labor Council], because it will do no good and may do harm. It seems that Mrs. Harris is stiff and can not reach the laboring people there." State and local suffrage leaders gave the matter of organizing working-class women their attention, corresponded with labor spokeswomen, and sought solutions on how to penetrate the labor pool. But Galveston suffragists, many of whom were traditional clubwomen, had great difficulty presenting their message to working-class women.[21]

Clearly, active suffragists in Galveston were middle to upper class, and many of the leaders came with persuasive powers attached to class status and prominence. Status and elitism cut two ways, however. Apparently Texas suffragists carried their strength borne of their respectability to the statehouse where they were well received by progressive assemblymen. But their middle- to upper-class respectability repelled working-class women whose voting menfolk

---

21. Annette Finnigan to Eva Goldsmith, July 7, 1914; Goldsmith to Finnigan, July 20, 1914, and February 3, 1916, all in McCallum Papers. There were virtually no farm women active in Galveston civic affairs, although there were truck farms and dairies on the island.

were most in need of education on the issue of woman suffrage.[22] Suffragists saw the immigrant vote as a "counterbalance [to] the intelligent vote of Galveston,"[23] and they discussed the suffrage rights of black women, as well as black men, only as problems that would have to be eliminated with disfranchisement measures. Indeed, Minnie Fisher Cunningham, Texas Equal Suffrage Association president, stated in 1917, "The same moral influence that prevents the negro man from gaining control of political matters can, and will, serve a similar purpose with respect to the negro woman." When a black woman requested admission to the Texas Equal Suffrage Association, Cunningham wrote in 1918 that the idea of affiliating with African-American women had never before been considered. Carrie Chapman Catt, NAWSA president, when asked about the matter retreated to a states' rights position. The petitioning black suffragist was hence denied admission to the Texas association. Belle Critchett of El Paso shed the best light on this sordid picture when she explained: "We want to help the colored people but just now it is a rather hard question." The hard question was, of course, whether southern men would ratify suffrage if suffragists aligned themselves with black women. Pervading racism kept the question of African-American women's voting rights out of the suffrage campaign.[24]

22. This was borne out in 1919 when the Texas legislature introduced a woman suffrage referendum to Texas voters. Working-class immigrant, Catholic, and antiprohibition voters rejected the amendment. One month later progressive assemblymen ratified the Nineteenth Amendment. Eva Goldsmith to Annette Finnigan, February 3, 1915, McCallum Papers.

23. Larry J. Wygant, "'A Municipal Broom': The Woman Suffrage Campaign in Galveston, Texas," *Houston Review* 6, no. 3 (1984): 117–34, quoting *Galveston Tribune*, June 14, 1913.

24. Nieuwenhuizen, "Minnie Fisher Cunningham and Jane Y. McCallum," 61–62, 63. Rosalyn Terborg-Penn finds that Anna Howard Shaw, Carrie Chapman Catt, and Ida Husted Harper, although in favor of voting rights for black women, acquiesced to southern cultural expectations regarding the black vote. Terborg-Penn, "Discrimination against Afro-American Women in the Woman's Movement, 1830–1910," in Sharon Harley and Rosalyn Terborg-Penn, eds., *The Afro-American Woman: Struggles and Images* (Port Washington, N.Y.: Kennikat Press, 1978), 17–27, 25–26. For a discussion of the strategies employed by southern suffragists with respect to race, see Aileen S. Kraditor, "Tactical Problems of the Woman-Suffrage Movement in the South," *Louisiana Studies* (Winter 1966): 289–307, and *The Ideas of the Woman Suffrage Movement, 1890–1920* (New York: Columbia University Press, 1965).

The tendency to repel or exclude the laboring classes poses the question whether there ever was much working-class support for suffrage. The fact is that prominently placed or highly educated urban white women waged the suffrage campaign in Texas by appealing mainly to progressive white men for financial support and to members of the Texas legislature for political support.

In Galveston the respectability of suffrage officers did not rest exclusively on age, occupation, and their husbands' economic and social status (hence their own status). Equally important were their impressive organizational histories. Twenty-one of the twenty-four officers were involved in other women's clubs and church societies. The three who had no activity besides suffrage were the youngest women, all in their twenties, who had not yet had time to amass a "civic leadership portfolio." It is a credit to the GESA that its members elected three eager but unproven workers. The remaining twenty-one give an impressive record of volunteer activism.

Logically, the older the woman the more associations and activities were to her credit. Among the twenty-one older women at least nineteen other clubs and societies were represented. Nine of the women were officers in four or more other associations. (Miss Bettie Ballinger, age sixty-one and the only Baptist, was an officer in six other clubs and associations. Single and independently wealthy, she cofounded both the literary Wednesday Club and the Daughters of the Republic of Texas.) Eleven of the leaders held offices in from one to three other clubs. Dividing the clubs and associations into such categories as church societies, boards of lady managers for benevolent institutions, literary and performing arts clubs, patriotic-hereditary associations, and civic associations, including the WHPA, YWCA, Red Cross, and Mothers Clubs, one finds, not surprisingly, that suffragists preferred active leadership in civic associations, followed by literary clubs, patriotic-hereditary associations, women's church societies, and benevolent institutions.

Clearly, this was an overwhelmingly active group of women. Mostly Texas-born, middle-aged, patriotic, educated, well informed, industrious, and convincingly civic-minded, Galveston suffragists projected an image of unblemished respectability—an image that at times masked their political goals. The *Galveston Tribune* gave what it considered high praise in 1915 when it wrote: "Galveston women are not the kind that go in for every fad that comes along. They are in some respects old-fashioned, meaning they are not feverishly new fashioned. They are inclined to proceed wisely, conservatively; and that is why they haven't been shouting their heads off these past 20 or 30 years about the ballot."[25]

The local women leaders may have appeared conservative to the *Tribune* editors, but the GESA differed from popular women's clubs in one respect: nine of its twenty-nine officers were professional women who, undoubtedly, had seen the inequality in their paychecks and were willing to campaign for the vote in order to gain equal earning opportunities. Minnie Fisher Cunningham, a pharmacist and president of the GESA and the Texas Equal Suffrage Association, said that in 1901 in her first position as a prescription clerk at a Huntsville drugstore, she earned "$75 a month and everybody else $150. And now you could see what made a suffragette out of me—Equal Pay for Equal Work, only it wasn't equal work, I was the professional!" The fusion of women professionals with women volunteers who had long been prominent in civic improvement gave the GESA both a more worldly composition and certainly a more strident feminist spirit.[26]

Although we have accounted for suffragists in other types of organizations, there is one group conspicuously absent from the list of civic organizations to which suffragists were linked—the Woman's Christian Temperance Union. Only one suffrage officer maintained membership in the WCTU, and the tension between the two groups was so intense that in 1915 she resigned from the GESA in a huff over perceived slights on the part of suffragists toward WCTU leaders.[27] The truth is that in Galveston suffragists and WCTU members moved in different circles bound by religion and economic status. The issues of class and religious preference in southern women's reform have often been overlooked, but in Galveston, and perhaps

25. *Galveston Tribune*, Special Edition, March 17 and 18, 1915.

26. R[onnie]. D[ugger]., "Spanning the Old to the New South: Minnie Fisher and Her Heroine Mother," *The Texas Observer*, November 21, 1958; Patricia Ellen Cunningham, "Too Gallant a Walk: Minnie Fisher Cunningham and Her Race for Governor of Texas in 1944" (Master's thesis, University of Texas, 1985), 24. Thanks to Patricia Cunningham for these citations. See also John Carroll Eudy, "The Vote and Lone Star Women: Minnie Fisher Cunningham and the Texas Equal Suffrage Association," *East Texas Historical Journal* 14 (Fall 1976): 52–59.

27. Mrs. J. S. Sweeny to Annette Finnigan, March 26, 1915, McCallum Papers.

in other urban areas, members of the WCTU belonged almost exclusively to evangelical (Baptist and Methodist) churches and were mostly middle to lower-middle class in economic status. As a rule WCTU members belonged only to Protestant associations such as church missionary societies and the YWCA. The WCTU and the YWCA were the only two women's civic organizations in which more than 50 percent of the officers came from evangelical churches. In other words, when entering the public sphere WCTU members tended to confine their activism to those organizations where Christianity provided the organizing principle.

The GESA, by contrast, was more heterogeneous in membership. The officers belonged to eight different denominations, and their record of service to the community, contributed mostly through secular organizations, was far broader. Economic status varied among the suffrage officers: Miss Etta Lasker, for example, came from a family that could afford to donate a park and $35,000 to the city school system; Miss Mary Gardner, who moved to Galveston in 1903 from Montana (a suffrage state), worked all of her life as a librarian. If any link can be established between religion and suffrage in the island city, it was to those churches that had long promoted women's societies concerned with clothing and feeding the poor and that continued to emphasize community service. The women of Trinity Episcopal and First Presbyterian churches as early as the 1880s had taken charge of relief for those citizens (mainly women and children) who were in no way served by any other rescue or relief agency. Finally, suffrage officers did not confine themselves to Protestant groups; rather, they expanded upon their religious bases to embrace secular and political associations.

The evidence gathered from Galveston challenges the prevailing notion that the southern suffrage movement sprang from evangelical Protestant roots, or that WCTU members who fell in line after Frances Willard's organizing tour of the South in the 1880s became suffragists when assemblymen "listened politely but refused to act" upon temperance legislation. The view that Anne Firor Scott and others have painted of an orderly progression from Methodist missionary society to WCTU to suffrage may well be true for suffrage leaders at the state level, but this view does not account for the origins of suffrage support among Galvestonians. The great storm of 1900 was a major catalyst for women's involvement in city reconstruction and political reform, but organizational experience among women had preceded the storm by twenty years. The origins of a suffrage movement in Galveston began not with Frances Willard's organizing tour of the South but with the advent of urban problems brought on by the rapid rise of the city's population, the discrepancy in wealth among citizens, and the attendant dislocations caused by a more mobile and industrialized society. Members of the Galveston Women's Health Protective Association and other groups that had fought city hall in order to ensure pure milk for children or parks and playgrounds for their families were the most anxious to preserve their gains by winning the vote and by entering into public office. Women in southern cities with strong progressive agendas for reform had the most to gain from access to the voting booth.[28]

Other cities need to be tested, of course. In a cursory review of the founding of suffrage societies in other southern states, a similar pattern of dependence on urban centers prevailed. In most cases urban suffrage societies preceded permanent and viable state equal suffrage associations. A majority of the states experienced the beginning of fledgling state suffrage leagues in the 1890s, but they sputtered and died only to be resurrected after permanent local societies formed, usually after 1910. (See Table 1.)

Although urbanization acted as a catalyst in advancing suffrage, it was not the only causative agent. If that had been so, then suffrage societies would have formed in cities of the South a decade or two earlier, especially in some cities where the population was sufficient to bring women together in cohesive groups. Other factors contributed to the advance of the movement in the South, most notably the level of activity of women's civic reform clubs and associations in every city where suffrage eventually appeared. Women had to experience some form of politicization of their goals and values before they were ready to take on the struggle for their own rights. This study argues that the WCTU was only one organization (and a weak one at that) among many by 1910 that helped women gain the political savvy necessary to mobilize. Because cities provided the most common arena for politicizing women's goals, they were essential to the

28. For a discussion of the links connecting Methodism, the WCTU, and suffrage see Scott, *Southern Lady,* 144–48; Jean E. Friedman, *The Enclosed Garden: Women and Community in the Evangelical South, 1830–1900* (Chapel Hill: University of North Carolina Press, 1985), 111–20; and Hall, *Revolt against Chivalry,* 22, 25, 36, 66.

Table 1. Suffrage Associations by State.

The following table shows the state, the date and location of permanent suffrage organizations, whether the first association was local or state level, and the city population at the time or at the decade closest to the time of incorporation.

State	When Formed	Local	First Cities	Population
Alabama	1910	yes	Selma	13,600 (1910)
	1911		Birmingham	132,600 (1910)
Arkansas	1911	yes	Little Rock	46,000 (1910)
Florida	1912	yes	Jacksonville	57,699 (1910)
Georgia	1890	yes	Columbus	17,300 (1890)
	1894		Atlanta	65,500 (1890)
Kentucky	1888	no	Lexington	21,500 (1890)
Louisiana	1900	yes	New Orleans	287,000 (1900)
Maryland	1894	yes	Baltimore	434,000 (1890)
Mississippi	1906	no	Jackson	21,000 (1910)
Missouri	1910	yes	St. Louis	687,000 (1910)
North Carolina	1913	yes	Morganton	2,712 (1910)
	1913		Charlotte	34,000 (1910)
South Carolina	1914	no	Spartanburg	17,500 (1910)
	1914		Columbia	26,300 (1910)
	1914		Charleston	58,800 (1910)
Tennessee	1910	yes	Knoxville	36,300 (1910)
	1911		Nashville	110,000 (1910)
Texas	1908	yes	Austin	29,000 (1910)
	1912		San Antonio	96,600 (1910)
Virginia	1909	no	Richmond	127,000 (1910)

Sources: Elizabeth Cady Stanton et al., eds., *History of Woman Suffrage* 6:1–3, 16–19, 113–16, 121–22, 207–9, 216–19, 248–50, 326–29, 342–44, 490–93, 579–80, 596–99, 630–33, 665–66. U.S. Bureau of the Census, *Thirteenth Census of the United States Taken in the Year 1910.* Vol. 1. *Population* (Washington, D.C.: GPO, 1913), 80–97.

suffrage movement, more essential than the ideals of the WCTU. Southern suffrage at the grass roots should perhaps be viewed first as an urban-based phenomenon supported and maintained by women with an investment in community building and only secondarily as a movement fueled by evangelical reforming sentiment.[29]

How women used their political know-how, their traditional club training, and the opportunities provided by an urban environment can be illustrated through the activities of the Galveston Equal Suffrage Association members after 1912. In the first year suffragists made arrangements for no fewer than six speakers—from a local judge to National American Woman Suffrage Association President

29. Stanton et al., eds., *History of Woman Suffrage*, 6:1–3, 16–19, 113–16, 121–22, 207–9, 216–19, 248–50, 326–29, 342–44, 490–93, 579–80, 596–99, 630–33, 665–66. In a few of the state histories of suffrage authors made reference to the importance of cities to the movement. "As Baltimore is the only large city and contains more than half the population of the State it is not surprising that this city has been the real battleground of the movement" (248). "The movement did not gain much impetus until the Nashville League was organized in the fall of this year [1911] and Chattanooga and Morrison soon followed" (597). The smaller towns cited as forming first suffrage societies (Selma, Ala.; Columbus, Ga.; Morganton, N.C.; Spartanburg, S.C.; Austin, Tx.) were soon followed by the state's more populous cities. For a similar table extracted from *The History of Woman Suffrage* that shows southeastern interest in suffrage at its earliest (before a network of permanent local societies formed), see Margaret Nell Price, "The Development of Leadership by Southern Women through Clubs and Organizations" (Master's thesis, University of North Carolina, 1945), 97, and Scott, *The Southern Lady*, 177 n. 21. Price also observes that "suffrage agitation in the South falls roughly into three periods of time": 1) Before 1885 with individual interest and isolated societies, 2) 1885 to 1912, when some state-level associations formed, and 3) 1912 to 1920 when organizations that had disappeared revived and permanent local suffrage societies spread (96). The period roughly between 1912 and 1920 also coincided with the culmination in major southern cities of women's progressive civic reform activities. Prior to 1912 women worked for the betterment of their communities, and at the state level fought for "progressive" goals to improve health, child labor, prison reform, and education. The rise of women's civic and state reforming activities actually precedes the formation of permanent local societies suggesting a logical progression (Dewey W. Grantham, *Southern Progressivism: The Reconciliation of Progress and Tradition* [Knoxville: University of Tennessee Press, 1983], 200–217). Jean Friedman in *The Enclosed Garden* also maintains that a strong suffrage movement in the South was not possible until modernization triumphed over ties of kinship that prevented women from forming independent women's societies.

Anna Howard Shaw and Mrs. Philip Snowden of Great Britain. As time went on, GESA members held teas, set up a booth at the annual cotton carnival, and established headquarters inside a downtown store—all in order to distribute literature and gain new members. They performed in a suffrage play that entertained, educated, and brought in revenue. They raised money for the state coffers by soliciting pledges from wealthy men and women supporters within the city. They canvassed door to door for signatures on petitions to the Texas legislature for a constitutional amendment that would enfranchise women. They placed a subscription to the *Woman's Journal* in the public library, persuaded the local press to feature weekly articles on suffrage, and edited a "Suffrage Edition" in the *Galveston Tribune*. A representative from Galveston went to the NAWSA national convention in 1913, and other delegates attended the state convention through the years. The Galveston association hosted the state suffrage convention in 1915 and sent several of its own members, including its chapter president, to proselytize those parts of Texas where no suffrage leagues existed. The GESA persisted in such activities for most of its seven years before 1919. GESA women with their broad range of experience could perform most of these tasks blindfolded; there was nothing new to them about holding conventions, entertaining speakers, or raising money. And because it was familiar, it was a safe expression of feminist goals, demanding change without resorting to militancy.[30]

As necessary as these activities were to the development of the movement at the local level, they alone could not bring voting rights to the women of Texas. It also took an intensive lobbying approach to push the Texas legislature in the direction of suffrage. This meant that a few women leaders within the state would need to give up their local agendas and assume state-level priorities. Here, local suffrage societies performed one of their most important yet unassigned tasks: the fostering and "training" of women who would make suffrage and politics their careers. The Galveston Equal Suffrage Association "promoted" several such women to the state level, but none was more important or influential to the movement than Minnie Fisher Cunningham.

30. In Galveston 1917 and 1918 were slump years for suffrage activity, especially when the war intervened. *Galveston Tribune*, June 14, 1913; Wygant, "'Municipal Broom,'" 117–27; Taylor, "Woman Suffrage Movement in Texas," 27–28.

Having come to Galveston initially as a student, Minnie Fisher took a degree in pharmacy from the University of Texas Medical Department and then left the city to work and to marry. She and her husband, Beverly J. Cunningham, returned to Galveston in 1907. Just how the Galveston suffrage society and other women's clubs influenced Cunningham's decision to advance from local to state work can be seen in a series of letters she wrote to the second state suffrage president, Annette Finnigan.

Cunningham joined the GESA at its inception in 1912 but at the same time was also invited to become a member of the Wednesday Club, an exclusive women's literary club founded in 1891 that held its active roll to twenty-five members. Although Cunningham served as secretary, remained a member until 1916, and addressed the club on woman suffrage, she suspected that clubwomen in general were holding back the suffrage movement. This was confirmed for her in 1914 when the Texas Federation of Women's Clubs met in Galveston. First, the Wednesday Club "declined to give the Suffragists any part whatever in the entertainment of the Federation." Then the federation refused to endorse suffrage and would not allow Cunningham and other suffragists to speak openly about it. "I feel black and blue all over about that business," she wrote Finnigan. "I feel so culpable in allowing myself to be bound to silence on such an important subject. . . . I can't help regretting that I didn't make a 'scene!'" Later she cast aspersions on Fort Worth's "miserable antediluvian clubwomen" but saved her most critical asides for Mrs. Percy V. Pennybacker, a Texan and president of the General Federation of Women's Clubs, whom Cunningham regarded as a latecomer to the suffrage movement. Clearly Mrs. Cunningham was not cut out to be a clubwoman, yet she belonged to an age when no other avenue for women's civic activism was available. So she joined women's clubs, used them where she could to promote equal suffrage, and moved on.[31]

31. Membership roll, 1903–1919, and Program, 1912–1913, Wednesday Club Records, Rosenberg Library, Galveston. Letters among McCallum Papers: Mary Fowler Bornefeld to Annette Finnigan [October or November 1914]; Minnie Fisher Cunningham (MFC) to Annette Finnigan [November or December, 1914]; MFC to Annette Finnigan, [January 1915]. MFC to Carrie Chapman Catt, April 27, 1917, Minnie Fisher Cunningham Papers, Houston Metropolitan Research Center, Houston Public Library. Thanks to Janelle Scott for showing me this letter regarding Pennybacker. It should be

In 1914 the GESA elected Cunningham its president. She brought efficiency and zest to the organization but was compelled to leave it too, not for its members' lack of commitment, for as already evidenced they proved their dedication to the cause, but for what seemed to her their old-fashioned methods influenced by years of traditional club work. At one time she was optimistic and wrote Finnigan that the state could "count on Galveston for teamwork." Cunningham simply brimmed over with energy and ideas for how to promote the cause in Galveston. Her enthusiasm for suffrage outdistanced even her most ardent sisters in the GESA. But one frustration after another caused her to reconsider her position in local work.[32]

The beach headquarters incident illustrates her frustrations with the GESA's foot-dragging. She wrote Finnigan in May 1914,

> The darling hope of my heart for three years has been a beach headquarters in the summer, and open air speaking on excursion days. It seems to me we are letting a glorious opportunity to reach all Texas slip right through our fingers. . . . Last year we had money in the bank which we had made for the express purpose of establishing a headquarters, and because the price was high we kept our money in the bank. . . . I wish you could come down . . . and see the potential readers of Suffrage literature and listeners to Suffrage speeches wandering up and down the Boulevard with nothing to do.

A little later in the summer she pleaded, "But O! *Please* worry about Galveston! We should be doing so much more than we are." The state president approved her plan for a beach headquarters but could not afford to help with even one-half the cost. The Galveston women turned down the idea again and opted instead for a less expensive booth at the Cotton Carnival for one week in August. Even then, organizers were unable to make suffrage speeches on

noted that Cunningham's association with the Women's Health Protective Association, a civic organization rather than a literary club, was a happier one. In 1913 she assumed chairmanship of the School Hygiene Committee, which made an inspection of all the public schools. As a consequence, "conditions have been remedied, and relief has been afforded the school room" (*Galveston Daily News*, February 4, 1914). The following year, under the auspices of the WHPA, she worked toward the establishment of restrooms for women on the beaches and in the downtown area (November 4, 1914).

32. MFC to Finnigan, July 15, 1914, McCallum Papers.

Sunday "on account of a few *very* strict Sabbath keepers" in the association. Minnie Fisher Cunningham made the most of it, but she was clearly disappointed with the GESA's fiscal and religious conservatism.[33]

Cunningham's belief that Galveston suffragists did not do enough or spend enough on the movement was typical of the conflicts that would arise between state-level and local officers, or, to put it in historical context, between women whose volunteer careers had been shaped by a "popular women's culture" found in club work and women whose lives were fully engaged in feminist politics. Actually, the GESA offered no less support than did other local groups, and its conservatism and respectability aided the cause in other ways. Cunningham, however, was unusually impatient, the mark of a leader ready to move on to larger projects. Her attitudes were bound to create tension among the more traditional suffragists, and yet recognizing her talents, they reelected her president. She confided to Finnigan, "The Galveston organization at its annual meeting Saturday did me the honor of returning me to office for another year. In spite of my stern determination not to be returned. It makes me feel like a 'spell' of sickness to think of another year, but please don't tell on me." Cunningham was rescued from local work by her election to the state presidency in May 1915. Annette Finnigan had nothing but praise for her successor: "She [is] the best one for the Presidency. She has the time to give to the work, the ability, and I believe, the deepest interest in the cause."[34]

By then Cunningham's personal life was such that she was able to become a full-time servant for suffrage. Childless, she virtually took a sabbatical from her thirteen-year marriage. Putting the best face on the situation, she explained, "Mr. Cunningham and I have agreed that the fight is well worth giving up a lot for, and we will simply close the house and he will board, for as long as the State organization needs my services." Thus freed from domestic responsibilities and from what was for her the cloying conservatism of the Galveston association, she became one of the South's most effective state presidents. Both she and NAWSA president Carrie Chapman

33. MFC to Annette Finnigan, May 8, 1914, June 2, 1914; MFC to Perle Penfield, [July 16, 1914].

34. Hall and Scott, "Women in the South," 491; MFC to Finnigan, [January 1915]; Annette Finnigan to Mrs. J. S. Sweeny, June 5, 1915.

Catt came into office the same year; together they provided new energy and winning leadership for the suffrage movement.[35]

The Galveston Equal Suffrage Association continued to do what it did best—educate, organize, and raise money. Although successive presidents were competent, none had Cunningham's unique leadership ability. This is not to say that the more traditional civic leaders were unnecessary to the suffrage movement; on the contrary, to mobilize for suffrage both types were critically necessary. White-gloved New Women, rooted in the soil of their native city, held the community respect that was essential to dispel the taint of radicalism. They also remained in the city to encourage and lead other women and men in the cause of suffrage while their more peripatetic sisters canvassed the state. Local suffragists provided the home support essential to the firm planting of the movement. Women such as Minnie Fisher Cunningham, who made gaining passage of women's right to vote a career, moved on to the state level, constantly traveling, organizing, stumping, lobbying. Her leadership, drive, sacrifices, and organizational skills not only sustained her life in politics (she later ran for United States senator and governor) but also pushed the movement to its successful conclusion in the state of Texas.

It is time to look beyond filiopietistic notions of solidarity among white women and see the campaign for the vote as it was—a complex political movement destined to bulldoze aside forever the staid traditionalism of the nineteenth century. Clearly Cunningham thought that there were major differences between individual suffragists; she felt some, after years of conventional club work, were too conservative for the good of the movement. In any such mobilization there are tensions, rifts, slights, and worse. The results of these differences were beneficial to the movement, however; eager and aggressive leaders rose to the state level while more traditional community activists supported suffrage from their home bases. There was, it seems, room for both types in the Texas woman suffrage movement.

Historians of woman suffrage in the South have long tended to

35. MFC to Finnigan, [January 1915]; Eleanor Flexner, *Century of Struggle: The Woman's Rights Movement in the United States* (1959; reprint, New York: Atheneum, 1968), 272-73; Michael McGerr, "Political Style and Women's Power, 1830-1930," *Journal of American History* 77 (December 1990): 876-78.

view the movement from the lofty altitudes of state and regional politics and have assumed that suffrage support stemmed from frustrated evangelical church and WCTU members determined to impose temperance reform and a women's agenda upon an unredeemed South. The Galveston case suggests that the movement for the vote among women in the South at the local level was an urban-based phenomenon and that southern or Texas women, who may have been slow to respond to the national suffrage campaign, were nonetheless stirred to action on behalf of their own communities and their equal political and economic involvement in them. Galveston was a city that inspired great devotion from its women activists; some of them in return asked for the right to full electoral equality.

ॐ *Roseanne V. Camacho*

Race, Region, and Gender in a Reassessment of Lillian Smith

"Lillian Smith was born female, white, southern, at the threshold of the twentieth century. This convergence of gender, color, place and time afforded her vantage (some might say disadvantage) points shared by few writers. Each contributed, in obvious or subtle ways, to her stature as artist and human being."[1] Thus Paula Snelling described her colleague and companion, a southern writer who, well in advance of her time, advocated social and racial change in the South. As a writer, Lillian Smith was committed to both the creative imagination and human rights, to racial justice and to the South, to the modern sexuality of her generation and the conservative tradition of southern churchwomen. With a lifelong desire to bridge the categories that fragment life—white and black, North and South, man and woman—she crossed and recrossed the lines between fiction and nonfiction, between disciplines and readerships, inadvertently promoting a fragmentation of her work that persists today.

Several recent studies of Smith discuss her as an exception in some way and isolate one aspect of her thought at the expense of the rest. Morton Sosna's *In Search of the Silent South* (1977) includes Smith in the southern liberal tradition, even though she "did not typify Southern liberalism." Fred Hobson's *Tell About the South* (1983), which excludes novelists, makes an exception for Smith. Both of these studies praise Smith as a courageous writer but also see her as limited intellectually by her moralism. Smith's commitment to

1. Snelling, preface to *The Winner Names the Age: A Collection of Writings by Lillian Smith*, ed. Michelle Cliff (New York: W. W. Norton, 1978), 11.

157

change, couched in evangelical language, leaves her vulnerable to negative assessments of women as moral arbiters. Daniel Joseph Singal's book on modernism, *The War Within* (1982), on the other hand, isolates Smith's views on sexuality and questionably lists her as an early modernist because she described Victorian sexuality as repressive. And finally, Richard King's *A Southern Renaissance* (1980) includes Smith in a primarily literary study (which does not include other southern white women writers) because Smith was (paradoxically for a woman) concerned with "larger cultural, racial and political themes."[2]

These disjunctures point to the need for a fresh reading of Smith that highlights her experience as a southern white woman writer and illuminates the continuities between both southern women's history and current changes in literary criticism. Women's history, especially southern women's history, helps elucidate Smith's polarized self-image and fragmented critical reception by shifting the analysis from Smith as an individual to her work's relationship to widely accepted social norms for women. Smith pinpointed the central polarity, as she saw it, when she compiled materials in the early 1960s for her biography. Seeing her life as a "conflict between my creative daemon and my conscience," she named it for the Biblical sisters Mary and Martha.[3]

Anne C. Loveland's *Lillian Smith* (1986), a full-length biography and the first to consult extensively Smith's many unpublished letters, acknowledges the Mary/Martha split and documents Smith's desire to be recognized as Mary. But Loveland's account reduces the polarization to a personal matter:

2. Sosna, *In Search of the Silent South: Southern Liberals and the Race Issue* (New York: Columbia University Press, 1977), 201, 172–97; Hobson, *Tell About the South: The Southern Rage to Explain* (Baton Rouge: Louisiana State University Press, 1983), 321; Singal, *The War Within: From Victorian to Modernist Thought in the South, 1919–1945* (Chapel Hill: University of North Carolina Press, 1982), 373–75; King, *A Southern Renaissance: The Cultural Awakening of the American South, 1930–1955* (New York: Oxford University Press, 1980), 9.

3. Lillian Smith prepared over one hundred pages of autobiographical notes for Louise Blackwell, Frances Clay, and Margaret Sullivan. These pages and several other biographical summaries and chronologies are in Box 1 of the Lillian Smith Papers, Hargrett Rare Book and Manuscript Library, University of Georgia, Athens. Hereafter this collection will be cited as LSP.

The Mary/Martha split continued to shape her life. Her childhood sensibilities—her empathy and feelings of rejection, her aware- ness of contradictions—may explain her later involvement in civil rights, but the Mary/Martha split, *which represented an internal rather than an external contradiction,* exerted even more influence not only on her attitude toward race and segregation but on the greater part of her life and thought [emphasis added].[4]

Loveland uses Smith's Mary/Martha construction extensively but without exceeding the limits of Smith's own perceptions.[5] Yet Smith's own conceptualization of Mary/Martha testifies to a specific histor- ical context, which Loveland does not read. That context is especially indicated in two forces affecting Smith's writing and the reception of her work: the New Criticism and the civil rights movement.

In Smith's view, the New Critics of the 1940s and 1950s, especially John Crowe Ransom, Allen Tate, and Robert Penn Warren, who had been Agrarians in the 1930s and Fugitives at Vanderbilt University in the 1920s, produced a new aesthetic that allowed a generation of intellectuals to avoid the imperative for racial change, which Smith considered essential to any southern writer. Yet Smith shared much with these southern men of letters: a generational relationship to southern history, a loyalty to the region, a reverence for the power of literature, and a background of the white, middle-class, non- aristocratic South. To understand her points of opposition to the Agrarians is to admit the relevance of women's history and gender in the Southern Renaissance, that flowering of southern writing dating from the 1920s to the 1960s.[6] Women's history, that is, the analytical account of women's experience, illuminates the para- doxes of Smith's position as a white southern woman writer of this period. Further, an analysis of gender opens such questions as how men and women's social relations bear on the language they use as writers, and how the southern context affects this interaction.[7] The

4. An earlier work by Louise Blackwell and Frances Clay, *Lillian Smith* (New York: Twayne Publishers, 1971), purports to concentrate on Smith's literary work but misplaces her in a tradition of naturalism. Loveland, *Lillian Smith, A Southerner Confronting the South: A Biography* (Baton Rouge: Louisiana State University Press, 1986), 21.

5. Margaret Rose Gladney, review of Loveland's *Lillian Smith* in *Southern Changes* (March 1987): 14.

6. The Southern Renaissance is defined here to include literature, his- tory, the social sciences, and journalism.

7. For a discussion of gender and historical analysis, see Joan Scott,

consequences of gender differences, for example, emerge clearly from a comparison of Smith and one of the Agrarians, John Crowe Ransom, on the specific case of religion. Southern religion, fundamentalist and unscientific, was at the center of the controversial Scopes Trial in 1925. That trial not only publicized the South as an intellectual desert but stimulated responses among southerners, including John Crowe Ransom, who would emerge as intellectual leaders in the Southern Renaissance.

Of all the Agrarians, Ransom most directly discussed religion and art. In addition, and more importantly, he dealt with religion in conformity with his, and consequently the New Criticism's, treatment of art. Both he and Lillian Smith were reared in southern Methodism, and both modified the religion of their upbringing to meet the challenges of the early twentieth century in significantly different ways. Both were young adults in the 1920s, children of Reconstruction-born parents, grandchildren of Civil War soldiers and/or survivors. Within living family memories, they reexperienced those enduring crises of southern history, the Civil War and Reconstruction. Born in the decades of the most violent repression of black Americans since the Civil War, when the era of Jim Crow opened, Smith and Ransom were children of a culture in which the survival of the social order depended on intense loyalty to a way of life. White writers of this period refashioned that loyalty to their particular view of southern history and their needs of the present. Any writer who accepted the label "southern," as Smith and Ransom did, needed a workable definition of "loyalty" that would not compromise aesthetics, and vice versa.[8]

Ransom, the son and grandson of Methodist ministers, wrote about his religious background at the same time that he helped write about Agrarian politics. In *God without Thunder*, published in 1930, the same year as the Agrarian manifesto *I'll Take My Stand: The South and the Agrarian Tradition*, he rejected the religion he said evolved with the rise of science, "one which adapt[ed] itself to the requirements of our aggressive modern science." According to Ransom,

---

"Gender: A Useful Category of Historical Analysis," *American Historical Review* 91 (December 1986): 1053–75.

8. Smith and Snelling, "Yes . . . We Are Southern," *South Today* 7 (Spring 1943): 41–44, esp. 42; "Introduction: A Statement of Principles," written primarily by John Crowe Ransom, in *I'll Take My Stand: The South and the Agrarian Tradition* (New York: Harper & Brothers Publishers, 1930), ix–xx.

the more appropriate contemporary religion would be one that respected the gap between man and God, between the supernatural and the natural, between the knowable and the unknowable. Making one's God a knowable one, he argued, was an unacceptable concession to science, for science would then define the powers to know, and in a denial of myth and belief it would assign religion "simply to attend to the morals of mankind."[9]

To Ransom, American Methodism had already confused this hierarchy of knowledge over moral conduct by affirming a policy of the social gospel. Ransom disdained religious "do-gooders" and outlined religion proper as the knowledge and worship of God. An uncannily similar distinction originates in the historical break between the churches of the North and South around the time of the Civil War. According to religious historian Samuel Hill, Jr., the South, remaining evangelical after the Civil War, resisted a religion of "good works." The result was that "morality is construed in ahistorical categories, for it is associated with *being*, rather than doing," an ethos without an ethic. But for Ransom, knowledge, and not just being, constituted the first order, correcting what he considered an undesirable emotional bias in southern evangelism.[10]

Southern Methodism, however, did include an ethic of social practice, commonly called "women's work," or missionary work, at home and abroad. Within the decades of the New Woman, roughly between 1880 and 1920, the missions offered many middle-class, southern white women romance, adventure, a public voice, and, most important, an autonomous structure within which to operate. For these women, the separation of proper religion from social action threatened their changing views of self, views shaped in varying degrees by their missionary activity, which was itself laced with gender conflict:

> The distinction between the spiritual and social spheres, so precious to much of southern religion, including Methodism, and so embedded in its history, was antithetical to these southern women's ideas. They believed that the work of women in other denomina-

9. John Crowe Ransom, *God without Thunder: An Unorthodox Defense of Orthodoxy* (New York: Harcourt, Brace and Co., 1930), 5, 12.

10. Hill, Jr., et al., *Religion and the Solid South* (New York: Abingdon Press, 1972), 35. See also Hill, *The South and the North in American Religion* (Athens: University of Georgia Press, 1980), 140–41.

tions had been seriously hampered by men who demanded a "strict separation of church and political activities," and they rejoiced that they, with more autonomy, had been able to bridge the separation.[11]

The philosophy of the social gospel, insofar as it existed in southern Methodism, influenced Lillian Smith. Women's participation in the social gospel in the South, however, touched her not through her mother, whose generation had created the separate woman's sphere of activity, but through her oldest sister, who went to the China missions in 1910 as a newlywed. Bertha "Birdie" Smith Barnett and her husband Eugene E. Barnett both joined the Student Volunteer Movement while in college and dedicated their lives to "the evangelization of the world in this generation."[12] Smith recalled the influence of her sister's regular letters to the family as widening everyone's vision beyond the Western world. She claimed that Birdie's experience in the East affected the family as fundamentally as their maternal grandfather's northern origins had: "We spoke of the world [and] we meant East and West; we spoke of Americans [and] we meant North and South."[13]

The missions, however, were in decline when Smith herself went to China in 1922. She called herself an agnostic and went to teach music, not to evangelize. Living in China, however, constituted an

11. John Patrick McDowell, *The Social Gospel in the South: The Woman's Home Mission Movement in the Methodist Episcopal Church, South, 1886–1939* (Baton Rouge: Louisiana State University Press, 1982), 27–28, quoting Mrs. J. W. Mill, "Vice-President's Report," *Twenty-sixth Annual Report of the Woman's Missionary Council,* 54–55. See also Noreen Dunn Tatum, *A Crown of Service* (Nashville: The Parthenon Press, 1960), for a history of Methodist Episcopal Church South's effort in the foreign missions. For women's participation in foreign mission activities of the Protestant church, see Patricia R. Hill, *The World Their Household: The American Woman's Foreign Mission Movement and Cultural Transformation, 1870–1920* (Ann Arbor: University of Michigan Press, 1985), and Jane Hunter, *The Gospel of Gentility: American Women Missionaries in Turn-of-the-Century China* (New Haven: Yale University Press, 1984).

12. Interview with Eugenie Schultheis, daughter of Bertha and Eugene Barnett, August 12, 1989. The Student Volunteer Movement, founded in 1886, was a national, interdenominational recruiting organization for the missions. It was strongest in the midwestern states but enrolled college students from all over the country for missionary service.

13. Lillian Smith, autobiographical materials, LSP.

intellectual awakening for her, as she recognized the divisive effects of colonialism. Although she was critical of the narrow prejudices of the mostly southern women with whom she worked, they were strong role models in a way that would become important to her as a southern writer: "Once this writer lived in China and worked in a mission school. Though she saw many mistakes made by missionaries, many instances of stupidity and ignorance, much blind following of inappropriate American cultural patterns, she never saw one act of fear."[14] Such a lack of fear would prove useful when Smith began to write about race at home.

The points of divergence, then, between Smith and Ransom are to be found in southern religious history and its gender conventions. While Ransom held to the already distinct southern theology of ethos or belief over behavior, Smith clearly aligned herself with the tenuous bridge between evangelism and social action in women's missionary work. Smith and Ransom not surprisingly drew different conclusions from the gender base of their religious upbringings. Ransom moved from the historical paradigm of knowledge over conduct to a corresponding hierarchy in his literary criticism: poetry over science. At eighty, when he wrote a new introduction to his essays, he remained true to his views of 1930:

> The true poetry has no great interest in improving or idealizing the world, which does well enough. It only wants to realize the world, to see it better. Poetry is the kind of knowledge by which we must know what we have arranged that we shall not know otherwise. We have elected to know the world through our science, and we know a great deal, but science is only the cognitive department of our animal life, and by it we know the world only as a scheme of abstract conveniences. What we cannot know constitutionally as scientists is the world which is made of whole and indefeasible objects, and this is the world which poetry recovers for us.[15]

Even though science is here alienating and inadequate as a means of knowledge, the New Criticism itself became known as a "sci-

14. Smith, "Humans in Bondage," in *Winner Names the Age*, 53, originally published in *Social Action*, February 15, 1944.

15. Ransom, *The World's Body* (1938; reprint Baton Rouge: Louisiana State University Press, 1968), x-xi.

ence." This development is sometimes called ironic, yet a consistency lies in the preexisting gender bias of science as male and emotion as female. For although southern male writers such as Ransom chafed against northern dominance over the South, their dissatisfaction did not undermine the gender bias in the concept of domination itself. Ransom's taking exception to the North-South relationship did not threaten the explanatory power of masculine as "subject" and feminine as "other" in the New Criticism. The language of male domination, for example, is evident in his description of woman as essentially emotion and man as intellect:

> A Woman lives for love, if we will but project that term to cover all her tender fixations upon natural objects of sense, some of them more innocent and far less reciprocal than men. Her devotion to them is more gallant, it is fierce and importunate, and cannot but be exemplary to the hardened male observer. . . . The minds of man and woman grow apart, and how shall we express their differentiation? In this way, I think: man, at best, is an intellectualized woman. Or, man distinguishes himself from woman by intellect, but it should be well feminized.[16]

While Ransom valued hierarchy and stability, Smith supported the motto of the Women's Missionary Council for whom she worked in China: "Grow we must, even if we outgrow all that we love."[17] Smith had already outgrown the missionary structure even as she was part of it, yet the rhetoric of growth, in which a future is implied, continued to attract her. As a construct through which she viewed all her experience, the concept of growth resisted the fixed natures that Ransom's philosophy prized. Ransom's comments on religion, southern politics, and his literary aesthetic, which span his career, affirm a static, not dynamic, tradition, for when Ransom left Agrarianism behind him he invested the stability of a civilized society in universal truths.

Smith, on the other hand, embraced change. In the very first

16. Ransom, "The Poet as Woman," *Southern Review* 2 (1937): 784. These sentiments in the 1937 essay on the poetry of Edna St. Vincent Millay were anthologized in *The World's Body* (1938) and reissued in 1968 without further comment.

17. On the Women's Missionary Council, see Tatum, *A Crown of Service*, 29–37.

issue of her magazine in 1936, she wrote to explain its name: "The name *Pseudopodia* was chosen . . . partly to give encouragement to certain of those whose attempts at artistic expression have met with obstacles and rebuffs." She defined a pseudopod as "a temporary and tender projection of the nucleus or inner-self, upon the success of whose gropings the nucleus is entirely dependent for its progress and sustenance."[18]

The "nucleus" was the climate of change within the South, which was sustained by the movements of writers already in progress. It was also Smith's changing self as a professional woman writer, moving tentatively but steadily into a public arena. The magazine's successive titles *Pseudopodia* (1936–1937), *North Georgia Review* (1937–1941), and *South Today* (1942–1945) reflect its expanding stages of growth and confidence.

Meanwhile, John Crowe Ransom's rhetoric reaffirmed the gender status quo; that is, his vision of poetry's new knowledge was a reformation of science-in-art, where he had tamed impersonal science with "feminization." Like other Agrarians, he affirmed the racial status quo by omission. Smith, in contrast, with her conception of the future, destabilized what the South had accepted as fixed and inevitable, especially concerning race. And just as Ransom reconstructed a science out of need, Smith leaned on the new sciences of psychology and sociology to reject religion's stark division of body and soul, its repression of body, and its endorsement of racial separation.[19] But she did not relinquish religion's affirmation of change through redemption and forgiveness, or more practically, women's work. The historical roles of men and women in nineteenth-century southern religion thus influenced both Smith's and Ransom's treatment of the twentieth-century South.

Playing the role of the biblical Martha, Smith turned her own domestic obligations into opportunities for growth and change. Martha's obligations arose from the family at crucial times in Smith's

18. Smith and Snelling, *Pseudopodia* 1 (Spring 1936): 6.

19. For the role of social sciences, especially sociology, in the changes in racial theory during this period from biological to culturally determined differences, see Vernon Williams, Jr., *From a Caste to a Minority: Changing Attitudes of American Sociologists toward Afro-Americans, 1896–1945* (New York: Greenwood Press, 1989).

life. Her father, for example, called her home from China in 1925 to direct a summer camp he had started. Ten years later, just as she had seriously begun writing, her mother needed constant care. Mary, the creative self, turned these obligations into intellectual challenges. She slowly modified the activities of Laurel Falls Camp to eliminate competition in favor of the creative arts, taught by college-educated women from all over the country. More significantly, she introduced and worked in a practical way with the theories of psychology that had interested her since her return from China. The result was a camp with a philosophy that encouraged maximum personal growth and supported a continuously developing group discussion of race and sexuality. It offered white, middle-class girls at Laurel Falls something besides the traditional southern belle as a role model.[20]

When Smith began to care for her widowed and invalid mother, she was Martha again. But with the help of Paula Snelling, who was her assistant camp director at Laurel Falls Camp, Smith turned the situation into Mary's work by creating the magazine *Pseudopodia*. The magazine took half their year's schedule and running the camp filled the other half. The two women continued this collaboration for nearly ten years. With no money and no backing, either organizational or academic, they set out to discuss southern writers and encourage unpublished ones—black or white—to voice their concerns about the South. It was unprecedented to publish black and white writers together, much less to assume that they would have common interests. The magazine recognized black authors of southern experience who had left the region, while covering the widest discussions of the period now called the Southern Renaissance: southern history, economics, sociology, religion, and literature. Writers for the magazine discussed virtually every new book on the

20. Margaret Rose Gladney, "A Chain Reaction of Dreams: Lillian Smith and Laurel Falls Camp," *Journal of American Culture: Studies of a Civilization* 5 (Fall 1982): 50–55. Paula Snelling, who was teaching math during the winters and working at the camp in summers, received an M.A. from Columbia Teachers College in 1925, studying psychology as well as education. It was no doubt her influence that prompted Smith's readings of Freud, Rank, Adler, and others. Smith also studied psychology in the semester she spent at Columbia Teachers College in the winter of 1927–1928.

South in this period, fiction and nonfiction, published in and out of the South. And through this forum, Lillian Smith was one of the earliest white southerners, if not the first, to denounce racial segregation in print.[21]

The camp and the magazine illustrate Mary, the "creative daemon," reworking the domestic obligations of Martha, the conscience, in Smith's personal life, but they can also represent expectations for women of Smith's generation who were held to traditional family obligations while attracted to the professions of modern women. The intellectual and creative Mary was Smith's primary identification, yet Martha inscribed all that Smith did for an understanding of race: magazine editorials, speeches, and writings dating from 1936 that advocated social change in the South. Martha embodies extended domesticity, a nineteenth-century justification of women's public activities, their involvement in social causes from sanitation to suffrage and temperance. Mary and Martha represent the opposite ends of a spectrum of shifting cultural norms, moving from a model of true womanhood to the New Woman, who could be independent, intelligent, and sexual.

Mary and Martha were in fullest harmony in the early years of Smith's career, from the first issues of *Pseudopodia* in the 1930s until the publication of *Killers of the Dream* in 1949. It is from this period, specifically 1939, that Hobson and Sosna derive their view of Smith as comfortable with her missionary image and reformist zeal. The debate on the South and its literature seemed open at that time, and Smith and Snelling were interested in southern literature as therapeutic for the region. They had planned a critical study of southern literature within its entire cultural and political context, but never completed the project because of the financial success of *Strange Fruit*, Smith's controversial novel dealing with interracial romance. Within two years of *Strange Fruit* (1944), the camp closed and the magazine ceased publication, in spite of a subscription list of nearly 10,000. Even through the *Strange Fruit* years, Mary and Martha remained in good balance, for commentators on the novel ranged from Malcolm Cowley to W. E. B. Du Bois, a suitable Mary/Martha mix. Smith became known as both spokesperson for the South on

21. Lillian Smith, "Buying a New World with Old Confederate Bills," *South Today* 7 (Winter 1942–1943): 7–30.

racial issues and as a popular novelist, and her reputation grew distinct from Snelling's.[22]

With the publication of *Killers of the Dream* five years later, Smith's treatment of race was no longer a literary issue but an unequivocal challenge to white supremacy. As Smith's best-known and some would argue best-written book, *Killers of the Dream* is confessional literature, distilled from her magazine's editorials and her memories of a segregated childhood in northern Florida. It converted Smith's childhood into an allegory of the reproduction of white supremacy in each generation, and aimed to move white southerners to a symbolic confession, a recognition of the evil of segregation.[23] With this book's reception, however, the harmony of Mary and Martha began to jar.

22. Lillian Smith, *Killers of the Dream* (New York: W. W. Norton, 1949). Both Hobson, *Tell About the South*, 314, and Sosna, *In Search of the Silent South*, 183, cite a report to the Rosenwald Fund in which Lillian Smith admits her desire to help the South reform. The Julius Rosenwald Fund fellowships, shared by Smith and Snelling in 1939–1940 and 1940–1941, were granted to support the joint literary study by Smith and Snelling, traveling for the magazine, and Smith's fiction writing. See Smith and Snelling, "Plans for Continuation of Work, Submitted with Application for Renewal of Joint Fellowship for Additional Half Year," in *South Today* Papers, Lillian Smith Collection, University of Florida Library, Gainesville. Snelling outlined this argument in "Southern Fiction and Chronic Suicide," *North Georgia Review* 3 (Summer 1938): 3–6, 25–28; esp. 3. *Strange Fruit* received attention from literary critics and social commentators. Bernard DeVoto gave *Pseudopodia* national attention in "Regionalism or the Coterie Manifesto," *Saturday Review* (November 28, 1936): 8. When *Strange Fruit* was banned in Boston, DeVoto covered the controversy in his column, "The Easy Chair," in *Harper's* (May 1944): 525–28; (July 1944): 148–51; (February 1945): 225–28. See also DeVoto, "The Decision in the *Strange Fruit* Case, The Obscenity Statute in Massachusetts," *The New England Quarterly* 19 (June 1946): 147–83. For other reviews of *Strange Fruit*, see Malcolm Cowley, "Southways," *New Republic* (March 6, 1944): 320–22, and William [E. B.] Du Bois, "Searing Novel of the South," *New York Times Book Review* (March 5, 1944): 1, 20.

23. Earlier titles for *Killers of the Dream* were *Mr. White Man* and *Give Them Tears*. See Smith's letter to Norman Cousins, May 9, 1936, Lillian Smith–Norman Cousins Correspondence, Hargrett Rare Book and Manuscript Library, University of Georgia, Athens; Smith letter to Motier Harris Fisher, [June 1940], and Fisher to Smith, July 24, 1940, in *South Today* Papers, Lillian Smith Collection; Lillian Smith, "Break Their Hearts, Oh God. Give Them Tears," *North Georgia Review* 4 (Winter 1939–1940): 22, and "No Easy Way—Now," in *Winner Names the Age*, 76–90, esp. 77.

After World War II, with racial advocacy argued increasingly in legal and democratic terms, *Killers of the Dream* too clearly pointed out the need for change in the basic social order of the South, namely legal segregation, in order to achieve southern democracy. Smith parted company at this point with southern moderates, who favored a slow, rational, evolutionary change and who positioned themselves precariously between what they called the two radical extremes of those who attacked segregation and those who upheld white supremacy.[24]

Southerners understandably resisted or ignored *Killers of the Dream*, although it remains unclear whether there was actually a conspiracy to stifle the distribution of Smith's next book, *Now Is the Time* (1955).[25] The point is, however, that for Smith the balance between Mary and Martha tipped as civil rights activity gained momentum. Beginning with *Killers of the Dream*, Smith's practical, Martha image dominated and continued to do so for virtually the rest of her life, creating tension and ambivalent feelings as she sought validation as a serious writer.

Leading southern liberal Ralph McGill was among those southern journalists who reviewed *Killers of the Dream*. He described Smith's "sin-sex-segregation" analysis thus: "I know Miss Smith to be a sincere, honest person, but also to be a zealot, burning with a bright blue flame, a person whose own psychological agony cries from her words; whose long service as a missionary across the seas has not assuaged the invisible spurs which obviously rowel her; which also has not quenched the passion of her fervent witnessing for the Savior." McGill's review suggested condescendingly that Smith was not only disturbed but a reformer hysterically bound by religious

24. Ralph McGill in particular represented the moderate position to Smith. Smith praised McGill, Virginius Dabney, and Jonathan Daniels as prominent liberal newspapermen, yet later disagreed with them over their reticence to condemn segregation. See *North Georgia Review* 6 (Winter 1940): 53. For a full discussion of Smith and southern liberals on segregation, see Loveland, *Lillian Smith*, 38–63.

25. Smith was convinced that there was a conspiracy to withhold distribution of *Now Is the Time*. See her letters to Frank Taylor, editor of *Strange Fruit*, December 15, 1955, and February 17, 1956; and Taylor to Smith, April 18, 1956. Concerning Smith's "smothering" after *Killers of the Dream*, see letters to Jerry Bick, in negotiations to movie rights to *Strange Fruit*, September 9, 1961, and William Targ, of World Publishing Company, February 24, 1963, LSP.

fervor. Smith indeed sought the effectiveness of an evangelical preacher in her appeal to the South, based on her psychological analysis of cultural reproduction. Her approach, unlike the predominantly economic analyses of southern liberals, allowed her to bypass the liberal's dilemma over segregation. She tapped the language of evangelism precisely because of her specific cultural audience: the white South. But her relationship to the South was an ambiguous one of privilege afforded her by race on one hand, and disloyalty to white supremacy on the other. She recognized that she was part of an oppressive order and thought that admission of guilt was a crucial bridge to change. As a woman she could be disloyal to such a past because she saw it not primarily as women's making, even as she used her whiteness for entry into southern discourse on race. Her use of evangelical rhetoric testified to her historical connection with women's work, not to Jesus Christ, whom she mentioned only to contrast Christian teachings with southern praxis.[26]

Like other women positioned between the Woman Movement, which waned in her childhood, and the Women's Movement, which emerged just after her death, Smith basically sought acceptance on human terms. She never considered herself either a churchwoman or a feminist.[27] In her chapter on women in *Killers of the Dream*, for example, she categorized white southern women on the basis of their response to the dilemma of being put on a pedestal, defended in the name of chivalry, and held above black women who served as mammies to their children and sexual objects to their husbands. A minority of white women, she said, avoided this dilemma by demanding equality with men. She described these women unflatteringly as "a kind of fibroid growth of sick cells multiplying aggressiveness in an attempt at cure." Most southern white women, however, she said, turned their attention to homes where "food and

26. McGill, "Miss Smith and Freud," *Atlanta Constitution* (November 24, 1949), 18-B.

27. Nancy F. Cott in *The Grounding of Modern Feminism* (New Haven: Yale University Press, 1987) argues that the term *feminism* came into use in the early twentieth century "when *the woman movement* began to sound archaic." Feminists had "vital connections with the suffrage movement. The meaning of Feminism (capitalized at first) also differed from the woman movement. It was both broader and narrower: broader in intent, proclaiming revolution in all the relations of the sexes, and narrower in the range of its willing adherents" (3).

flowers were cherished, and old furniture, and the family's past (screened of all but the pleasing and the trivial)."[28]

But there was yet another minority of white women who protested their dilemma by organizing the Association of Southern Women for the Prevention of Lynching (ASWPL). "These women worked like the neat, industrious housewives they really were, using their mops and brooms to clean up a dirty spot here and there but with no real attempt to change this way of life which they dimly realized had injured themselves and their children as much as it had injured Negroes, but which they nevertheless clung to." In Smith's own metaphor of domesticity, these women were "Marthas," and they included women whom Smith admired, like Jessie Daniel Ames, who founded the ASWPL, and her successor Dorothy Tilly. Yet Smith considered herself a generation apart from these women. She brought sexuality to the analysis of the South in *Killers of the Dream:* "Few of them had disciplined intellects or giant imaginations and probably no one of them grasped the full implications of this sex-race-religion-economics tangle, but they had warm hearts and powerful energy and a nice technic for bargaining, and many an old cagey politician, and a young one or two, have been outwitted by their soft bending words."[29]

Richard King, in *A Southern Renaissance,* argues that by the mid-1950s, after the reaction to *Killers of the Dream,* Smith had turned entirely to the civil rights movement. Smith was in fact intent on withdrawing her creative energies, although not her support, from civil rights to focus on writing her last novel, *One Hour,* in which she wanted

28. Smith, *Killers of the Dream,* 137–38.
29. Ibid., 143. Smith's concerns were framed in the white southerner's experience. Although she read black literature extensively, she did not credit black women's organized protest as she did white women who organized against lynching. She wrote about Jessie Daniel Ames, for example, and Dorothy Tilly but not about black clubwomen such as Ida B. Wells, Mary Church Terrell, and Josephine St. Pierre Ruffin, who had organized to protest lynching before Smith was born. In the first year of publication, *Pseudopodia* listed groups in which the numbers of women predominated— the interracial movement, the YWCA, and the Student Volunteer Movement—calling them "sugar-coated but nonetheless worthy efforts," as liberal forces, along with the Southern Regional Committee, the Social Science Research Council, and liberal journalists (*Pseudopodia* 1 [Fall 1936]: 8).

to move beyond the South and race.[30] Within literary circles, where she sought legitimate recognition, the success of her southern contemporaries as New Critics had confirmed a separation of literature and aesthetics from politics or social action. In the 1950s Smith strove to accommodate a growing tension between a literary aesthetic that minimized the validity of historical difference and the civil rights movement that confronted difference. While she suppressed both race and gender in *The Journey* (1954), a philosophical essay and personal narrative of her search for meaning, she described *Now Is the Time* (1955) as propaganda for school desegregation. *One Hour* would continue to avoid both race and region, sources of Smith's politics. The gap widening between Smith's Mary and Martha in the 1950s cannot be credited to Smith's paranoia about literary recognition but demonstrates the political as inseparable from her in all her writing.[31]

When the novel *One Hour* (1959) was not a success, Smith revised *Killers of the Dream* for reissue in 1961. She took the opportunity to criticize openly her southern literary contemporaries, something she had not done publicly for decades:

> No writers in literary history have failed their region as completely as these did. They called themselves Fugitives; some preferred the name, Agrarians. . . . [They] recognized the evils of industrialized society; they saw clearly the increasing anonymity of men's activities, they recognized the overesteem of the scientific method. . . . But instead of confronting these new realities the Fugitives turned away, after some eloquent denunciations, and sought the ancient "simplicities." In their search most of them ended up on northern campuses. . . . And because their tones were cultured, even though their minds were not wholly so, they had great influence on the youngsters, sensitive, bright, who were their students: persuading many of them to refuse commitment to a future that was bound to be difficult.[32]

Near the end of her career, Smith saw that her primary identification as a creative writer, as she had conceptualized it over a lifetime,

30. King, *Southern Renaissance*, 4; Smith to Denver Lindley, editor of *One Hour*, October 27, 1956, LSP. The novel was published by Harcourt, Brace and Co., 1959.

31. The personal as inseparable from the political eludes Loveland's analysis, *Lillian Smith*, 21.

32. Smith, *Killers of the Dream* (New York: W. W. Norton, revised edition, 1961; reprinted by Anchor Books, 1963), 199–200.

did not conform with race, region, or gender as they were delineated in literary circles. In 1963 she wrote in frustration to her publisher: "The literary people never mention my name: if they write about books on race they never mention *Strange Fruit*; if they write about southern novelists or writers they never mention me; if they write about women writers they ostentatiously leave me out."[33]

Smith's desire to be recognized as a serious writer, regardless of her race, sex, or region, conforms to her philosophy of liberal humanism as a dream of the resolution of differences. In practice, however, "universal" models are more often grounded in experiences of a dominant gender, race, or class, leaving those of difference with an unequal imaginative access to what is the perceived as "universal" art. Smith's imagination was not captured by the southern yeoman model of independence, Jeffersonian agrarianism, or the Old South. She was primarily engaged in what she hoped was a process of change, the goals of which would threaten white male supremacy, not only in the South, but in the Western world. She had written, for example, in 1943 of "old minorities [which] are combining to form the new world majority" and that "it is just possible that the white man is no longer the center of the universe," as she argued for a world democracy of cooperation over competition.[34]

Her imagination was spurred primarily by the possibilities of emotion and reason together, of the union of art and science; she claimed both reason and a "mythic mind" were necessary for great art. Her contemporaries, the Agrarians, dismissed this dream because of the hostility of science, arguing that the gap, if anything, deserved widening.[35] Smith, however, brought her own history and experience to this long-established debate over the threat science posed to religion or literature. Her preference for synthesis rather than separatism no doubt derived in part from southern women's historical role as survivors in the face of catastrophic defeat, whether war or slavery, but also from her unspoken determination that "New Women," professional and intellectuals like herself,

33. Smith to William Targ, February 24, 1963, LSP.
34. Smith, "Buying a New World with Old Confederate Bills," 11, 23, 29.
35. Allen Tate, "The Present Function of Criticism," in *Collected Essays* (Denver: Alan Swallow, 1959), 3–15. See also Matthew Arnold, "The Function of Criticism at the Present Time," in *The Norton Anthology of English Literature*, 2 vols., ed. M. H. Abrams (New York: W. W. Norton, 1962), 2:908–29.

would assume their part in any public discourse. In spite of her lack of gender consciousness per se, Smith pursued a lifelong project of making the terms of the "universal" discourse—the rhetoric of democracy, individualism, and humanism—work for her experiences, even though that selfsame rhetoric had historically served to exclude.

Bridging the gaps, in other words, was always Smith's solution, beginning with her treatment of race and ending with her own inclusion as an intellectual. Her literary magazine had included black southern writers and southern social scientists. By the 1950s, the Mary/Martha split put Smith herself as a writer in jeopardy. Yet she continued to subscribe to liberal humanism as the philosophical bridge between the polarities that organize thinking:

> I wonder why it is so hard for us to accept these two partners out of which comes life, this dualism out of which unity is created. There is always a question, and an answer, before knowledge is found. We know everything creative that concerns human existence comes in pairs: freedom and responsibility, faith and doubt, the question and the answer, risk and security, the child and his grown-up self, past and future, wonder and certainty, pain and pleasure, male and female, sex and love, the dream and reality, victory and defeat, man and God. Keep them together, we have a whole, we have life; cut them apart, we find death at the center.[36]

Accepting the dualities theoretically meant inclusion and egalitarianism. Representative "man" remained her point of reference, and groups in her work were either alienating or ruled by the irrationality of a mob. Smith did not challenge polar differences but tried to rotate the hierarchical axis to an egalitarian, horizontal plane.

Smith's essays and speeches counterpoint the deceptively placid surface of this humanistic philosophy that was her real religion. In *Winner Names the Age*, some of these works illustrate the tensions and points of difference between Smith and other southerners of her time. The book's first section concerns the South in the years from World War II to the civil rights movement and contrasts starkly with the work of moderate southern liberals. For at a time when southern liberals talked of postponing claims of rights for black Americans for the sake of a national solidarity in the war effort, Smith

36. Lillian Smith, *The Journey* (Cleveland: The World Publishing Co., 1954), 56.

supported them. She spoke of the fears and warped perceptions of whites about blacks and the origins of these fears in childhood, and included a speech given in 1960, "The Moral and Political Significance of the Students' Non-Violent Protests."[37] That no others championed these views so pointedly or so early in the southern white liberal press, underscores Smith's historical significance.

The book's second section, on creativity and language, reveals the contrast between Smith and her contemporaries, the Agrarians. All of these entries were written after 1950 when the Mary/Martha split emerged. She insisted on the need for commitment among writers and the need to bridge the deep divisions in Western culture, especially the division between reason and feeling. And a third section, on women and men, shows Smith with a pre-feminist consciousness in the last years of her life, wondering why no Western woman had written a representative autobiography and asking, "Whom, among the mighty, have I so greatly offended!"[38]

Once Smith had taken her stand on race, her relationship to the literary and political worlds was unalterably fixed as long as the arbitrary lines of racial separation held. She linked race and gender in her criticism of the South without endorsing strategic separatism for either blacks or women; she used all of her resources to construct new meanings for the old rhetorics of democracy, liberalism, and humanism, much as women constructed every possible argument for suffrage when the point of resistance would not give. But for her as a writer, the strategy ended in ambiguities and silences.

In this perspective, Smith's stand on race, far from being an anomaly, can be understood in the context of historical and gender-specific structures in religion, enhanced by her generation's modern—that is, sexual—agenda. Her work and its reception illustrate the difficulties she had bridging the gap between her own and the preceding generations. In 1963, with an eye to the coming generation of women, Smith reviewed Betty Friedan's *The Feminine Mystique* for the *Saturday Review*. She predicted to her editor that the book would "stir up an enormous amount not of controversy but of fresh thinking on what is actually a situation which pales out the racial situation." Understandably, fresh thinking did not come without

37. Smith, *Winner Names the Age*, 91–99.
38. Smith, "Extracts from Three Letters," in *Winner Names the Age*, 212–18, esp. 218.

controversy, and it has not solved the private/public dilemma of Mary/Martha. But Smith also once said that human dilemmas are not really solved, just abandoned to redefinition.[39]

In time new theories, new explanations of gender and racial difference have not only provided leverage for social change, which Smith frequently lacked, but have also undermined the validity of the many dualities Smith tried unsuccessfully to reconcile. Such "fresh thinking" can now help define the tension, ambiguities, and silences that gathered ominously in the last ten years of Lillian Smith's life, as the civil rights movement progressed. Her well-established reputation as a courageous southerner can be enhanced by analyzing gender in her work and consequently in the Southern Renaissance, already defined by race and region.

39. Letter to Rochelle Girson, book review editor of *Saturday Review,* January 1, 1963, LSP; Smith, review of *The Feminine Mystique,* by Betty Friedan, *Saturday Review* 23 (February 1963): 34; Letter to Gerda Lerner, January 22, 1961, LSP.

❧ Darlene Clark Hine

Rape and the Inner Lives of Southern Black Women
Thoughts on the Culture of Dissemblance

One of the most remarked upon but least analyzed themes in the history of southern black women deals with black women's sexual vulnerability and powerlessness as victims of rape and domestic violence. Author Hazel V. Carby put it baldly when she declared,

> The institutionalized rape of black women has never been as powerful a symbol of black oppression as the spectacle of lynching. Rape has always involved patriarchal notions of women being, at best, not entirely unwilling accomplices, if not outwardly inviting sexual attack. The links between black women and illicit sexuality consolidated during the antebellum years had powerful ideological consequences for the next hundred and fifty years.[1]

1. Carby, *Reconstructing Womanhood: The Emergence of the Afro-American Woman Novelist* (New York: Oxford University Press, 1987), 39. For a discussion of the relationships between suffrage, rape, and lynching, see Bettina Aptheker, *Woman's Legacy: Essays on Race, Sex, and Class in American History* (Amherst: University of Massachusetts Press, 1982), 53–76. It is interesting to note, as Neil R. McMillen points out in his study of black Mississippians, that of the 476 recorded lynchings in the state between 1889 and 1945 at least fourteen were black women, two of whom were well advanced in pregnancy (*Dark Journey: Black Mississippians in the Age of Jim Crow* [Urbana: University of Illinois Press, 1989], 229). Joel Williamson offers another rather problematic assertion about sexual relations between the races that begs credibility: "The myth arose that Negro women were especially lusty creatures, perhaps precisely because white men needed to think of them in that way. With emancipation, however, white men's access to black women virtually ended. Miscegenation, contemporary observers agreed, prac-

I suggest that rape and the threat of rape influenced the development of a culture of dissemblance among southern black women. By dissemblance I mean the behavior and attitudes of black women that created the appearance of openness and disclosure but actually shielded the truth of their inner lives and selves from their oppressors.

In a poignant and insightful compilation of oral histories of southern black domestics and their white employers, editor Susan Tucker asserts, "The culture of women in general, which includes that of both black and white, has been hidden within our dreams, deemed not worthy of consideration in a male-dominated society, and obscured even to women themselves."[2] While dissemblance may very well be an integral feature of general southern women's culture, it exists in an even more complex fashion among black women who endured the combination of race, gender, and class oppression.

Most women in American society fear rape. Yet black and white women dealt with this fear in radically different ways, which reinforced the silences between them and obscured their vision of each other. Southern white women, as Susan Tucker argues, were taught from childhood that "black men were their potential rapists and that only in aligning themselves with white men could they be spared." These early teachings, added to their fear and economic dependence on white males, made it virtually impossible for southern white women to believe or admit that white men were capable or guilty of raping black women. Thus southern white women attributed the presence of mulattoes in their communities to the lax moral standards of black women.[3]

Now, only recently, are black women beginning to break the silence surrounding the long history of their rape and economic exploitation. Themes of rape and sexual vulnerability have received considerable

---

tically stopped." Ignoring the fact that black women continued to work as domestic servants in white households, Williamson asserts, "Mulatto women and black went with their husbands, and dark Victoria was no longer easily available in either body or imagination to upper-class white men" (*The Crucible of Race: Black-White Relations in the American South since Emancipation* [New York: Oxford University Press, 1984], 307).

2. Tucker, *Telling Memories among Southern Women: Domestic Workers and Their Employers in the Segregated South* (Baton Rouge: Louisiana State University Press, 1988), 248.

3. Ibid., 18.

attention in the recent literary outpourings of black women novelists. Of the last six novels I have read and reread, for example, five contained a rape scene or a graphic description of domestic violence.[4] Moreover, this is not a recent phenomenon in black women's literary and autobiographical writing.

Virtually every known nineteenth-century female slave narrative contains a reference to, at some juncture, the ever-present threat and reality of rape. Two works come immediately to mind: Harriet Jacobs's *Incidents in the Life of a Slave Girl* (1861) and Elizabeth Keckley's *Behind the Scenes, or Thirty Years a Slave, and Four Years in the White House* (1868). Yet there is another thread running throughout these slave narratives, one that concerns these captive women's efforts to resist the misappropriation of and to maintain the integrity of their own sexuality. The combined influence of rape (or the threat of rape), domestic violence, and a desire to escape economic oppression born of racism and sexism is the key to understanding the hidden motivations of major social protest and migratory movements in African-American history. Historian David Katzman declared in his study of domestic service, "Although the mark of caste would follow them north, conditions there were different enough to

---

4. See Terry McMillan, *Mama* (Boston: Houghton, Mifflin, 1987); Grace Edwards-Yearwood, *In the Shadow of the Peacock* (New York: McGraw-Hill, 1988); Alice Walker, *The Color Purple: A Novel* (New York: Washington Square Press, 1982); Toni Morrison, *The Bluest Eye* (New York: Holt, Rinehart and Winston, 1970); Gloria Naylor, *The Women of Brewster Place* (New York: Viking Press, 1982); Maya Angelou, *I Know Why the Caged Bird Sings* (New York: Random House, 1969). Descriptions of interracial rape of black women abound in non-fiction writings. In his autobiography Robert Parker, maitre d' of the Senate Dining Room from 1964 to 1975, recalls a white planter's rape of his sister in Montgomery County, Texas, and his own futile efforts at revenge. He wrote, "Robbie was never the same again. The white man had stolen her dignity and dirtied a precious corner of her self when he had taken her, at dusk, on the leaves in the woods" (*Capitol Hill in Black and White* [New York: Dodd, Mead & Company, 1986], 6). For a painful and poignant account by a black woman of the rape of her mother, see Daisy Bates, *The Long Shadow of Little Rock: A Memoir* (New York: David McKay Co., 1962), 14–15. Bates wrote, "Daddy, who killed my mother? Why did they kill her?" Her father replied, "Your mother was not the kind to submit, so they took her. They say that three white men did it. There was some talk about who they were, but no one knew for sure, and the sheriff's office did little to find out."

promote a steady migration of young Southern black women north-ward between the Civil War and the Great Depression of the 1930s."[5]

Second only to black women's fear of sexual violation is the pervasive theme of the frustration attendant to finding suitable employment. Oral histories and autobiographical accounts of twentieth-century southern black women who moved north are replete with themes about work. Scholars of black urban history and black labor history agree that migrating black women faced greater economic discrimination and had fewer employment opportunities than did black men. Black women's work was the most undesirable and least remunerative of all work available to migrants.

As late as 1930 a little over three thousand black women, or 15 percent of the black female labor force in Chicago, were unskilled and semiskilled factory operatives. Thus, over 80 percent of all employed black women continued to work as personal servants and domestics. Historian Allan H. Spear noted, "Negro women were particularly limited in their search for desirable positions. Clerical work was practically closed to them and only a few could qualify as school teachers. Negro domestics often received less than white women for the same work, and they could rarely rise to the position of head servant in large households—a place traditionally held by a Swedish woman." Given that many southern black women migrants were doomed to work in the same kinds of domestic service jobs they held in the South, one wonders why they bothered to move in the first place. There were some significant differences that help explain this phenomenon. A maid earning $7 a week in Cleveland perceived herself to be, and probably was, much better off than a counterpart receiving $2.50 a week in Mobile, Alabama. A factory worker, even one whose work was dirty and low-paying, could and did imagine herself better off

5. Rennie Simson, "The Afro-American Female: The Historical Construction of Sexual Identity," in *Powers of Desire: The Politics of Sexuality,* ed. Anne Snitow, Christine Stansell, and Sharon Thompson (New York: Monthly Review Press, 1983), 229–35. For a fascinating discussion of Harriet Jacobs's *Incidents in the Life of a Slave Girl* (New York: Oxford University Press, 1988), see Elizabeth Fox-Genovese, *Within the Plantation Household: Black and White Women of the Old South* (Chapel Hill: University of North Carolina Press, 1988). Katzman, *Seven Days a Week: Women and Domestic Service in Industrializing America* (1978; reprint, Urbana: University of Illinois Press, 1981), 203–4; Aptheker, "Domestic Labor: Patterns in Black and White," in *Woman's Legacy,* 111–28.

than domestic servants who endured the unrelenting scrutiny, interference, and complaints of household mistresses and the untoward
advances of male family members. But one black woman migrant to
New Jersey from a small town in North Carolina actually favored
performing domestic service work in the South. She explained, "You'd
go about workin'—when I was down home—at eight o'clock; you
was workin' till about two- or two-thirty. Then you was goin' home.
And it wasn't as hard as jobs in the North, not as hard as here." In
spite of the difference and her obvious love of the South, still she
admitted that not all was rosy, adding, "When I was there the colored
wasn't allowed to ride in the bus with white people."[6]

I believe that in order to understand this historical migratory trend
we need to understand the non-economic motives propelling black
female migration. I believe that many black women quit the South out
of a desire to achieve personal autonomy and to escape both from
sexual exploitation from inside and outside their families and from
the rape and threat of rape by white as well as black males. To focus
on the sexual and the personal impetus for black women's migration
in the first several decades of the twentieth century is not to dismiss
or diminish the significance of economic motives. Rather, as historian
Lawrence W. Levine cautioned, "As indisputably important as the
economic motive was, it is possible to overstress it so that the black
migration is converted into an inexorable force and Negroes are seen
once again not as actors capable of affecting at least some part of their
destinies, but primarily as beings who are acted upon—southern
leaves blown North by the winds of destitution." It is reasonable to
assume that some black women were indeed "southern leaves blown
North," and that there were many others who were self-propelled
actresses seeking respect, control over their own sexuality, and access
to better-paying jobs. In *Children of Strangers*, Kathryn L. Morgan
recounts the story of how her female ancestors migrated to Philadelphia from Lynchburg, Virginia, and passed for white during the
day in order to secure decent paying jobs in downtown restaurants.[7]

6. Spear, *Black Chicago: The Making of a Negro Ghetto, 1890–1920* (Chicago:
University of Chicago Press, 1967), 34; Kathryn L. Morgan, *Children of
Strangers: The Stories of a Black Family* (Philadelphia: Temple University
Press, 1980), 18; Audrey Olsen Faulkner et al., *When I Was Comin' Up: An
Oral History of Aged Blacks* (Hamden, Conn.: Archon Books, 1982), 58.
7. Levine, *Black Culture and Black Consciousness: Afro-American Folk Thought*

My own research on the history of black women in the Middle West has led me to questions about how, when, and under what circumstances the majority of them settled in the region. These questions have led to others concerning the process of black women's migration across time, from the flights of runaway slaves in the antebellum period to the great migrations of the first half of the twentieth century. The most common, and certainly the most compelling, motive for running, fleeing, or migrating was a desire to retain or claim some control of their own sexual beings and the children they bore. In the antebellum period hundreds of slave women risked their lives and those of their loved ones to run away to the ostensibly free states of the Northwest Territory in quest of an elusive sexual freedom for themselves and freedom from slavery for their children.

Two things became immediately apparent as I proceeded with researching the history and reading the autobiographies of late nineteenth- and early twentieth-century migrating, or fleeing, black women. First, that these women were sexual hostages and domestic violence victims in the South (or in other regions of the country) did not reduce their determination to acquire power to protect themselves and to become agents of social change once they settled in midwestern communities. Second, the fundamental tensions between black women and the rest of the society—especially white men, white women, and to a lesser extent, black men—involved a multifaceted struggle to determine who would control black women's productive and reproductive capacities and their sexuality. At stake for black women caught up in this ever evolving, constantly shifting, but relentless war was the acquisition of personal autonomy and economic liberation. Their quest for autonomy, dignity, and access to opportunity to earn an adequate living was (and still is) complicated and frustrated by the antagonisms of race, class, and gender conflict, and by differences in regional economies. At heart, though, the relationship between black women and the larger society has always been, and continues to be, adversarial.

Because of the interplay of racial animosity, class tensions, gender role differentiation, and regional economic variations, black women as a rule developed a politics of silence and adhered to a cult of secrecy, a culture of dissemblance, to protect the sanctity of the

---

From Slavery to Freedom (New York: Oxford University Press, 1977), 274; Morgan, *Children of Strangers*, 11.

inner aspects of their lives. The dynamics of dissemblance involved creating the appearance of disclosure, or openness about themselves and their feelings, while actually remaining enigmatic. Only with secrecy, thus achieving a self-imposed invisibility, could ordinary black women acquire the psychic space and gather the resources needed to hold their own in their often one-sided and mismatched struggle to resist oppression.

The honing of dissemblance skills was perfected during black women's work as domestic servants. Young Florence Grier, for example, left Oklahoma for California in 1942 and later recalled the sexual politics of domestic service. In a scene that probably resonates in the memories of thousands of black domestics, Grier described her encounter with a white female employer: "When I said, 'I'm not getting a half day, and this is what you promised me when I took this job,' she said, 'Well, you're just a bit too smart! For your smartness . . . you're just gonna get a dollar, ninety-five cents!' And I said, 'if that nickel will do any good, you keep it! But I'm gonna be sure to tell every other negro maid in the town the kind of person you are.'" Grier admitted that she was afraid to have been so outspoken. She explained, "To hit back or to do too much talking you could get murdered. You just don't look a white woman in the face and tell her that she was doing you wrong!"

On many occasions Grier had to fight the untoward advances of white men in the homes. She declared with wisdom born of resistance: "A man is a man. And I really haven't found any difference in 'em. Only that the white man will want an undercover situation. It's not to be talked about or anything." She elaborated on the variety of approaches or overtures made, such as, "If you're nice to me— you're getting, say you're getting a dollar an hour—wouldn't you like to make your check a little bit bigger?"[8]

The inclination of the larger society to ignore them as elements considered "marginal" actually enabled subordinate black women to fashion the veil of secrecy and to perfect the art of dissemblance. Yet it could also be argued that their secrecy or "invisibility" paradoxically contributed to their failure to realize equal opportunity or to receive respect in the larger society. There would be no room on

8. Bob Blaunder, *Black Lives, White Lives: Three Decades of Race Relations in America* (Berkeley: University of California Press, 1989), 24–25; see John Dollard, *Caste and Class in a Southern Town* (New Haven: Yale University Press, 1937), 142.

the pedestal for the southern black lady, nor could she join her white sisters in the prison of "true womanhood." In other words, stereotypes, negative images, and debilitating assumptions filled the space left empty due to inadequate and erroneous information about the true contributions, capabilities, and identities of black women.

This line of analysis is not without problems. To suggest that black women deliberately developed a culture of dissemblance implies that they endeavored to create, and were not simply reacting to, widespread misrepresentations of themselves in white minds. Clearly, black women did not possess the power to eradicate negative social and sexual images of their womanhood. Rather, what I propose is that in the face of the pervasive stereotypes and negative estimations of the sexuality of black women, it was imperative that they collectively create alternative self-images and shield from scrutiny these private empowering definitions of self. I would argue that a secret, undisclosed *persona* allowed the individual black woman to function, to work effectively as a domestic in white households, to bear and rear children, endure the domestic violence of frequently under- or unemployed mates, to support churches, found institutions, and engage in social service activities—all while living within a clearly hostile white, patriarchal, middle-class America.

The problem that this penchant for secrecy presents to the historian is readily apparent. Deborah Gray White has commented about the difficulty of finding primary source material for the personal aspects of black female life.

> Black women have also been reluctant to donate their papers to manuscript repositories. That is in part a manifestation of the black woman's perennial concern with image, a justifiable concern born of centuries of vilification. Black women's reluctance to donate personal papers also stems from the adversarial nature of the relationship that countless black women have had with many public institutions, and the resultant suspicion of anyone seeking private information.[9]

White's allusion to "resultant suspicion" speaks implicitly to one important reason why so much of the inner lives of black women remain hidden. Indeed, the concepts of "secrets" and "dissemblance" as I

9. Deborah Gray White, "Mining the Forgotten: Manuscript Sources for Black Women's History," *Journal of American History* 74 (June 1987): 237–42.

employ them hint at those issues that black women believed better left unknown, unwritten, unspoken except in whispered tones. Their alarm, their fear, or their Victorian sense of modesty implies that those who broke the silence provided grist for detractors' mills and, even more ominously, tore the protective cloaks from their inner selves. Undoubtedly, these fears and suspicions contribute to the absence of sophisticated historical discussion of the impact of rape (or the threat of rape) and incidences of domestic violence on the shape of black women's experiences.

However, the self-imposed secrecy and the culture of dissemblance, coupled with the larger society's unwillingness to discard tired and worn stereotypes, have also led to ironically misplaced emphases. Until quite recently, for example, when historians talked about the rape of slave women they often bemoaned the damage that this act did to the black male's sense of esteem and self-respect. He was powerless to protect his woman from white rapists. Few scholars probed the effect that rape, the threat of rape, and domestic violence had on the psychic development of the female victims. In the late nineteenth and twentieth centuries, as Carby has indicated, lynching, not rape, became the most powerful and compelling symbol of black oppression. Lynching, it came to be understood, was one of the major non-economic reasons why southern black men migrated North.

The culture of dissemblance assumed its most institutionalized form in the founding, in 1896, of the National Association of Colored Women's Clubs (NACW). This association of black women quickly became the largest and most enduring protest organization in the history of African-Americans. Its size alone should have warranted the same degree of scholarly attention paid to Marcus Garvey's Universal Negro Improvement Association. By 1914 the NACW had a membership of 50,000, far surpassing the membership of every other protest organization of the time, including the National Association for the Advancement of Colored People and the National Urban League. In Detroit in 1945, for example, the Detroit Association of Colored Women's Clubs, federated in 1921, boasted seventy-three member clubs with nearly three thousand individual members.[10] Not surprisingly, the primary targets of NACW attack were

10. Robin S. Peebles, "Detroit's Black Women's Clubs," *Michigan History* 70 (January/February 1986): 48; Cynthia Neverdon-Morton, *Afro-American Women of the South and the Advancement of the Race, 1895–1925* (Knoxville: University of Tennessee Press, 1989), 191–201.

the derogatory images and negative stereotypes of black women's sexuality.

Mary Church Terrell, the first president of the NACW, declared in her initial presidential address that there were objectives of the black women's struggle that could only be accomplished by the mothers, wives, daughters, and sisters of this race. She proclaimed, "We wish to set in motion influences that shall stop the ravages made by practices that sap our strength, and preclude the possibility of advancement." She boldly announced, "We proclaim to the world that the women of our race have become partners in the great firm of progress and reform. . . . We refer to the fact that this is an association of colored women, because our peculiar status in this country . . . seems to demand that we stand by ourselves."[11]

At the core of essentially every activity of NACW's individual members was a concern with creating positive images of black women's sexuality. To counter negative stereotypes many black women felt compelled to downplay, even deny, sexual expression. The twin obsessions with naming and combating sexual exploitation tinted and shaped black women's support even of the woman's suffrage movement. Nannie H. Burroughs, famed religious leader and founder of the National Training School for Women and Girls at Washington, D.C., cajoled her sisters to fight for the ballot. She asserted that with the ballot black women could ensure the passage of legislation to win legal protection against rapists. Calling the ballot a "weapon of moral defense," she exploded, "When [a black woman] appears in court in defense of her virtue, she is looked upon with amused contempt. She needs the ballot to reckon with men who place no value upon her virtue."[12]

Likewise, determination to save young unskilled and unemployed black women from having to bargain sex in exchange for food and

11. Darlene Clark Hine, "Lifting the Veil, Shattering the Silence: Black Women's History in Slavery and Freedom," in Darlene Clark Hine, ed., *The State of Afro-American History: Past, Present, and Future* (Baton Rouge: Louisiana State University Press, 1986), 223–49.

12. Evelyn Brooks Barnett, "Nannie Burroughs and the Education of Black Women," in Sharon Harley and Rosalyn Terborg-Penn, eds., *The Afro-American Woman: Struggles and Images* (Port Washington: Kennikat Press, 1978), 97–108; Rosalyn Terborg-Penn, "Woman Suffrage: 'First because We are Women and Second because We are Colored Women,'" *Truth: Newsletter of the Association of Black Women Historians* (April 1985): 9.

shelter motivated some NACW members to establish boarding houses and domestic service training centers, such as the Phillis Wheatley Homes and Burroughs' National Training School. Their efforts to provide black women with protection from sexual exploitation and with dignified work inspired other club members in local communities around the country to support or to found hospitals and nursing training schools.

At least one plausible consequence of this heightened mobilization of black women was a decline in black urban birth rates. As black women became more economically self-sufficient, better educated, and more involved in self-improvement efforts, including participation in the flourishing black women's club movement in southern and in midwestern communities, they had greater access to birth control information. As the institutional infrastructure of black women's clubs, sororities, church-based women's groups, and charity organizations sank roots into black communities, it encouraged its members to embrace those values, behaviors, and attitudes traditionally associated with the middle class. To urban black middle-class aspirants, the social stigma of having many children did, perhaps, inhibit reproduction. To be sure, over time the gradually evolving male-female demographic imbalance meant that increasingly significant numbers of black women, especially those employed in the professions in urban midwestern communities, would never marry. The point stressed here, however, is that not having children was, perhaps for the very first time, a choice enjoyed by large numbers of black women.

There were additional burdens placed upon and awards granted the small cadre of single, educated, professional black women who chose not to marry or to bear children. The more educated they were, the greater was their sense of being responsible for the advancement of the race and for the elevation of black womanhood. They held these expectations of themselves and found a sense of racial obligation reinforced by the demands of the black community and its institutions. In return for their "sacrifice of sexual expression," the community gave them respect and recognition. Moreover, this freedom and autonomy represented a socially sanctioned, meaningful alternative to the uncertainties of marriage and the demands of raising children. The increased employment opportunities, whether real or imagined, and the culture of dissemblance enabled many migrating black women to become financially independent and simultaneously to fashion socially useful and autonomous lives while reclaiming control over their own sexuality and reproductive capacities.

This is not to say that black women, once settled into midwestern communities, never engaged in sex for pay or occasional prostitution. Sara Brooks, a black domestic servant from Alabama who migrated to Cleveland, Ohio, in the 1930s, could not disguise her contempt for women who bartered their bodies. As she declared, while commenting on her own struggle to pay the mortgage on her house, "Some women woulda had a man to come and live in the house and had an outside boyfriend, too, in order to get the house paid for and the bills." She scornfully added, "They meet a man and if he promises em four or five dollars to go to bed, they'd grab it. That's called sellin your own body, and I wasn't raised like that."[13] What escaped Brooks in this moralizing moment was that her poor and powerless black female neighbors were extracting value from the only thing the society now allowed them to sell. As long as they occupied an enforced subordinate position within American society this "sellin your own body," as Sara Brooks put it, was rape.

At some fundamental level all black women historians are engaged in the process of historical reclamation, but it is not enough simply to uncover the hidden facts, the obscure names of black foremothers. Merely to reclaim and to narrate their past deeds and contributions risks rendering a skewed history focused primarily upon the articulate, relatively well-positioned members of the aspiring black middle class. In synchrony with the reclaiming and narrating must be the development of an array of analytical frameworks that allow us to understand why black women of all classes behave in certain ways and how they acquired agency. The culture of dissemblance is one such framework.

The migration of hundreds of thousands of black women out of the South between 1915 and 1945, the formation of thousands of black women's clubs, and the activities of the NACW are actions that enabled these women to formulate and put into place an infrastructure of protest and resistance: a culture of dissemblance. This

13. Thordis Simonsen, ed., *You May Plow Here: Narrative of Sara Brooks* (New York: W. W. Norton, 1986), 218, 219.

culture born of rape and fears of rape shaped the course of black women's history. It was this culture, grounded on the twin prongs of protest and resistance, that enabled the creation of positive alternative images of black women's sexual selves and facilitated their mental and physical survival in a hostile world.

CONTRIBUTORS

Roseanne V. Camacho received her Ph.D. in American Civilization from Brown University in 1992, after teaching fourteen years at Gordon School in East Providence, Rhode Island. She completed her dissertation, "Woman Born of the South: Race, Region and Gender in the Work of Lillian Smith," with the support of a Charlotte W. Newcombe Doctoral Dissertation Fellowship, which encourages the study of ethical or religious values in all fields. She teaches currently at the University of Rhode Island.

Kathy Roe Coker holds the doctoral degree from the University of South Carolina where she wrote a dissertation on "The Punishment of Revolutionary War Loyalists in South Carolina." Since 1985 she has been historian-archivist with the Department of the Army at Fort Gordon, Georgia. She has published in a number of journals, including *American Archivist,* the *South Carolina Historical Magazine,* and *Army Communicator.* She co-authored *A Concise History of the U.S. Army Signal Corps.*

Jacquelyn Dowd Hall is Julia Cherry Spruill Professor of History at the University of North Carolina at Chapel Hill. Her numerous publications include *Revolt against Chivalry: Jessie Daniel Ames and the Women's Campaign against Lynching* (1979); the prize-winning volume, *Like a Family: The Making of a Southern Cotton Mill World* (1987), written with James Leloudis, Robert Korstad, Mary Murphy, Lu Ann Jones, and Christopher B. Daly; and "Private Eyes, Public Women: Images of Class and Sex in the Urban South, Atlanta, Georgia 1913–1915," in *Work Engendered: Toward a New History of American Labor,* edited by Ava Baron (1991).

Darlene Clark Hine is John A. Hannah Professor of History at Michigan State University. She has edited and written widely on African-American history, particularly on black women in the nursing profession and in the Midwest. Her books include the prize-winning volume *Black Women in White: Racial Conflict and Cooperation in the Nursing Profession, 1890–1950* (1989), *Women's Culture and Community in Indiana, 1875–1959* (1981), and *Black Victory: The Rise and Fall of the White Primary in Texas* (1979). She has also published over fifty research articles on black history and is the editor of the sixteen-volume series, *Black Women in United States History: From Colonial Times to the Present*. Hine has also edited *The State of Afro-American History: Past, Present, and Future* (1986).

Kent Anderson Leslie received her doctoral degree from the Graduate Institute of the Liberal Arts at Emory University in 1990. Her dissertation is entitled "Woman of Color, Daughter of Privilege: Amanda America Dickson, 1849–1893" and will be published by the University of Georgia Press. In 1986 she published "A Myth of the Southern Lady: Antebellum Pro-Slavery Rhetoric and the Proper Place of Woman" in *Spectrum*. Leslie is presently an assistant professor and fellow of the Institute for Women's Studies at Emory University.

Mary Martha Thomas has retired as professor of history at Jacksonville State University, Jacksonville, Alabama. She completed her doctoral studies at Emory University and is the author of a history of her undergraduate institution, Southern Methodist University. Her books *Riveting and Rationing in Dixie: Alabama Women and the Second World War* was published in 1987, and *The New Woman in Alabama: Social Reform and Suffrage, 1890–1920* was published in 1992.

Cheryl Thurber is a doctoral candidate in history at the University of Mississippi. The title of her dissertation is "'Dixie': The Cultural History of a Song and Place." She is the founding editor of *Rejoice! Gospel Music Magazine* and a member of the governing board of the Presbyterian Historical Society. She presented a paper, "'Belongin' to the White Folks': Slavery in Marshall and DeSoto Counties, Mississippi," at the 1988 meeting of the American Historical Association and is currently teaching at Union University in Memphis.

Elizabeth Hayes Turner has taught at the University of North Carolina at Charlotte, Queens College (Charlotte, N.C.), and is currently assistant professor of history at the University of Houston-Downtown. She received her doctoral degree in American history from Rice University and has served as associate editor of *The Journal of Southern History.* Her dissertation is entitled "Women's Culture and Community: Religion and Reform in Galveston, 1880–1920." In 1991 she presented a paper, "Southern Suffragists and the Progressive Era," at the meeting of the Organization of American Historians.

Susan Westbury wrote on "Colonial Virginia and the Atlantic Slave Trade" for her doctoral degree from the University of Illinois, Urbana-Champaign. She has undergraduate degrees from the University of Melbourne and the University of Alberta. Her article, "Virginia Slaves: Where They Came From," appeared in the *William and Mary Quarterly* in 1985. She has also written "Analysing a Regional Slave Trade: The West Indies and Virginia 1698–1775" for *Slavery and Abolition* (1986). Since 1982 she has taught at Illinois State University.

❧ INDEX